P9-AFZ-641

Additional Praise for *Retire Secure!*
by James Lange, CPA/Attorney

"… Jim delves into topics that few lay people are aware of and most professionals don't address. Protect yourself and your family with the excellent comments of *Retire Secure!*"

— **Martin M. Shenkman, Attorney, CPA, MBA**
Author, *Inherit More*

"*Retire Secure!* shows you how to make your money last longer and go further than you ever imagined possible."

— **Brian Tracy, Strategic Planner**
Author, *Something for Nothing*

"*Retire Secure!* does a fine job of explaining why, when, and how folks should move money into, out of, and between the myriad tax-advantaged employer-sponsored retirement savings plans and IRAs. The key points are summarized clearly, but a more thorough, equally clear explanation is also offered for those who want it.

The book is well-organized, with plenty of practical examples. It will be a valuable resource to people in both the accumulation and distribution of their retirement assets - and to their advisors, as well."

— **Michael T. Palermo, Attorney**,
Certified Financial Planner™
Author, *AARP Crash Course in Estate Planning*

"The frequent mini case studies throughout *Retire Secure!* are very beneficial. They help give readers a full understanding of a complicated topic and how to apply that topic to their own situation."

— **Paul Richard, RFC**
Exec. Director Institute of Consumer Financial Education

"I hope this book will be a blessing for readers."

— **Rev. Dr. Robert H. Schuller**
Minister, *The Hour of Power*
Author, *If it is Going to Be it is Up to Me*

"Jim offers the best advice I've read on making your dollars go the longest distance, for you and your loved ones."

— **John A. Tracy, Ph.D., CPA**
Author, *Accounting for Dummies*

"Keeping your investment expenses low and following Jim Lange's tax savings strategies are the surest routes to a comfortable retirement."

— **Burton G. Malkiel, Ph.D.**
Professor of Economics, Princeton University
Author, *A Random Walk Down Wall Street*

"Nice girls eventually become old women who want to retire. Let this book help you to ensure you have all the money you need to live your life the way you want at retirement."

— **Lois P. Frankel, Ph.D.**
Author, *Nice Girls Don't Get Rich: 75 Avoidable Mistakes Women Make with Money*

"I recommend Retire Secure! above all other books on retirement planning. No other work features the famous Lange's Cascading Beneficiary Plan™."

— **Norman G. Levine, CLU, ChFC , RFC**
Author, *A Passion for Compassion* and *Selling With Silk Gloves*

"James Lange is a genius at making the most difficult subject of estate/retirement planning easy to understand. His book is an absolute must for anyone who wants the peace of mind that comes from knowing they will retire secure."

— **Eleanor Schano**
Former TV News Anchor
Host, "LifeQuest" WQED Multimedia

Praise for *Retire Secure!—Geared Towards Professionals*

"We recognize *Retire Secure!* by tax attorney Jim Lange of Pittsburgh, PA, as the definitive work available. We have rated this volume as the most complete and the most authoritative retirement guide serving our industry."

— **Fred R. Kissling, CLU, MSPA, AEP, RF**
Publisher, *Financial Services Advisor* magazine

"More than useful, *Retire Secure!* is an absolute essential for advisors because it helps you best deal with the many risks involved. Attorney James Lange did most of the difficult planning work for you."

— **Louisa M. Montecalvo, CEP, CCPS**
College Advisors Group, LLC

"Jim created the most flexible and effective estate guide for IRA and retirement plan owners."

— **Charles "Tremendous" Jones, RFC**
CEO, Executive Books
International speaker, sales trainer
Author, *Life Is Tremendous*

"Every financial advisor ought to have a copy of *Retire Secure!* at his or her fingertips, plus copies to give more serious clients. After clients have been taught how to save and where to place their investments, James Lange's book, *Retire Secure!* is the definitive answer to the very important tax considerations."

— **Vernon D. Gwynne, CFP, RFC**
Former Executive Director of the IAFP now FPA

"Distribution planning is where every financial advisor needs to be who is serious about helping clients and getting their professional practice to the next level."

— **Peter M. Vessenes, RFC**
Author, *Building Your Multi-Million Dollar Practice*

"*Retire Secure!* will help provide the education that financial advisors need to reduce their potential liabilities."

— **Jerry Reiter**, **CEO/Chairman**
Financial Advisors Legal Association

"*Retire Secure!* is one of the best educational tools and reference manuals ever available! *Retire Secure!* serves as a text for a comprehensive financial planning course on retirement. *Retire Secure!* will certainly have a long shelf life."

— **Al Coletti, CLU, ChFC, RFC**
Chairman, Institute for Financial Education

"*Retire Secure!* is absolutely "essential" reading for all practitioners in the estate and retirement planning field."

— **Jack Gargan, Founder**
Intl. Assoc. of Registered Financial Consultants (IARFC)

"Jim Lange's book is a must in the retirement library of anyone with a large IRA. Not only does it provide thorough coverage of a difficult topic, but it does so with crisp writing, surrounded with charts and tables to help you understand your options."

— **Robert S. Keebler, CPA, MST**
Editor in Chief, Journal of Retirement Planning
Author, *A CPA's Guide to the New IRAs*

"Only in *Retire Secure!* will you learn how to better accumulate wealth in a logical, realistic, practical, and legally structured (protected) way. You will also learn when trusts in estate planning documents can be a disaster!"

— **Lew Nason, RFC**
Speaker, Marketing Consultant/Insurance Pro Shop

Additional testimonials (37 and counting) available at www.RetireSecure.com/testimonial

RETIRE
SECURE!
PAY TAXES LATER

RETIRE SECURE!

PAY TAXES LATER

The Key to Making Your Money Last As Long As You Do

James Lange
CPA/Attorney

John Wiley & Sons, Inc.

Published by John Wiley & Sons, Inc., Hoboken, New Jersey.
Published simultaneously in Canada.

For general information about our other products and services, please contact our Customer Care Department within the United States at (800) 762-2974, outside the United States at (317) 572-3993 or fax (317) 572-4002.

Wiley also publishes its books in a variety of electronic formats. Some content that appears in print may not be available in electronic books.

For more information about Wiley products, visit our web site at www.wiley.com.

Cartoons by Michael McParlane.

Library of Congress Cataloging-in-Publication Data:

Lange, James, 1956-
Retire secure! : pay taxes later : the key to making your money last as long as you do / by James Lange.
p. cm.
Includes index.
ISBN-13: 978-0-470-04354-7
ISBN-10: 0-470-04354-7
1. Tax planning--United States. 2. Individual retirement accounts--Law and legislation--United States. 3. Pension trusts--Law and legislation--United States. I. Title.

KF6297.Z9L265 2006
343.7305'238--dc22

2005048766

Printed in the United States of America.
10 9 8 7 6 5 4 3 2 1

Contents

Foreword

Retire Secure! is written for consumers and advisors who worry about these essential questions: "Will I have enough *income* when I retire?" and "Will it last as long as I might?" These questions might have additional significance for the wife of a male retiree because she is statistically likely to survive her husband.

Jim has properly identified the three stages of retirement planning: accumulation, distribution, and estate planning, and readers will find the organization extremely helpful. They can quickly place themselves along the continuum of the retirement process and find excellent recommendations for each stage of their journey.

Understanding the implications of various retirement planning decisions requires looking at the numbers. There is no getting around that. Comparing and contrasting different options guides the consumer into making the right choices. Jim takes all the work out of this by providing numerous comparisons. Gradually the reader is educated and informed—and making the right choices becomes easier.

An important issue is, "Which account (Roth, IRA, 401(k), 403(b), after tax, etc.) is the best to make withdrawals from first?" This is very clearly addressed in the book despite the fact that the explanation cannot be simple or the response universal. It depends on an individual's particular circumstances, and Jim avoids giving the reader the simplified, and often wrong, answer.

The mini case studies are a real eye-opener for all readers, both consumers and financial advisors, because they mathematically prove Jim's assertions. Each comparison and mini case study is based on several assumptions, which Jim is careful to point out in a clear fashion. I particularly enjoyed Mini Case Study 5.2 about the disastrous execution of beneficiary forms and the decision of Junior not to sue the careless estate administrator—his mother.

Jim is the first financial writer to point out the problems of trying to make plan withdrawals in December. Most advisors suggest executing them late in December—but he brings a reality check—it is tough to get them accomplished when folks are on holiday breaks—not to mention the risk of the consumer simply forgetting to trigger the withdrawal and remembering only when relaxing on the beaches of Cancun.

Financial planning books and authors frequently choose to focus primarily on one aspect of planning: accumulation, distribution, or estate planning. This can easily lead the reader into making inappropriate decisions, and it fails to present the complete picture. While life expectancies are growing longer—that is only a statistical probability—it does not reflect the risk of meeting a drunk driver head on late at night. So while the preretiree should be focusing on accumulating the largest account, he cannot ignore the need for a careful beneficiary arrangement.

Fortunately *Retire Secure!* carefully considers all the options in a balanced fashion, and it does not declare a universal solution. Why? Because solutions depend on very careful fact-finding specific to the individual. But this book gives you the road map, and that is indispensable.

Retire Secure! repeatedly makes the point, in case after case, that comprehensive beneficiary designations accurately completed are critical to saving money. This repetition is important because millions of Americans have already made the wrong type of passage arrangements for their qualified plan accounts and IRAs.

If readers learn nothing more than the importance of creating a new beneficiary arrangement using "Lange's Cascading Beneficiary Plan™," then this book will save hundreds of millions for American families.

Edwin P. Morrow, CLU, ChFC, CEP, CFP®, RFC®
Chairman and CEO, the International Association of Registered Financial Consultants
Author, Speaker, Consultant

Acknowledgments

This book could not have been written without the work and dedication of many others. I am indebted to a few individuals whose contributions were invaluable.

Steven T. Kohman, Certified Public Accountant, Certified Valuation Analyst, Certified Specialist in Estate Planning, has worked with me for over eight years and has coauthored many articles with me. Steve is a superb number cruncher and combines his extensive tax background with superb quantitative and computer skills. Steve's quantitative analysis, evidenced in the graphs and charts throughout the book, presents compelling proof of the fundamental concepts that make up the backbone of *Retire Secure!*

Matt Schwartz, Esq., is an exceptionally bright and capable IRA and estate attorney. I am proud to have him as a colleague. Matt has made many original contributions to the book, as well as many corrections. If there are any remaining errors, then they are mine and not his. He works closely with my clients and me to complete the documentation necessary to implement our recommended planning solutions.

Cynthia Nelson has been working with me for over five years. During that period, she has had full editing and writing responsibilities for all of my published works. She is a rare find. Her editing and writing skills are only surpassed by her ability to come through in the eleventh hour.

Geraldine Skupien, Esq., C.F.P., has an LL.M. in Taxation from New York University. She has written several articles with me and has provided original ideas, drafting help, and tax research.

Camille Brubach, Esq., created the first flowchart of Lange's Cascading Beneficiary Plan™ and helped with the early stages of editing.

Jillian Manus, my "rock star agent," thank you for your patience with a difficult client. Debra Englander, my Wiley editor, thank you for selecting *Retire Secure!* for publication and for all of your subsequent help.

Special thanks to Dae Scott and Ed Helvey who helped enormously in the early stages of the book.

Wally Cato, my media advocate, thank you for believing in me from day one.

I also want to thank all the prerelease readers and reviewers of *Retire Secure!* Special thanks to Charles Schwab and Seymour Goldberg who both provided insight and suggestions to the original manuscript. Many of you offered thoughtful testimonials that have been included inside the book or on its covers. Your support means more than I can adequately express. Unfortunately, there was not room to include all the fine testimonials offered, so I will also thank those of you who offered testimonials that did not appear.

I also want to thank Ed Morrow for writing such a thoughtful foreword.

I must also convey my gratitude to my full-time coworkers (in addition to Steve and Matt) who provided me with so much help in my practice that without them the book could never have been written: Glenn Venturino, CPA (how can I properly thank you for 18 years of superb service to our clients); Sandy Proto, our office manager (without Sandy the office would cease to function); Alice Davis, who is superb with our clients and has become an integral part of the office because she makes things happen; Donna Master, who keeps my books, which would certainly be a nightmare without her dedicated precision; and Daryl Ross, our legal administrative assistant/master tax return compiler who rolls up her sleeves and gets it done year after year.

Finally, to matters of the heart, a special thanks to my mother, Barnetta Lange, Ph.D., Professor Emeritus of Journalism. Out of her love for the English language, she tried to keep me from too many clichés and "ize" words as well as improving the language and correcting grammatical errors.

And closest to my heart, I have to thank my beloved wife, Cindy Lange, who surely is one of the few women alive who could put up with me. Her imprint is on every page of the book. Cindy has been enormously resourceful in many areas and has made both direct and indirect contributions to the book. This book would have never happened without her help, support, and love. And to my daughter Erica, who gives me a reason to smile (almost) every day.

Thank you all.

How to Read This Book

I recommend you start with "The Big Retirement Question" and "A Summary of Tax Reduction Strategies" so that you can begin to apply the underlying theme of "pay taxes later" to your own situation. Then, please look at the detailed table of contents and pick out the chapters that grab your attention.

Virtually every chapter contains proof that my recommendations have been tested and proven worthy. You may want to skip over portions of the proof and just read the advice. Sometimes, when I am looking for information or advice, I want to scream, "Don't tell me why, just tell me what to do." If you feel similarly, or you find yourself moving in that direction after realizing there is enormous support for virtually every recommendation made, the book's sidebars and summaries at the end of the chapters will serve you well.

Obviously, you would benefit greatly if you read the book cover to cover, and then took action on the recommendations appropriate for you and your family. I do, however, live in the real world and recognize that you may only read or even skim portions you know are personally relevant.

I have tried to "spice up" the content by including some true stories (modified for confidentiality), an occasional sarcastic comment, at least one witty quote per chapter, and perhaps the most fun, the eleven cartoons. I hope you enjoy them.

What *Retire Secure!* Does Not Cover

Retire Secure! does not provide direct investment advice nor do I recommended any specific stocks, bonds, mutual funds, or even asset allocation models. Obviously, choosing appropriate investments is critical, but this book is not the place for direct investment advice.

I also do not address the issue of determining an appropriate withdrawal rate for retirement.

Finally, though there is some analysis on Roth IRAs and Roth IRA conversions, the coverage is not complete. (I am preparing a new book on Roth retirement plans and IRAs.)

Additional Resources for the Reader

My goal is to provide you, my readers, with the best information I know and establish a continuing dialogue with you. I hope you would not stop with this book. I offer other information and services, and my hope is that for many readers this book will be the beginning, not the end, of a good relationship. Much of that information will be free in the form of an e-mail newsletter and the audio CD and the offer of several free reports.

Of course as time goes on, the tax code will change, creating new opportunities and pitfalls. One wonderful source of free information is my e-mail newsletter. It will keep you up to date on the best ways to secure a comfortable retirement and the latest tax planning strategies. Please go to www.PayTaxesLater.com/book/newsletter.htm to sign up.

In addition, I would recommend you visit my blog. To do so, please go to www.PayTaxesLater.com/book/blog.htm.

Feel free to use my blog to send comments, questions, and/or ideas you would like to relay to me. I will try to post questions and answers on a regular basis. Your thoughts are most appreciated. In addition to tax updates, I expect to continue improving this book for the next edition, and most of the improvements will come from your comments.

When you purchased this book, you qualified for a free CD. To receive your CD visit www.PayTaxesLater.com/book/freecd.htm or refer to the back of the book for ordering information. This audio CD will supplement and reinforce some of the most important points in the book as well as provide some new material. It is quite advantageous to listen to the material as well as to read it. Furthermore, you can play it in your car—make good use of that downtime! It would be a major mistake not to take advantage of this free offer.

Thank you for making this purchase. I appreciate that the investment of your time is more precious than the money spent on the book. I have given everything I have to make this book worthy of your valuable time. I hope you will be pleased and preferably absolutely delighted.

A Note Specifically for Financial Professionals

If you are a financial professional (financial planner, CPA, attorney, banker, stockbroker, insurance professional, CFP, money manager, et al.), then I would encourage you to actually read this book. I don't say this lightly. I fully realize that your time is a precious commodity. If you choose to do some strategic skipping of material because you understand the concepts and don't need to have the concepts proved, then strategic skipping is fine.

I think we have a sacred trust as advisors to give our clients the best advice we can. Taking the time to read this book is a critical step toward fulfilling that trust. After all, isn't becoming your clients' most trusted advisor the absolute best way to secure referrals and recommendations that expand your business? The entire direction of the industry is to distinguish ourselves by the quality of our advice and service and to provide our clients "added value." The information in this book is likely to radically improve the scope and quality of the advice you give your clients regarding IRA and retirement plans.

Before reading this book, I urge you to print out a list of your clients and keep it with the book. As you read, please think about how the different strategies could be used by individual clients to significantly improve their financial picture—I would hazard a guess that every one of your clients could benefit from at least one of the tax saving strategies that I talk about. Make a notation next to the client's name and then make the call to schedule a meeting with your client to discuss your latest personalized recommendations. There isn't a client who doesn't appreciate the personalized touch. By the time you are done reading the book, chances are you will have a good reason to call and schedule a meeting with the majority of your clients.

Then, please don't stop there.

Please sign up for my free email newsletter geared towards financial professionals at www.PayTaxesLater.com/book/finprof.htm.

Every financial professional who has clients with significant IRAs and/or retirement plans should have a copy of *Retire Secure!* If you are a department manager or you oversee other financial professionals, I urge you to read this book with an eye to purchasing a copy for all the financial professionals in your organization as well as using it as a premium for your clients.

I hope you will enjoy great benefits from reading and implementing the ideas in *Retire Secure!*

The Big Retirement Question

"Do I have enough money to last for the rest of my life?"

That's the $64,000 question.

While you can never answer that question with 100% certainty, you can take action on two fronts which will dramatically improve your odds.

1. *Develop an appropriate portfolio.* With the exception of several observations interspersed throughout, I leave the discussion of building a portfolio to another day.

2. *Take action to drastically reduce your taxes.* This is easier than you may think. With this book in hand you have the tools to significantly reduce your and your family's tax burden. Reducing your taxes will dramatically increase your chances of financial success.

The U.S. tax structure rewards certain actions and punishes others. The difference can mean, literally, millions of dollars.

Retire Secure! examines how you can use IRAs, retirement plans, and other tax-favored investments to let Uncle Sam subsidize your lifestyle and increase the odds you will have sufficient income for the rest of your and your spouse's life.

Retire Secure! is the culmination of the best advice that I have to offer from 27 years as a practicing CPA and 22 years as an estate attorney. Though the optimal treatment of IRAs and retirement plans is the focus of this book, even readers with IRAs and retirement plans as their primary assets have other concerns besides planning for their retirement assets. Therefore, this book isn't limited to IRA and retirement plan advice but contains my best advice in many related areas as well. *Retire Secure!* provides critical advice for all stages of IRA and retirement plan saving and spending. We cover the best strategies for accumulating wealth while you are working, as well as the distribution of IRAs and retirement plans when you are retired.

In addition, *Retire Secure!* gives you a *uniquely flexible* solution for disbursing the IRA or retirement plan after the death of the IRA owner. The inherent flexibility of Lange's Cascading Beneficiary Plan™ provides the maximum flexibility for your survivors. We think it is highly likely you will prefer this plan to the more traditional, fixed-in-stone type of estate planning. Flexibility is important because we can't predict the future; changes in investments and in the tax environment are likely to affect the best plans. If we provide flexibility in our estate planning, we will often get a better result for the family.

Retire Secure! is supported with peer-reviewed mathematical proof that these strategies result in more dollars—sometimes millions of additional dollars—to you and your family.

A Summary of Tax Reduction Strategies

For the reader who wants to take what I have to say on faith and wants several of the most important strategies in five pages or less, here you go.

The Clear Advantage of IRA and Retirement Plan Savings during the Accumulation Stage

If you are working or self-employed, to the extent you can afford to, please contribute the maximum to your retirement plans.

Mr. Pay Taxes Later and Mr. Pay Taxes Now had identical salaries, investment choices, and spending patterns, but there was one big difference. Mr. Pay Taxes Later invested as much as he could afford in his tax-deferred retirement plans even though his employer did not match his contributions. Mr. Pay Taxes Now contributed nothing to his retirement account at work but invested his "savings" in an account outside of his retirement plan.

Please look at Figure A. Mr. Pay Taxes Later's investment is represented by the gray curve, and Mr. Pay Taxes Now's by the black curve. Look at the dramatic difference in the accumulations over time—nearly $2 million versus less than $1 million (and ultimately nothing if Mr. Pay Taxes Now lives long enough).

There you have it. Two people in the same tax bracket who earn and spend an identical amount of money and have identical investment rates of return. Based on the simple application of the "Pay Taxes Later" rule, the difference is poverty in old age versus affluence and a $2 million estate. (Details are spelled out in Chapter 1.) "Pay taxes later" is a concept to embrace for a lifetime of earning, living, and estate planning.

"Pay taxes later" is a concept to embrace for a lifetime of earning, living, and estate planning.

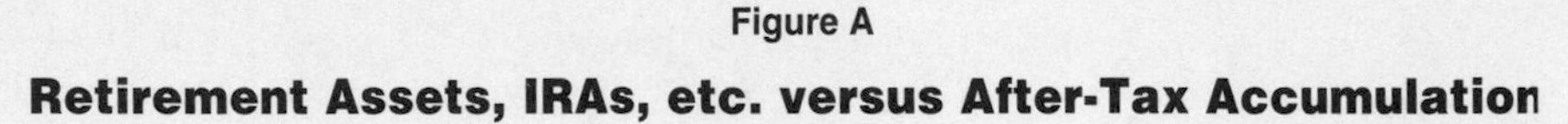

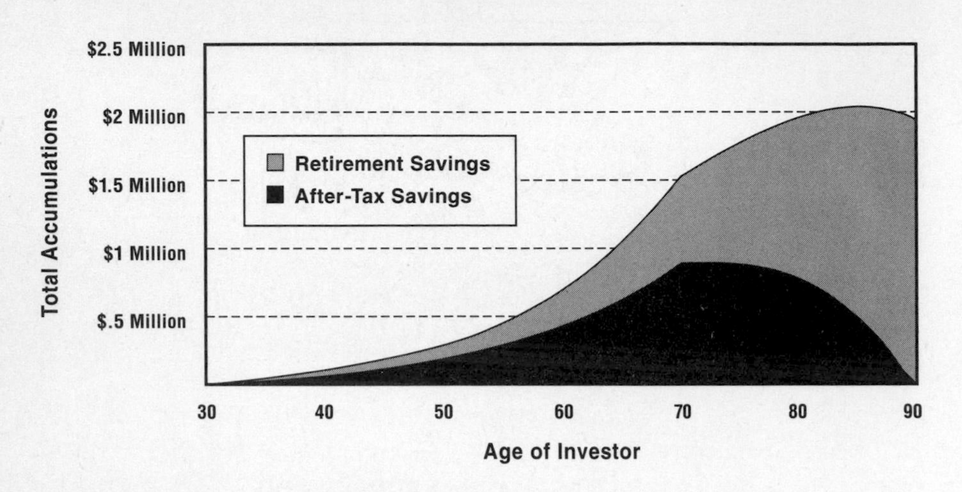

Spend Your After-Tax (Nonretirement or Non-IRA) Money First during the Distribution Stage

Mr. Tax-Efficient and Mr. Tax-Inefficient, both aged 65, start with identical investments inside and outside of their IRAs and retirement plans.

Mr. Tax-Inefficient refuses to spend any of his after-tax funds (non-IRA and nonretirement plan funds) until all his IRA and retirement funds are depleted. Each withdrawal of his IRA and retirement plan triggers income taxes. Because he is spending the IRA and retirement plan money first, he is *paying tax now*. (See Figure B.)

Mr. Tax-Efficient does the opposite. He spends nothing of his IRA or retirement plan until he runs out of money from his nonretirement sources or until he is required to take minimum required distributions when he reaches 70½. In the accompanying figure, Mr. Tax-Efficient is represented by the upper curve and the unfortunate Mr. Tax-Inefficient by the lower curve.

Which scenario looks better to you? The principle of don't pay taxes now—pay taxes later also applies to retirees' spending decisions. Making the correct decisions will have a dramatic impact on your lifestyle and your ability to provide for your family. (Details are spelled out in Chapter 1.)

Figure B

Benefits of Spending After-Tax Savings Before Tax-Deferred Retirement Accounts

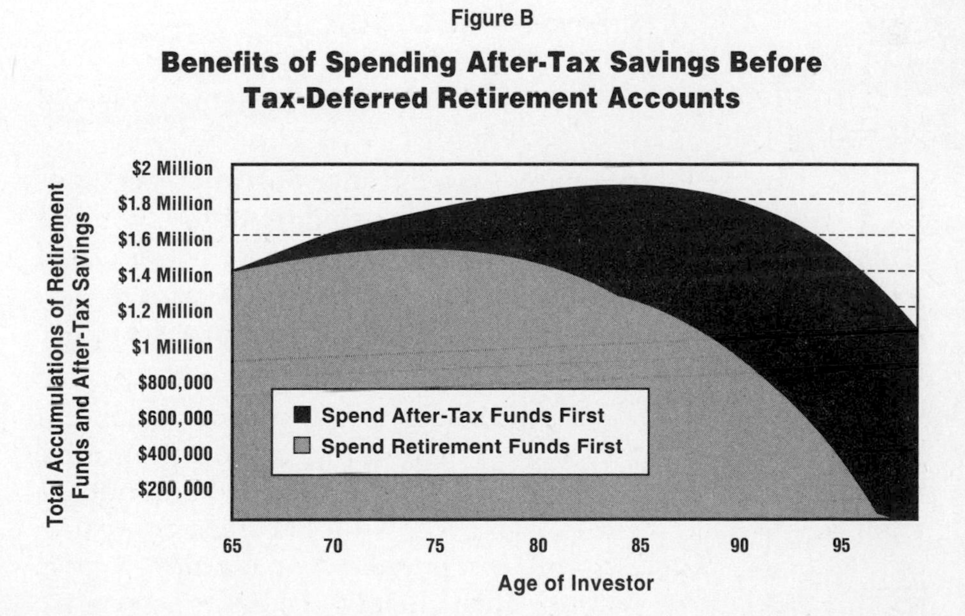

My Best Advice—Read This Book

Whether you do it on your own or hire a professional advisor, pay attention to your investments and develop an appropriate portfolio. Also, please determine a safe spending or withdrawal rate.

To discover tax-efficient strategies for retirement planning, read this book. Then act on my suggestions, finding professional help when necessary. Subject to a couple of exceptions, which I will identify and explain, don't pay taxes now—pay taxes later and reap the rewards of a richer life. Under most circumstances, you and/or your family will be better off, potentially by millions.

An Outline Overview of the Whole Process

Don't pay taxes now—pay taxes later:

- As you are saving for retirement
- During your retirement
- Through the estate planning process

Here is the lifetime outline:

While still working, that is, during the accumulation stage:

1. Contribute the maximum amount to your retirement plan. (Chapter 1)
2. Allow the account to accumulate tax-deferred while continuing to make new contributions. (Chapter 1)

At retirement, that is, during the distribution stage:

3. First, spend the money on which you have already paid income tax. (Chapter 3)
4. Second, spend any retirement plan or IRA money (tax-deferred or tax-free). (Only make withdrawals from your IRA, etc., after you have exhausted your nonretirement plan assets.) (Chapter 3)

5. At 70½, you will have to take minimum required distributions (MRDs). If you can afford it, take only the minimum required distributions and allow the rest of the account to continue to accumulate tax-deferred. (Chapter 4)

When you are planning for your heirs:

6. Develop an estate plan that continues the tax-deferred status of your IRA or retirement plan long after your death. Some variation of Lange's Cascading Beneficiary Plan™ is probably the best solution for the IRA beneficiary form for most readers. (Chapter 12)

Finally, know when to make an exception to the "pay taxes later" rule. Notable exceptions include:

7. Roth IRAs, Roth 401(k)s and Roth 403(b)s (better than nonmatched 401(k) or 403(b) or traditional IRAs). (Chapter 2)
8. Roth IRA Conversions (often the best move, but violate the spirit of don't pay taxes now—pay taxes later). (Chapter 3)
9. Distributions of IRA and retirement plan money at targeted income tax brackets. (Chapter 3)
10. In large estates, sometimes it does pay to withdraw money from IRAs prematurely to avoid the dreaded combination of estate tax and income tax on the IRA within the estate. (Chapter 9)

That's it in a nutshell, but there is so much more. So, jump on board and enjoy the ride.

What's New for 2006

The Roth 401(k) and Roth 403(b)

The biggest change in the tax law that will have an impact on present workers with existing 401(k) and/or 403(b) plans is the addition of two new types of retirement plans—the Roth 401(k) and the Roth 403(b) plan effective January 1, 2006. True, all the traditional retirement plans have increased contribution limits. Please see page 18 for the increased contribution limits. This means that starting January 1, 2006, employees and even self-employed individuals will be able to contribute more money to their retirement plans. The hot news, however, is the new Roth 401(k) and Roth 403(b).

The following explanation may not be clear before reading the descriptions of the traditional 401(k) and 403(b) and Roth IRA plans. All three of these plans are described in detail in the main body of the book. Therefore, it may make more sense to read about the existing law before reading this section. For those of you who, like me, want to know the changes right now, here they are.

As detailed in *Retire Secure!* employees with either a traditional 401(k) or 403(b) retirement plan have the option of contributing a portion of their salary to these plans. If an employer makes a contribution to the plan, there will be an employer portion (often a match based on the employee's contribution) and an employee portion. I always have and probably always will recommend contributing to your retirement plan whatever an employer will match. Traditionally I also recommended employees contribute as much to their 401(k) or 403(b) plan as they can afford and are allowed to contribute.

The one exception I made for this recommendation for reasons detailed in *Retire Secure!*, is I generally preferred Roth IRAs to contributions to a deductible 401(k) or 403(b) plan that is not matched by the employer. This preference for Roth IRAs to nonmatched traditional 401(k)s and the reasons for my preference for Roth IRAs are well documented in the main body of text. If there are sufficient funds to allow a Roth IRA contribution and the maximum 401(k) contribution, I generally recommended making both a Roth contribution and the maximum 401(k) contribution.

The new Roth 401(k) and Roth 403(b) plan is really a hybrid between the traditional 401(k) or 403(b) and the Roth IRA. That is, an employer that now offers a 401(k) plan or a 403(b) plan could choose to expand the options it gives its employees to include a Roth 401(k) or Roth 403(b) contribution that will be taxed like a Roth IRA.

This change provides an unprecedented ability for employees to expand or, in some cases, begin their tax-free investments. The new 401(k) and 403(b) employee contribution limits will go up to $15,000 (or $20,000 if you are 50 or older) per year. The same contribution limits apply to the Roth 401(k) and the Roth 403(b) plans. It is important to note that the *total* employee contribution limit will be $20,000 in 2006 if you are 50 or older. In other words, you cannot make a $20,000 contribution to the traditional portion of the 401(k) plan and a $20,000 contribution to the Roth portion of the 401(k) plan. If you take my advice and contribute to a Roth 401(k) or Roth 403(b) your contributions and the growth on those contributions will not be subject to income tax.

Perhaps an example will clarify: Joe, a prudent 50-year-old employee, is a participant in his company's 401(k) plan. He has dutifully contributed the maximum allowable contribution to his 401(k) plan since he started working. Until he heard about the new Roth 401(k), his expectation was to continue contributing the maximum into his 401(k) for 2006 and beyond.

Now, Joe has a choice. He could continue making his regular deductible 401(k) contribution (which has increased to $20,000 for 2006), elect to make a $20,000 contribution to the new Roth 401(k), or split his $20,000 contribution between the regular

401(k) portion and the Roth 401(k) portion of the plan. His decision will not have an impact on the employer's contribution, either by amount or the way the employer's contribution is taxed.

With Joe's contribution, however, there is a fundamental difference in the way his traditional 401(k) is taxed and the way his new Roth 401(k) is taxed. The new Roth 401(k) is basically taxed like a Roth IRA. That is, Joe will not get a tax deduction for making the contribution to the Roth 401(k), but the Roth 401(k) portion will grow income tax-free. With the traditional 401(k), Joe would get an income tax deduction for his contribution to the 401(k). However, after Joe retires and takes a distribution from his traditional 401(k), he will have to pay income taxes on that distribution. When Joe takes a distribution from his Roth 401(k) portion of the account, he will not have to pay income taxes. In the main body of the book, I analyze and compare the traditional retirement plan with the Roth IRA. The Roth IRA almost always comes out on top. For the same reasons that I prefer a Roth IRA to a traditional IRA, I prefer a Roth 401(k) and Roth 403(b) to a traditional 401(k) and 403(b).

Please note that I make this recommendation knowing full well it is a contradiction to the subtitle of the book—*Pay Taxes Later*. With a traditional retirement plan, you get a tax deduction now and pay taxes later. This is good. With the Roth, you don't get a tax deduction now but you don't have to pay tax later. This is better. Perhaps it would have been more accurate, though less appealing, to have the subtitle read *Pay Taxes Later, Except for a Roth.*

Now back to Joe. Assuming Joe takes my advice and switches his new 401(k) contributions to the Roth 401(k) portion of the plan, he will have three components of his 401(k) plan at work. He will have the employer's portion of the plan that remains unchanged. He will have his own (the employee's) traditional portion of the plan, which consists of all his previous contributions plus the interest, dividends, and appreciation on those contributions. Then, starting in 2006, he will have a Roth 401(k) portion.

If Joe is married and his adjusted gross income is less than $150,000, then he may have already been making contributions to a Roth IRA outside of his employer's retirement plan. As long as Joe is working, the Roth 401(k) will remain separate from any Roth IRA he may have outside of his employer's plan. If his adjusted gross income was more than $160,000, he was not eligible to make any Roth IRA contribution, but he will be eligible for a Roth 401(k) for $20,000. Thus high-income earners will now be offered their first entrée into the tax-free world of the Roth, but it will be in the form of a Roth 401(k) or a Roth 403(b).

Married taxpayers with earned income and adjusted gross incomes of less than $150,000 have been eligible to make maximum Roth IRA contributions outside of their employer's retirement plan. The maximum contribution for 2006 is $4,000 for employees under 50 and $5,000 for employees 50 and older. What is much different for these employees that were able to make some contributions to the tax-free Roth IRA is that the amount of money that they will be allowed to contribute into the income-tax-free world via the Roth 401(k) or 403(b). These taxpayers could still contribute $4,000 or $5,000 to a Roth IRA outside of work and $15,000 or $20,000 to the Roth 401(k) plan at work.

This tax change could dramatically increase your tax-free wealth. Subject to a few exceptions contained in the book, if you have access to a Roth 401(k) or Roth 403(b), I highly recommend you take advantage of that option and if you can afford it, contribute the maximum.

Notice, however, there is a caveat. I said "if you have access." Though Congress has now created these Roth 401(k)s and Roth 403(b)s, that doesn't mean your employer will adopt these plans. Before, a retirement plan administrator only had to keep track of the employer's portion and the employee's portion. Now, the administrator must keep track of the employer's portion, the traditional employee's portion, and the employee's Roth portion.

The additional cost of changing the terms of the retirement plan should not be significant. The cost of the extra accounting should also not be too significant. Many smaller employers may choose never to offer employees the Roth 401(k) or Roth 403(b) options. Many other employers will eventually offer Roth 401(k)s and Roth 403(b)s, but will not do so immediately. You may have to wait until 2007 or 2008 for your employer to adopt the changes.

If you are an employee who is not given the option of a Roth 401(k) or Roth 403(b), I would gently (or not so gently depending on your personality and the office politics) suggest your employer adopt the Roth 401(k) or Roth 403(b) plan and allow you to participate.

If you are a retirement plan administrator or business owner, and if you have not already considered implementing a Roth 401(k) or Roth 403(b), I would strongly consider it.

For most readers, however, the expansion or entrée into the tax-free world with Roth 401(k)s and Roth 403(b)s will be one of the best things you can do for yourself and your family.

Please see the back of the book for the free report: *Save $20,000/Year Tax-Free Using the New Roth 401(k).*

For Tax Years after 2009 Roth IRA Conversions Will Be Open to All IRA Owners Regardless of Income

The May 17, 2006 tax act, the *Tax Increase Prevention and Reconciliation Act* (TIPRA) presents wealthy Americans with an outstanding lifetime-and-beyond tax break. TIPRA extends the favorable capital gains rate and dividends rate of 15% from 2008 through 2010. It also gives 15.3 million taxpayers a small break on the alternative minimum tax for tax year 2006. The law raises taxes by expanding the kiddie tax provisions to include 14-17 year old children. Those changes, however, pale in comparison to the new provision regarding Roth IRA conversions. In 2010, wealthy Americans will be granted a wonderful, new opportunity. They will, for the first time, qualify for a Roth IRA conversion regardless of their income.

Previously, taxpayers with a modified adjusted gross income of $100,000 (or more) were not permitted to make Roth IRA conversions. The compelling reason to pay attention to the change is that individual IRA owners who have modified adjusted gross incomes of more than $100,000 can enjoy a huge, potential windfall by taking advantage of the opportunity to convert their traditional IRA to a Roth IRA.

The Roth IRA Changes in a Nutshell

For tax years after 2009, the Tax Reconciliation Act permits all taxpayers to make Roth IRA conversions, *regardless of income level*. If you make the Roth IRA conversion in 2010 you will be given the option to pay all the taxes on the conversion in 2010, or average the taxes owed on the conversion over two years, i.e., in 2011 and 2012. However, it is important to be aware that 2010 is the last year for the current low income tax rates. Current law provides for an increase in tax rates in 2011, therefore, if you were to choose to average your tax payments over the two year period, in 2011 and 2012, you might be hit with higher tax rates.

What Happens when You Make a Roth IRA Conversion?

When you make a Roth IRA conversion, you pay income tax on the amount you choose to convert. When you take advantage of this provision, you will pay income taxes "now" on all or a portion of your traditional IRA.

While my standard advice "to pay taxes later" still represents my strongest recommendation for successful long-term planning, I have always made a "philosophical exception" for Roth IRAs. With respect to Roth IRA conversions, the better advice for many individuals and their families is pay taxes now. While each case will benefit from an individualized analysis on the merits of the conversion, the critical feature of the Roth is that, once the initial taxes are paid on the conversion and other technical requirements are met, income taxes will never be due on its growth, capital gains, dividends, interest, etc. or for withdrawals of principle. This will be particularly advantageous to high-income taxpayers.

For the very high income family, the benefit of a Roth IRA conversion is potentially phenomenal. An estimate is that a taxpayer's family could benefit by as much as twice the amount converted. That is an estimate of the potential long-term benefit of making a Roth IRA conversion.

Here is a simple example: Assume you are in the top tax bracket of 35% (earning well over $100,000) and you have $1,000,000 in your IRA. Previously, you were not allowed to make a Roth IRA conversion. Under TIPRA you can make a Roth IRA conversion. If we assess the advantage of the $1,000,000 conversion, measured in purchasing power, you would be $517,298 better off in 20 years. However, in today's dollars, as adjusted for 3% annual inflation, this advantage is $286,416. If you don't spend your Roth IRA and leave it to your children, who spend it modestly using the previous assumption, they will be better off by $11,742,363 in their lifetime. Making the comparison in terms of today's dollars, this advantage translates into $2,000,000 for the child by the time he or she turns 85. This advantage is about twice the original amount converted. Clearly the potential advantages are significant, and for wealthy individuals, the legacy advantage of the Roth is difficult to beat.

The assumptions used in this simple analysis are as follows:

- All funds are invested and grow annually at the rate of 7%.
- Ordinary income tax rates are the maximum 35% for the owner and beneficiary.
- Half of the annual growth of after-tax funds is taxed at an estimated long-term capital gains rate of 19% for federal and 3% for state.
- Half of the annual growth of after-tax funds is taxed at the ordinary income tax rates of 35% for federal and 3% for state.
- During the owner's lifetime, the traditional IRA minimum required distributions are taxed at the ordinary federal rate of 35% and the balance is reinvested in the after-tax funds. These IRA distributions are not subject to state income taxes.
- The original owner converts his IRA at age 60 and dies at age 80. The benficiary inherits all funds at age 95. No

federal estate taxes or state inheritance taxes are taken in to account.
- The beneficiary inherits all funds at age 45. No federal taxes or state inheritance taxes are taken into account.
- The beneficiary is taxed annually on the traditional IRA minimum required distributions at ordinary rates and the balance is spent.
- Under the Roth conversion alternative, the beneficiary withdraws the minimum required distributions tax free, spends the same amount as under the traditional IRA alternative, and reinvests the difference in after-tax funds.
- The owner starts with a balance of $1,000,000 in an IRA and $350,000 of after-tax funds so that in the conversion alternative, the taxes on the conversion can be paid in full.
- In the following graphs, we have shown the net balances after allowances for income taxes and future inflation of 3% per year, so that the differences can be measured in spending power in today's dollars.

How much better off are you during your lifetime? Assuming you have the funds to pay the income tax on the Roth IRA conversion from money outside of the IRA, if you convert $1,000,000 today, then in 20 years, you are $286,416 ahead in today's dollars. In 30 years, you are $725,616 ahead. See Figure C (on the following page).

But, then please consider the scenario for the beneficiary. If you die 20 years after you make the conversion and you opt to leave the Roth IRA to your 45-year-old child, how much better off is your child? See Figure D (on the following page).

By age 85, he is $11,742,363 better off in actual dollars or $1,993,067 in today's dollars, as adjusted for 3% inflation. To be fair, that is in future dollars.

This example is simple so that the potential advantages can be easily quantified. There are many factors that should be taken into account in your own situation that may make the Roth IRA conversion more or less advantageous to you than in this example. In addition, there are risks inherent in this long-term analysis that may reduce the

Figure C
Should You Convert?
High Income Taxpayer

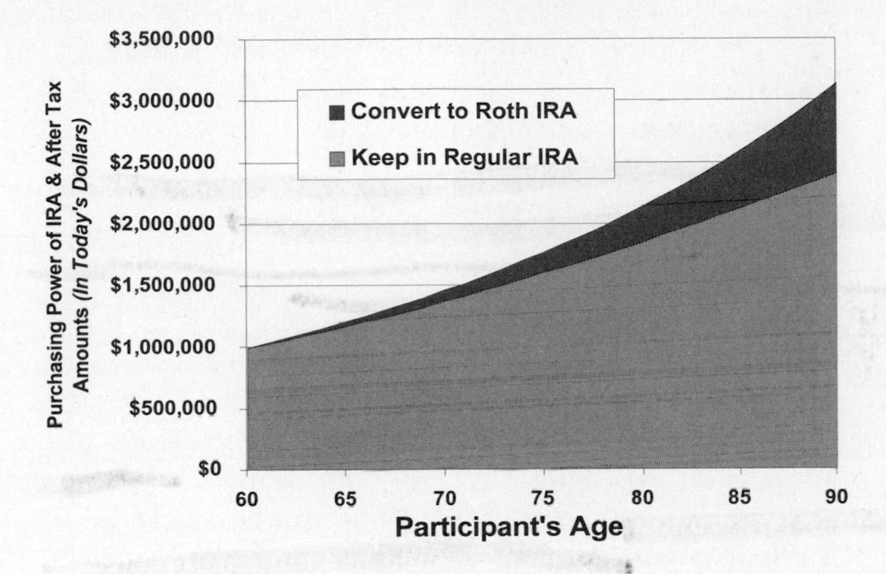

Figure D
Roth IRA Advantage to Child Beneficiary

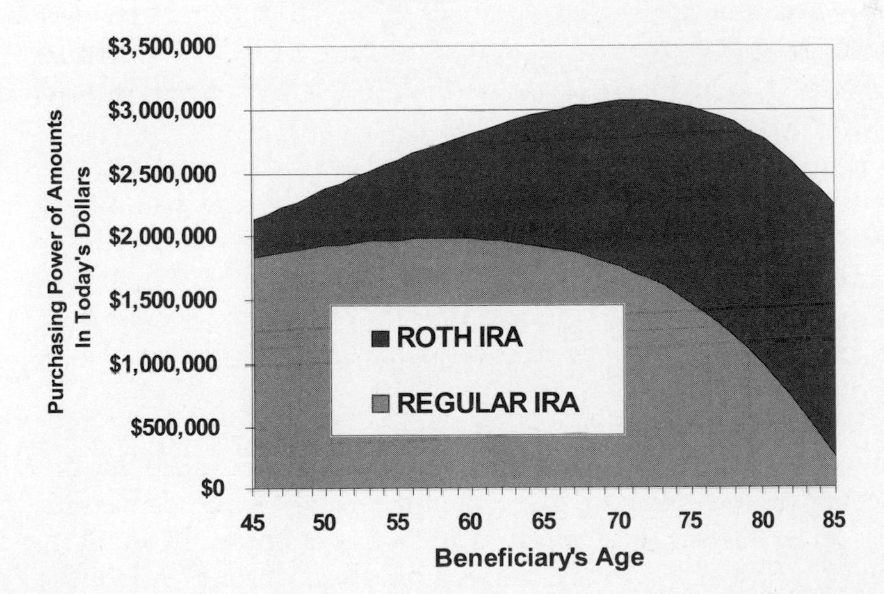

potential advantages. However, there are also unknown future events that may make the conversion even more valuable than shown.

Important Roth IRA Conversion Considerations

Please keep in mind this is not an all or nothing proposition. You can make a Roth IRA conversion of a portion of your IRA. We generally recommend a partial conversion or multiple smaller conversions over an extended time frame.

Remember, making the conversion does require paying taxes on the amount you convert to a Roth IRA. To make matters worse, the income from the conversion is added to your current taxable income. This means you pay income tax on the Roth IRA conversion in your current income tax bracket, but if you convert an amount in excess of the top of your current income tax bracket, you will have to pay income taxes at the higher tax rate. The optimal amount to convert, (a full analysis of this topic is beyond the scope of this chapter) is often estimated by how much more taxable income you could have at your current marginal tax rate. That amount then reflects the amount you should convert from your IRA to a Roth IRA—without the risk of jumping to a higher tax bracket. Keep in mind that there are many other factors to consider beyond your current tax rate, not the least of which is your future tax rates. These are the rates of tax you (and potentially your heirs) would have paid on your IRA if you had not counted it.

But, even taking into account the additional taxes due on the conversion, even if they are potentially at a higher rate, the conversion can provide dramatic increase in long-term benefits to your family.

Please note that I used a high conversion amount and a high income tax rate for this example because the new law opens the doors for taxpayers with incomes of over $100,000. That doesn't mean the Roth IRA conversion isn't a great deal for taxpayers with incomes of less than $100,000 or less than $1,000,000 to convert. However, for a family that is always in the top tax bracket, the conversion is taxed at a rate that is no higher than the normal tax rate.

The math in the previous analysis is not in and of itself controversial. It is a straight forward and intellectually honest attempt using relatively reasonable assumptions to measure the results of two identically situated taxpayers with this one difference: one makes a Roth IRA conversion and the other does not. There are many assumptions in this case example that may be appropriate in your own individual case, however. Your potential benefits maybe more or less than in this example.

Even though a simple analysis such as this shows potential advantages there are still plenty of financial advisors who say that making a Roth IRA conversion is a bad idea, especially for older IRA owners. With all due respect to these advisors, I would ask if they had ever "run the numbers." The results speak for themselves. It may or may not be appropriate for the owner and their families.

Wait, the nay-sayers scream. What if they change the tax law? Let's examine that possibility because that is everyone's greatest fear and, perhaps, the greatest threat to the potential long term benefit of making a Roth IRA conversion.

- True, they can eliminate Roth IRAs and Roth IRA conversions, but I think grandfathering legislation would be passed to protect taxpayers who have already made the conversion.
- They could also reduce or eliminate the income tax. If they do, the conversion, in retrospect, will reduce the conversion's value and possibly prove it to have been a mistake.
- Likewise, they could reduce or eliminate income taxes on traditional IRA withdrawals. This also would work against the Roth conversions.
- They may also reduce or eliminate income taxes on after-tax investment income. This will reduce or minimize the conversion advantages.
- They could attempt to indirectly tax Roth IRAs by making them preference items for the alternative minimum tax. That might change the math some, but I am willing to take that chance.

What I see as *more likely* than anything I have mentioned so far is the prospect of *higher* tax rates in the future. If for no other reason, the government will have to make up the taxes they will not receive from readers who take my advice and make the Roth IRA conversion and enjoy 60 years of tax-free growth!

Imagine this scenario: You make a Roth IRA conversion in 2010 when the highest tax rate is 35%. Down the line, maybe not even until your children are the beneficiaries of your Roth, the tax rate has jumped to 50% or even 70%. Think how grateful your children will be when they are withdrawing those funds tax-free, and everyone else is paying 50-70% tax on their inherited IRAs.

If I were an individual making more than $100,000, who previously did not have this opportunity for a Roth conversion, I would be starting to think ahead to determine if a Roth IRA conversion in 2010 will be advantageous for me and my family. And if so, how much of my traditional IRA I should convert to a Roth IRA and when I should do it.

Will Making a Roth IRA Conversion Stop the Required Minimum Distribution Rules of a Regular IRA when I Reach 70½?

There *are no* minimum required distribution rules for Roth IRAs for either the Roth IRA owner or the surviving spouse of the Roth IRA owner. If the Roth IRA is then left to a non-spousal heir, the heir will have to take required minimum distributions, but the distributions will *still be* income tax free. That is quite a boon to the child who inherits a Roth IRA.

There is no doubt that individuals should be keeping Roth IRA conversions on their radar screen. Advance planning and strategizing should be on your agenda.

Please see the back of the book to order your free CD: *The Secrets to a Secure Retirement* as well as the special report which will have more information on opportunities created with the new Roth IRA conversion provisions.

THE ACCUMULATION YEARS

The Best Way to Save for Retirement

Fund Retirement Plans to the Maximum

The most powerful force in the universe is compound interest.
— Albert Einstein

Main Topics

- Why contributing the maximum to a retirement plan is so valuable
- The clear advantage of pre-tax IRA and retirement plan savings
- Why you ***must*** always contribute to plans with employer-matching
- The two principal categories of retirement plans
- Eight major types of retirement plans and their contribution limits
- Running the numbers for an employer matching program
- Nonmatched contributions
- Tax-deferred accumulations versus after-tax accumulations
- Options for contributing to more than one plan
- Making contributions when you think you can't afford it

KEY IDEA

Every employee who has access to a retirement plan should contribute the maximum his or her employer is willing to match or even partially match. If you can afford more, make nonmatched contributions.

Why Contributing the Maximum to a Retirement Plan Is So Valuable

A trusted client of mine recently referred to me as "her guardian angel." At first I was totally taken aback—no one had ever called me their guardian angel before. She continued, "Twenty years ago you advised me to put the maximum into my retirement plan. I didn't know if it was a good idea or not but I trusted you and did what you recommended. Now I have a million dollars in my retirement plan. What should I do now?"

Her question is ultimately answered by this book. But her comment also compelled me to complete a comprehensive analysis of why it was such good advice. I wanted to be able to persuasively convince anyone who harbored the least little doubt about the advantages of saving in a retirement plan over saving outside of a retirement plan.

I set myself the challenge of evaluating the outcomes of two different scenarios:

1. You earn the money, you pay the tax, you invest the money you earned, and you pay tax on the dividends and interest, perhaps capital gains.
2. You put money in your retirement plan and you get a tax deduction. Looked at another way, you don't pay income taxes on that money when you invest it. The money grows tax deferred. You don't have to pay taxes on that money until you take it out.

The first question is: is it better to save inside the retirement plan or outside the retirement plan? The answer: it is better to save within the retirement plan. Why? This isn't a touchy-feely issue. It comes down to numbers. Let's look.

MINI CASE STUDY 1.1

The Clear Advantage of Pre-Tax IRA and Retirement Plan Savings

Mr. Pay Taxes Later and Mr. Pay Taxes Now are neighbors. Looking at them from the outside, you wouldn't be able to tell them apart. They own the same type of car; their salaries are the same; and they are in the same tax bracket. Their savings have the same investment rate of return. They even save the same percentage of their gross wages every year.

They have one big difference. Mr. Pay Taxes Later invests as much as he can afford in his tax-deferred retirement plan, his 401(k), even though his employer does not match his contributions. Mr. Pay Taxes Now feels that putting money in a retirement account makes it "not really his money," as he puts it. He doesn't want to have to pay taxes to take out his own money, or put up with the other limits to his access of "his money." Thus he contributes nothing to his retirement account at work but invests his savings in an account outside of his retirement plan. Mr. Pay Taxes Now invests the old-fashioned way: earn the money, pay the tax, invest the money, and pay the tax on the income that the invested money generates (dividends, capital gains, etc.).

Both men begin investing at age 30.

- They start saving in 2005 with $5,000 per year of their earnings, indexed for inflation.
- Mr. Pay Taxes Later has his entire $5,000 withheld from his paycheck and deposited to his tax-deferred 401(k). (The analysis would be identical if he contributed the money to a traditional IRA.)

- Mr. Pay Taxes Now chooses not to have any retirement funds withheld but rather to be paid in full. He has to pay income taxes on his full wages, including the $5,000 he chose not to contribute to his retirement plan. He has to pay income tax immediately on the $5,000. After the 25% income tax is paid, he has only 75% of the $5,000, or $3,750, left to invest.

Now, look at Figure 1.1. Mr. Pay Taxes Later's investment is represented by the gray curve, and Mr. Pay Taxes Now's by the black. Look at the dramatic difference, over time, in the accumulations.

Figure 1.1

Retirement Assets, IRAs, etc. versus After-Tax Accumulations

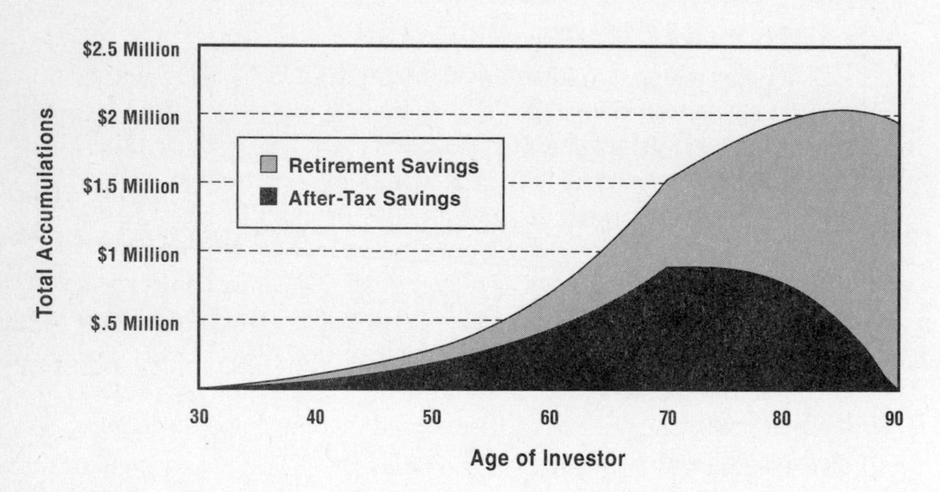

The assumptions for this graph include the following:

1. Investment rate of return is 7% including 70% capital appreciation, with 15% portfolio turnover rate, 15% dividend income, and 15% interest income.

2. Mr. Pay Taxes Later makes retirement savings contributions of $5,000 per year. Mr. Pay Taxes Now invests 25% less due to taxes. Both amounts are indexed for 2.5% annual raises, starting at age 30, until age 70.

3. Starting at age 71, spending from both investors' accounts is equal to the Minimum Required Distributions (MRD) from Mr. Pay Taxes Later's retirement plan.
4. Mr. Pay Taxes Later withdraws and spends only the minimum required distribution (MRD) and pays 25% income tax due on his distribution. Mr. Pay Taxes Now spends the same amount plus pays income taxes due on his interest, dividends, and realized capital gains.
5. Ordinary tax rates are 25%.
6. Capital gains tax rates are 15% for 2005 to 2008 and 19% thereafter.
7. Dividends are taxed as capital gains during 2005 to 2008 and as ordinary income thereafter.

Now, to be fair, Mr. Pay Taxes Later will have to pay the taxes eventually. When he is retired, for every dollar he wants to withdraw, he has to take out $1.33. He pockets the dollar and pays $0.33 in taxes (25% of $1.33). If Mr. Pay Taxes Now withdraws a dollar, subject to some capital gains taxes, it's all his, just as he wanted. At age 90, however, Mr. Pay Taxes Now has depleted his funds entirely while Mr. Pay Taxes Later has $1,946,949 left in his retirement plan.

... all things being equal, following the adage "don't pay taxes now—pay taxes later" can be worth almost $2 million over a lifetime.

Given reasonable assumptions and all things being equal, following the adage "don't pay taxes now—pay taxes later" can be worth almost $2 million over a lifetime.

Make Those Non-Matched Contributions to Retirement Accounts

What conclusion can we draw from Mini Case Study 1.1? Don't pay taxes now—pay taxes later. Even putting aside the additional advantage of matching contributions, you should contribute the maximum to your retirement plan, assuming you can afford

After spending your life working hard, paying the mortgage, paying the bills, raising a family, and putting your kids through college, you may never have expected to have such a substantial IRA or retirement plan and be so well off in retirement. To many of my clients, it seems like a fantasy.

A realistic and common emotional reaction is fear. It could be fear of the unknown, or fear because you're not sure what to do next. Many readers are scared they will make costly mistakes and/or mismanage their retirement money. The fear is paralyzing, so they do nothing—literally, nothing. They procrastinate, and avoid doing important planning for their IRA and retirement plan. That may have been you till now.

You have already made a great start by buying this book. Now, please read it and know that I have done everything in my power to provide you with the best information available on planning for your IRA and/or retirement plan. After all, your future and your financial security depend on you handling your retirement finances properly. After reading this book, *don't do nothing*. Promise yourself that reading this book will be more than an academic exercise, it will motivate you to take action—take the critical steps that will put you and your family in a much better position than you are in today.

it. Money contributed to a retirement plan, whether a 401(k), 403(b) SEP, SIMPLE, 457, deductible IRA, or another type of retirement plan, is a pre-tax investment that grows tax-deferred. There are no federal income taxes on the wages contributed. Some taxpayers look at it as a deduction. Either way you look at it, you are getting a tax break for the amount of the contribution multiplied by the tax rate for your tax bracket. In addition, once the contribution is made, you do not have to pay income taxes on the interest, dividends, and appreciation *until you take a distribution* (i.e., withdrawal) from the retirement plan. In other words, you pay taxes later.

In my practice the clients who usually have the most money saved at retirement are the ones that religiously contributed to a retirement plan during their long career.

By not paying the taxes up front on the wages earned, you reap the harvest of compounding interest on the money that would have gone to paying taxes—both on the amount contributed and on the growth had the money been invested outside of the retirement plan.

In the real world, not only is there a tax advantage to saving in a retirement plan, but there is the built-in discipline of contributing to your retirement plan every paycheck. The example above assumes that if you don't put the money in your retirement plan, then you will save and invest an amount equivalent to your contribution. But can you trust yourself to be a disciplined saver? Will the temptation to put it off till the next paycheck undermine your resolve? Even if it is put away for savings, knowing you have unrestricted access to the money, can you be confident that you would never invade that fund until you retire?

In my practice, the clients who usually have the most money saved at retirement are the ones who religiously contributed to a retirement plan during their long career.

The idea of paying taxes later and contributing the maximum to your retirement plan(s) is something that I have preached for over 20 years. Many of my long-standing clients took my advice 20 years ago—even if they didn't completely understand why—and now they are thanking me.

The Employer Matching Retirement Plan

With all due respect, broadly speaking, you have to be pretty "simple" (that's a nice word for "stupid") not to take advantage of a retirement plan where the employer is making a matching contribution.

The Cardinal Rule of Saving for Retirement

Money won is twice as sweet as money earned.

— Paul Newman, *The Color of Money*

If your employer offers a matching contribution to your retirement plan, the cardinal rule is: contribute whatever the employer is willing to match—even if it is only a percentage of your contribution and not a dollar for dollar match.

Imagine depositing $1,000 of your money into the bank, but instead of getting a crummy toaster, you receive an extra $1,000 to go along with your deposit. To add to the fun, imagine getting a tax deduction for your deposit and not having to pay tax on your "gift." Furthermore, both your $1,000 and the gift $1,000 grow (it is to be hoped), and you don't have to pay income tax on the interest, dividends, capital gains, or the appreciation until you withdraw the money. When you withdraw the money, you will have to pay taxes, but you will have gained interest, dividends, and appreciation in the meantime. That is what employer matching contributions to retirement plans are all about. If the employer matches the employee contribution, it offers a *100% return on the investment in one day* (assuming no early withdrawal penalties apply and the matched funds are fully vested).

Over the years, I have heard hundreds of excuses for not taking advantage of an employer-matching plan. All those reasons can be summarized in two words: ignorance and neglect. If you didn't know that before, you know now. If you are not currently taking advantage of your employer-matching plan, run—don't walk—to your plan administrator and begin the paperwork to take advantage of the employer match. Matching contributions are most commonly found within Section 401(k), 403(b), and 457 plans. Many eligible 403(b) plan participants also may have access to a 457 plan. You can, in effect, enjoy "double" the ability to tax defer earnings through participation in both the 403(b) and 457 plans. Even if your employer is only willing to make a partial match up to a cap, you should still take advantage of this opportunity. For example, a fairly common retirement plan may provide that the employer contribute 50 cents for every dollar up to the first 6% of salary you contribute. Keep in mind: this is free money!

Many eligible 403(b) plan participants also may have access to a 457 plan. You can, in effect, enjoy "double" the ability to tax defer earnings through participation in both the 403(b) and 457 plans.

Again, this isn't touchy-feely stuff. It is backed by hard numbers.

MINI CASE STUDY 1.2

Running the Numbers for Employer-Matched Retirement Plans

Scenario 1

- Bill earns $75,000 per year and is subject to a flat 25% federal income tax (for simplicity, I ignore other taxes and assume a flat federal income tax).
  25% × $75,000 = $18,750 tax

- He spends $50,000 per year.
- He doesn't use his retirement plan at work, so he has $6,250 available for investment:
  ($75,000 income – [$18,750 tax and $50,000 spending] = $6,250 available cash).

Scenario 2

Bill's dad is very wise. He bought *Retire Secure!* After reading this chapter, he advises his son Bill to contribute the maximum amount that Bill's employer is willing to match. Uncharacteristically, Bill listens to his dad and contributes $4,500 (6% times $75,000) to his retirement account. Bill is fortunate because his employer matches his contribution 100%. Thus $9,000 goes into his retirement account.

Under current tax laws, Bill will not have to pay federal income tax on his retirement plan contribution or on the amount his employer is willing to match.

By using his employer's retirement plan, Bill's picture changes for the better as follows:

- Bill pays tax only on $70,500
  ($75,000 income – $4,500 tax-deferred)
  25% × $70,500 = $17,625 tax.
- He now has $57,375 ($75,000 income – $17,625 taxes).
- He makes his 6% contribution of $4,500, leaving him with $52,875 outside the plan.
- His employer matches the $4,500 (also tax deferred).
- He now has $9,000 in his retirement plan (growing tax deferred).
- He spends $50,000 per year.
- He is left with $2,875 in cash.

Which scenario strikes you as more favorable: Scenario 2 with $9,000 in a retirement plan and $2,875 in cash, or Scenario 1 with no retirement plan and $6,250 in cash? The heckler can figure out situations why he may prefer a little extra cash and no retirement plan. For the rest of us, we will take advantage of any employer matching retirement plan.

Please remember that the money in the retirement plan will continue to grow, and you will not have to pay income taxes on the earnings, dividends, interest, or accumulations until you or your heirs withdraw your money. Even without the future deferral, at the end of the first year, assuming the employer-matched funds are fully vested, the comparative values of these two scenarios are measured by after-tax purchasing power as follows:

	Scenario 1	Scenario 2
After-tax cash available	$6,250	$2,875
Retirement plan balance	0	$9,000
Tax on retirement plan balance	0	($2,250)
Early withdrawal penalty	0	($900)
Total Purchasing Power	$6,250	$8,725

Obviously, it is better to take advantage of the retirement plan and the employer's matching contributions. Let's hope you can afford to do this and maintain the tax-deferred growth for many years, thus avoiding early withdrawal penalties altogether.

There is an interesting option if you want to see your child's retirement plan grow, but your child claims not to have sufficient cash flow to contribute to his retirement plan, even though his employer is matching 100%. You may consider making a gift to your child in the amount that your child would be out of pocket by making a contribution to his retirement plan. In this example, you could make a gift of $3,365 ($6,250 – $2,875).

For your $3,365 gift, your adult child would end up with $9,000 in his retirement plan. That is an example of a leveraged gift. Lots of bang for your gifted buck.

The long-term advantages of the employer match are even more dramatic. Using the same facts and circumstances as in Mini Case Study 1.1 with the addition of a 100% employer match of annual contributions, Figure 1.2 compares stubborn Bill who refuses to use the retirement plan versus compliant Bill who contributes to his retirement plan:

Figure 1.2

Retirement Assets Plus an Employer Match versus After-Tax Accumulations

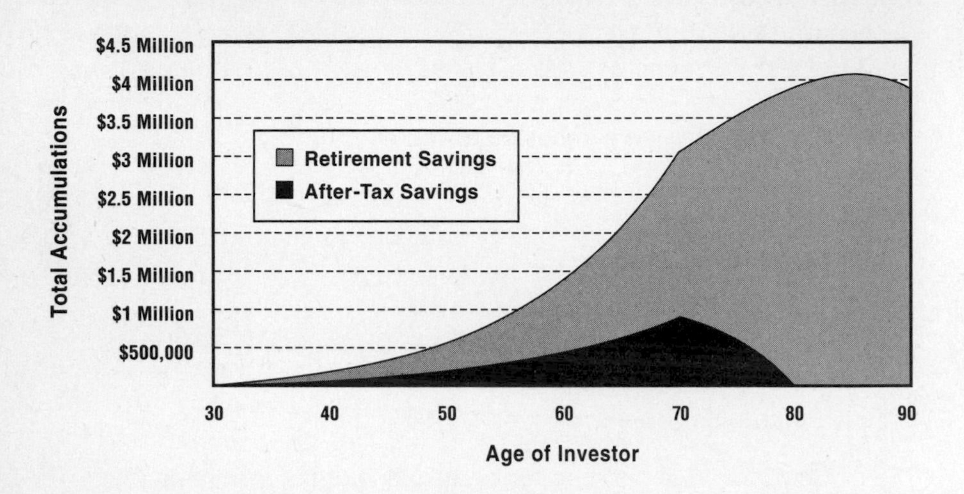

Figure 1.2 reflects higher spending from both accounts since the retirement plan's larger balance requires larger distributions. The higher distributions deplete stubborn Bill's unmatched funds even faster. He would run out at age 80 instead of 90 (in Mini Case Study 1.1), while compliant Bill' s matched retirement savings has $3,908,093 remaining, and despite the large distributions being made after age 80, compliant Bill's savings are still growing when he reaches 80. The obvious conclusion again is, if you are not already taking advantage of this, run—don't walk—to your plan administrator and begin the paperwork to take advantage of the employer match.

Occasionally, clients moan that they literally can't afford to make the contribution, even though their employer is willing to match it. I am not sympathetic. I would rather see you borrow the money to make matching contributions, especially if a home equity line of credit is available where the interest is tax deductible.

Two Categories of Retirement Plans

Generally all retirement plans in the workplace fall into two categories: defined-contribution plans and defined-benefit plans. The plan in the previous example is a defined-contribution plan.

Defined-Contribution Plans

In a defined-contribution plan, each individual employee has an account that can be funded by the employee or the employer or both. At retirement or termination of employment, subject to a few minor exceptions, the account balance represents the funds available to the employee. In a defined-contribution plan, the employee bears the investment risks. In other words, if the market takes a downturn, so does the value of your investments. Conversely if the market does well, you are rewarded with a higher balance.

The most common defined-contribution plans are 401(k) plans, 403(b) plans, and 457 plans. The Roth 401(k) and 403(b) are new options that many employees have for tax-free growth. The Simplified Employee Pension plan (more commonly known as a SEP plan) and the Savings Incentive Match Plans for Employees (more commonly known as SIMPLE plans) are attractive defined-contribution plan options for small employers or self-employed individuals. For self-employed individuals with higher incomes, consider the relatively new, one-man "Super-K," which is basically a 401(k) plan on steroids. More detailed descriptions of these plans appear below.

At retirement or service termination, I usually recommend transferring funds from defined-contribution plans to an individual retirement account (IRA).

Defined-contribution plans often offer a wide array of tax-favored investment options. Defined-contribution plans are relatively easy to understand. Most employees with defined-contribution plans usually can tell you the balance in their account—at least to the nearest $100,000. Most employees with defined-benefit plans have no idea how much their plan is worth.

Common Defined-Contribution Plans

Defined-contribution plan accounts often become substantial and are often the biggest asset in the estate. Typically they are rolled into an IRA at retirement. Therefore the planning for the defined contribution plan, or the IRA that the defined-contribution plan is eventually rolled into, becomes the most important part of the retirement and estate planning process. The following paragraphs discuss some of the more common defined contribution plans.

401(k) Plans: This type of plan usually includes both employee and employer tax-deferred contributions. No federal income taxes are paid until the money is withdrawn. Some states, however, will tax the employee's contribution in the year that the contribution is made. Employer contributions to 401(k)s are usually determined as a percentage of earnings, and the deductible employee contribution is usually limited to a prescribed amount ($20,000 in 2006 for someone 50 or older). The company—that is, the employer—is responsible for providing the employee with investment choices, typically 6 to 10 choices in either one or two families of mutual funds. The employer is also responsible for the investments and administration of a 401(k) plan. Many employers will be implementing Roth 401(k) plans beginning in 2006. The Roth 401(k) combines the features of a Roth IRA and a 401(k). When given a choice, I usually recommend the Roth 401(k).

403(b) Plans: This plan is similar to a 401(k) plan but is commonly used by certain charitable organizations and public educational institutions such as universities, colleges, and hospitals. One of the biggest differences between a 401(k) plan and a 403(b) plan is that 403(b) plans can only invest in annuities and mutual funds. TIAA-CREF is the best known 403(b) provider. The new Roth 403(b) combines the features of a Roth IRA and a 403(b). When given a choice, I usually recommend the Roth 403(b).

457 Plans: After recent changes passed with the Economic Growth and Tax Relief Reconciliation Act of 2001 (EGTRRA), 457 plans have become more similar to 401(k) plans. They are commonly used by state and local governmental employers and certain tax-exempt organizations. Typical 457 employees are policeofficers, firefighters, teachers, and other municipal workers.

An interesting side note is that many eligible 457 plan participants don't even know about the plan. They may have a 403(b) plan and don't know they can in effect enjoy "double" the ability to tax defer earnings through participation in both the 403(b) and 457 plans.

The New Roth 401(k) and 403(b): Starting in 2006 many employers will give employees the option of contributing either into their traditional 401(k) or 403(b) or to a new Roth 401(k) or Roth 403(b). I prefer readers take the Roth option for the same reasons that I prefer a Roth IRA to a traditional IRA. At retirement, a Roth 401(k) or 403(b) can be rolled into a Roth IRA. The Roth 401(k) and 403(b) options apply only to the employee's contribution. Any contributions made by the employer would be put into a traditional 401(k) account.

SEP: SEP is an acronym for Simplified Employee Pension. These plans are commonly used by employers with very few employees and self-employed individuals. Under a SEP, an employer makes contributions to IRAs, which are not taxable for federal income tax purposes, on behalf of employees. Contribution limits are higher with SEPs than with IRAs. Maximum contributions equal 25% of compensation. (You must be careful to look at how "compensation" is defined. After you go through the technical hoops, the contribution actually works out to about 20% of what most self-employed people think is compensation.)

Super-K or One-Man 401(k): The Super-K is commonly used by self-employed individuals (with no employees) who want to contribute the most money possible to their own retirement plan. You can contribute a deferral portion (up to $20,000 in 2006 for someone 50 or older) plus the 25% contribution amount subject to limitations. (As with a SEP plan, be careful to define compensation accurately.) For an example of the power of the Super-K and a calculation, please see Judy's example in Mini Case Study 1.3.

Deferral Contribution Limits

As a result of a series of tax law changes starting with EGTRRA (Economic Growth and Tax Relief Reconciliation Act of 2001), the new deferral contribution limits for employees and owners of many of these individual and defined-contribution plans have grown substantially more generous. The government now allows us to put more money in our retirement plans and provides greater tax benefits. I recommend that we take the government up on its offer to fund our own retirement plans to the extent we can afford it.

The maximum deferral contribution limits since 2005 and through 2008 are as follows:

Maximum Contributions for Individuals Younger than 50

Maximum Contributions for Those 50 and Older (in italics)

	2005	2006	2007	2008
Simple Plans [b]	$10,000	$10,000	$10,000 [a]	$10,000 [a]
50 and older	*12,000*	*12,500*	*12,500* [a]	*12,500* [a]
401(k), 403(b), 457 [c]	$14,000	$15,000	$15,000 [a]	$15,000 [a]
50 and older	*18,000*	*20,000*	*20,000* [a]	*20,000* [a]
Roth 401(k) + Roth 403(b)	N/A	$15,000	$15,000 [a]	$15,000 [a]
50 and older		*20,000*	*20,000* [a]	*20,000* [a]
Super K [d]	$56,000	$59,000	$59,000 [e]	$59,000 [e]
50 and older	60,000	64,000	64,000 [e]	64,000 [e]

[a] Plus inflation adjustment in $500 increments.

[b] SIMPLE Plans are for enterprises with 100 or fewer workers.

[c] 403(b) plans are for nonprofits; 457 plans are for governments and nonprofits. In the last three years before retirement, workers in 457 plans can save double the "under age 50" contribution limit.

[d] Wages (for corporations) must be at least:

$168,000 $176,000 $176,000 [e] $176,000 [e]

or Schedule C Net income (for sole proprietors) must be at least:

$218,506 $229,163 $229,163 [e] $229,163 [e]

[e] Plus amounts for inflation related adjustments.

Please note that with the exception of the Roth 401(k) and Roth 403(b), every one of the listed retirement plans works basically the same way. Subject to limitations, the participant in each plan receives a tax deduction on the contribution to the plan. The employer's contribution is not subject to federal income taxes, nor is the employee's deferral contribution. The employee pays no federal income tax until the funds are withdrawn; funds can only be withdrawn according to specific rules and regulations. Ultimately the distributions are taxed at ordinary income tax rates. These plans offer tax-deferred growth because as the assets appreciate, taxes are deferred—or delayed—until there is a withdrawal or a distribution.

Please note that the taxation of retirement plans differs for state income tax purposes. Some states, such as Pennsylvania, will not give employees a tax deduction for the contribution to their retirement plan. On the other hand, Pennsylvania doesn't tax IRA or retirement plan distributions. Other states will give you a state income tax deduction for a contribution, but will require you to pay income tax on the distribution.

The employee's contributions to Roth 401(k) and Roth 403(b) plans are similar to Roth IRAs in many respects. Just as with a Roth IRA, the participant does not receive a tax deduction on their contributions to the plan. Instead, the employee pays the federal and state taxes up front and their investments grow tax free. As long as the employee does not make a withdrawal during the first five years, there will not be any taxes to pay when the money is withdrawn. There are restrictions similar to those of a regular 401(k) regarding when the funds can be withdrawn. Unlike a Roth IRA, there are minimum required distributions for the Roth 401(k)s and Roth 403(b)s, but transferring the money to a Roth IRA upon retirement could help you avoid these required distributions. Any matching contributions made by the employer would be made with pre-tax dollars and the federal taxes would not be paid until those funds are withdrawn.

Timing and Vesting of Defined-Contribution Plans

It is important to understand when employers are required to make their contribution and when your interest becomes "vested."

Employers must make their contributions to an employee's retirement plan by the due date of their federal tax return. As a result, if your employer is on a calendar-year-end, you might not see the match portion of your 401(k) until well after year-end. Other employers match immediately when a contribution is made.

Also, just because the money is credited to your account doesn't necessarily mean it is all yours immediately. The portion you contribute will always be yours, and if you quit tomorrow, the contribution remains your money. The employer's contribution will often become available to you only after working a certain number of years. A common vesting schedule is 20% per year that an employee remains with the company until five years have passed. At that point, the employee is 100% vested. This is called *graded vesting*. Other plans allow no vesting until the employee has worked for a certain number of years. Then, when he or she reaches that threshold, there is a 100% vest in the employer's contributions. This is called *cliff vesting*.

Defined-Benefit Plans

With a defined-benefit plan the employer contributes money according to a formula described in the company plan to provide a monthly benefit to the employee at retirement. Many people refer to these types of plans as "my pension." The amount of the benefit is determined based on a formula that considers the number of years of service, salary (perhaps an average of the highest three years) and age. Defined-benefit plans usually do not allow the employee to contribute his or her own funds into the plan, and the employer bears all of the investment risk. When it is time for the employee to collect his monthly benefit, the employer is responsible for paying the benefit—regardless of how the investments have done from the time of the employer's contribution to the time of employee's distribution.

At retirement, the employee is often given a wide range of choices of how he would like to collect his pension. Distribution options generally involve receiving a certain amount of money every month for the rest of one's life. Receiving regular payments for a specified period, usually a lifetime, is called an "annuity." (Please don't confuse this type of annuity with a tax-deferred annuity or a 403(b) plan, which is also often called an annuity.) The annuity period often runs for your lifetime and that of your spouse. Or it might be defined with a guaranteed period for successor beneficiaries, such as a guaranteed 10-year term regardless of when you die. (A further discussion of annuities can be found in Chapter 6.)

The failure of companies to make their promised payments and announcements of reduced payments has reached crisis proportions and is getting worse. For example, retirees in the airline industries and many other industries now face a likely reduction in their pension income.

There is often an important need for life insurance for many married owners of defined-benefit plans, and you have some important decisions to make at the time of your retirement. For example, let's assume that the plan owner is in good health and wants the highest annuity income for his or her life. That is often the best option. If, however, the owner dies, the spouse is out of luck. Sometimes owners choose a lower monthly payment because it will last through their life and their spouse's life. Sometimes the owner will take a large payment and his or her spouse will receive a fraction, perhaps half or two-thirds.

The most prudent course might be to take a one-life (not two-life) annuity and use the additional income to purchase life insurance on the owner's life. Should the owner die, the life insurance death benefit can go toward the surviving spouse's support. This is an important decision to be made at your retirement. In these situations, "running the numbers," that is, comparing different potential scenarios, can provide guidance in making a decision. Please note that if you have already retired and already decided to take the highest pension without a survivorship feature, it is not too late, if you are still insurable. If you are retired and are now concerned that by taking a one-life annuity with the highest monthly payment that you did not sufficiently provide for your surviving spouse, you could still purchase life insurance.

Cash Balance Plan

A relatively new and unique version of a defined benefit plan is known as a *cash balance plan.* Technically, this is a defined-benefit plan, but it has features similar to defined-contribution plans. Though on the rise, this type of plan is not common. Each employee is given an "account" to which the employer provides contributions or "pay credits," which may be a percentage of pay and an interest credit on the balance in the account. The account's investment earnings to be credited are usually defined by the plan, and the employer bears all downside risk for actual investment earning shortfalls. The increase in popularity of the cash balance plan has been spurred by the country's increasingly mobile workforce. Employees may take their cash balance plans with them to a new employer when they change jobs or roll them into an IRA.

There is a good possibility that you have the opportunity to invest more money in your retirement plan or plans than you realize.

Defined-benefit plans were far more popular 20 years ago than today. For people with defined-benefit plans there are limited opportunities to make strategic decisions, during the working years, to increase retirement benefits. It might be possible to increase the retirement benefit by deferring salary or bonuses into the final years, or working overtime to increase the calculation wage base. These opportunities, however, depend on the plan's formula, and they are often not flexible and not significant.

How Many Plans Are Available to You?

There is a good possibility that you have the opportunity to invest more money in your retirement plan or plans than you realize. For many readers who are still working, applying the lessons of this mini case study could save you thousands of dollars every year.

MINI CASE STUDY 1.3

Contributing the Maximum to Multiple Retirement Plans

Tom and his wife, Judy, both 55, want to make the maximum retirement plan contributions allowed. Tom earns $44,000 per year as a secretary for a school district that has both a 403(b) plan and a Section 457 plan. Judy is self-employed, has no employees, and shows a profit on Schedule C of $80,000 per year. Tom and Judy have a 16-year-old computer-whiz child, Bill, who works weekends and summers doing computer programming for Judy's company. Bill is a legitimate subcontractor, not an employee of Judy's company. Judy pays Bill $14,000 per year. What is the maximum that Tom and Judy and Bill can contribute to their retirement plans for calendar year 2006?

Tom: Calculating Maximum Contributions to Multiple Plans

Under EGTRRA, Tom could contribute $20,000 to his 403(b) plan in 2006 ($15,000 normal limit plus another $5,000 because he is over 50). Please note that under EGTRRA, Tom's retirement plan contribution is not limited to 15% of his earnings as it would have been under prior law. Under a special rule specifically relating to only 457 plans, assuming Tom's employer has a 457 plan, he could also contribute another $20,000 to the plan in 2006 (same $15,000, plus $5,000). In addition, he could also contribute $5,000 in 2006 to a Roth IRA ($4,000 per year limit plus $1,000 because he is over age 50) by using the remaining $4,000 of his income (his income is $44,000 less $20,000 for the 403(b) less $20,000 for the 457, which leaves $4,000) and using $1,000 of Judy's income. (Roth IRAs are discussed in more detail in the next chapter.) Please note the new law allows contributions to all three plans—something not previously allowed. Tom was able to contribute the entire amount of his income into retirement plans. In addition, he could use $1,000 of Judy's income to maximize his Roth IRA contribution for 2006.

Judy: Calculating Maximum Contribution to a "Super K"

After rejecting a more complicated defined-benefit plan, Judy chooses the newly introduced one-person 401(k) plan, or the "Super-K" plan. These plans are now available as a result of the tax law changes effective in 2002. Judy could contribute as much as $34,870 into her 401(k) plan. This amount comes from two components. The first component is the 401(k) elective deferral amount that is limited to $20,000 (the same limits as Tom's 403(b) plan). The second component is a $14,870 discretionary profit-sharing contribution. To arrive at this figure, Judy's net self-employed income of $80,000 must be reduced by one half of her computed self-employment tax, which is $80,000 × .9235 ×.153 = 11,304 × 50%, or $5,652. The $74,348 ($80,000 – $5,652) is multiplied by the 20% contribution rate limit (for self-employed individuals, and equal to 25% of earnings net of the contribution itself) to compute the maximum profit-sharing contribution amount of $14,870. Judy also can make an additional $5,000 contribution to her Roth IRA.

Bill: For Parents Who Are Considering Funding Retirement Plans for Their Children

Though Bill is young, he should use his $14,000 income to begin making contributions to his retirement plan.

Bill could open up a SIMPLE plan and contribute $10,000. In addition, he could contribute his remaining $4,000 of earned income to a Roth IRA. If he already spent some of the $4,000, his parents could make him a gift of the money.

The tax-free benefit of the Roth IRA and the tax-deferred benefit of the SIMPLE plan is so important to the child during his lifetime that some parents who have sufficient funds—and who are willing to fund their child's retirement plan—will be tempted to create a sham "business" for their child or even put their child on the payroll as a sham transaction. I do not recommend this approach. I advocate that the child do legitimate work, complying with all child labor laws. All retirement plan contributions should stem from legitimate businesses and, if based on self-employed earnings, be a real business.

I have seen parents paying infants to model, characterizing the payment to the infant as "self-employed income" and making a retirement plan contribution for the infant. I think that goes too far. Any situation where a child younger than 11 years old receives employment compensation is highly suspect. Even at age 11, legitimate compensation should not be too high.

Let's assume that Tom, Judy, and Bill "max out." Though Tom and Judy earned only $124,000 and Bill earned only $14,000, the family could contribute over $98,000 into their retirement plans and Roth IRAs. For subsequent years, the contribution limits are even more generous. Is this a great country or what?

This example intentionally exaggerates the family's likely contributions. The point is to show maximum contribution limits and the variety of plan options. In this particular case, Tom and Judy may choose not to maximize their contributions because they may not receive any income tax benefits beyond a certain level of contribution. It is worthwhile to review this case study to help with choosing and implementing a new plan. In addition, Bill's Roth IRA may be considered an asset for financial aid purposes by universities that use the Institutional Method for determining financial aid.

Many people—perhaps you—feel they cannot afford to save for retirement. The truth is you may very well be able to afford to save, but you don't realize it.

When You Think You Can't Afford to Make the Maximum Contributions

Many people—perhaps you—feel they cannot afford to save for retirement. The truth is you may very well be able to afford to save, but you don't realize it. That's right. I am going to present a rationale to persuade you to contribute more than you think you can afford.

Let's assume you have been contributing only the portion that your employer is willing to match and yet you barely have enough money to get by week to week. Does it still make sense to make nonmatched contributions assuming you do not want to reduce your spending? Maybe.

If you have substantial savings and maximizing your retirement plan contributions causes your net payroll check to be insufficient to meet your expenses, I still recommend maximizing retirement plan contributions. The shortfall for your living expenses from making increased pre-tax retirement plan contributions should be withdrawn from your savings (money that has already been taxed). Over time this process, that is to say, saving the most in a retirement plan and funding the shortfall by making after-tax withdrawals from an after-tax account, transfers money from the after-tax environment to the pre-tax environment. Ultimately it results in more money for you and your heirs. Another way to squeeze blood from a stone is to consider an interest-only mortgage. The reduced mortgage payment (in contrast to what you would be paying on a 30-year fixed rate mortgage) is deductible as a home interest expense. The additional cash flow from the reduced payment could be used to pay credit card debt or fund one or more tax favored investments. You could open a Roth IRA, make additional retirement contributions, and/or purchase a tax-favored life insurance plan. In the long run, you could be better off, often by hundreds of thousands of dollars. Of course there are risks with this strategy. I will keep coming back to the primary theme: don't pay taxes now—pay taxes later.

MINI CASE STUDY 1.4

Changing Your IRA and Retirement Plan Strategy after a Windfall or an Inheritance

Joe always had trouble making ends meet. He did, however, know enough to always contribute to his retirement plan the amount his employer was willing to match. Because he was barely making ends meet and had no savings in the after-tax environment, he never made a nonmatching retirement plan contribution. Tragedy then struck Joe's family. Joe's mother died, leaving Joe $100,000. Should Joe change his retirement plan strategy?

Yes. Joe should not blow the $100,000. If his housing situation is reasonable, he should not use the inherited money for a house—or even a down payment on a house. Many planners and people will disagree. Of course it depends on individual circumstances. Instead, Joe should increase his retirement plan contribution to the maximum. In addition, he should start making Roth IRA contributions (see Chapter 2). Many of you who live in areas that have seen huge real estate appreciation think he should use the money to invest in real estate. You may have been right yesterday. You might even be right today. It is, however, a risky strategy, unsuitable for many if not most investors.

Assuming he maintains his pre-inheritance lifestyle, between his Roth IRA contribution and the increase in his retirement plan contribution, Joe will not have enough to make ends meet without eating into his inheritance. That's okay. He should then cover the shortfall by making withdrawals from the inherited money. True, if that pattern continues long enough, Joe will eventually deplete his inheritance in its current form. But his retirement plan and Roth IRA will be so much better financed that in the long run, the tax-deferred and tax-free growth of these accounts will make Joe better off by thousands, possibly hundreds of thousands, of dollars. The only time this strategy would not make sense is if Joe needed the liquidity of the inherited money, or he preferred to use the inherited funds to improve his housing.

A Key Lesson from This Chapter

You should contribute the maximum you can afford to all the retirement plans to which you have access.

Traditional IRAs and Nonmatched Retirement Plan Contributions versus Roth IRAs

The question isn't at what age I want to retire, it's at what income.

—George Foreman

Main Topics

- How traditional IRAs and Roth IRAs differ
- The principal advantages and disadvantages of a Roth IRA
- Eligibility rules for both Roth and traditional IRAs
- Contribution limits for both Roth and traditional IRAs
- Choosing between opening a Roth IRA and a traditional IRA
- Choosing between a Roth IRA and a nonmatched 401(k)
- Distribution regulations for Roth IRAs and traditional IRAs

KEY IDEA

The Roth IRA is usually preferable to a traditional IRA or a nonmatched contribution to a retirement plan.

What Is the Difference between an IRA and a Roth IRA?

IRAs allow individuals who earn income to make contributions to their own retirement accounts. IRA owners can deduct IRA contributions if they meet either of these two requirements:

- They (and their spouse if married) do not have a retirement plan at work.
- They earn less income than the adjusted gross income ("AGI") limit for deducting IRA contributions (please see discussion below regarding traditional IRA eligibility rules).

Within limits, the IRA owner deducts the contribution to the IRA and the IRA grows tax-deferred. That is to say, the owner does not pay income taxes until money is withdrawn, at which point the distribution will be subject to federal income taxes. With the exception of the Roth and the defined benefit plan, all the other plans mentioned in chapter 1 can usually be "rolled" into an IRA, income tax-free, at retirement or service termination.

The main advantage of the Roth IRAs is that the investment grows tax-free, and is not taxed when withdrawals are made. Roth IRAs differ from traditional IRAs in the following ways:

	Roth IRA	IRA
Investment	Grows tax-free	Grows tax-deferred
Withdrawals	Tax-free	Taxed as income
Contributions	Not deductible	Deductible
Income limits	Much higher than for an IRA	Much lower than for a Roth IRA
Contribution limits	Same as IRA	Same as Roth IRA
Required distributions at 70½	No	Yes

The Roth IRA income limit is much higher than the traditional IRA income limit, allowing many higher income earners who are not eligible for a deductible IRA to participate in a Roth IRA. Individuals who earn less than the maximum Roth IRA income limit (please see discussion below regarding Roth IRA eligibility rules) can make annual contributions without the benefit of a tax deduction.

What Makes a Roth IRA So Great?

One of the few things in life better than tax-deferred compounding is tax-free compounding. If you are eligible and can afford it, after making your matching contribution to a retirement plan, I generally recommend making additional annual contributions to a Roth IRA.

With a Roth IRA you contribute after-tax money. Looked at another way, you don't get an income tax deduction for your contribution to a Roth IRA. As with a traditional IRA, you don't pay income tax while the Roth IRA is invested. The striking advantage, however, is that when you eventually do make a withdrawal from your Roth IRA (or even when your heirs make a withdrawal) the distribution from the Roth IRA is income-tax-free. The distribution from a traditional IRA will be taxable.

One of the few things in life better than tax-deferred compounding is tax-free compounding.

The essence of a Roth IRA (in contrast to a traditional IRA) is that you pay tax on the seed (the contribution because you don't get a deduction) but reap the harvest (the distribution) tax-free. With a traditional IRA, you deduct the seed, but pay tax on the harvest.

The principal advantages of Roth IRAs are as follows:

- With limited exceptions, they grow income-tax-free.
- They are not subject to the minimum distribution rules requiring withdrawals at age 70½. You will never be required to take distributions during your lifetime. You

may choose to, but you don't have to. When you die and if you leave your Roth IRA to your spouse, your spouse will not have to take minimum distributions either.

- More liberal contribution rules.
- If needed, all of your after-tax annual contributions are always eligible for withdrawal at any time without tax consequences.
- If you have earned income after age 70½, you can keep contributing money to your Roth IRA (and so can your spouse, based on your income)—which is not an option for a traditional IRA—contributions must stop at 70½.

The essence of a Roth IRA is that you pay tax on the seed (the contribution because you don't get a deduction) but reap the harvest (the distribution) tax-free.

In many if not most cases, the biggest advantage of the Roth IRA is that the heirs receive income-tax-free distributions for their entire lives.

The principal disadvantages of Roth IRAs are:

- You do not receive a tax deduction when you make a contribution. If your tax bracket goes down, you may do better in some circumstances with a traditional IRA.

- If Congress ever eliminates the income tax in favor of a sales tax or value-added tax, you will have given up your tax deduction on the traditional IRA, and since the distribution will be tax-free anyway, in retrospect, the choice of a Roth IRA would have been a mistake.

What follows is a primer comparing traditional IRAs or nonmatched retirement plan contributions versus Roth IRAs. This section covers eligibility rules, limitations, and analysis.

Roth IRA Eligibility Rules

1. As with any IRA, an individual must have earned income in order to contribute to a Roth IRA. Earned income includes wages, commissions, self-employment income, and other amounts received for personal services, as well as taxable alimony and separate maintenance payments received under a decree of divorce or separate maintenance.
2. Individuals must meet the income tests, which exclude higher income-taxpayers from contributing to Roth IRAs.
3. A married individual filing a joint return may make a Roth IRA contribution for the nonworking spouse by treating his compensation as his spouse's, but must exclude any of his own IRA contributions from the income treated as his spouse's. (Total contributions cannot exceed your income. For example: if you make $7,000, you can contribute $4,000 to your Roth, but only $3,000 to your spouse's Roth.)

Eligibility Rules for Roth IRAs

	Full Contribution	Reduced Contribution	No Contribution
Single & Head of Household	Up to $95,000	$95,001–$109,999	$110,000+
Married Filing Jointly	Up to $150,000	$150,001–$159,999	$160,000+

Traditional IRA Eligibility Rules

1. All taxpayers with earned income are allowed to contribute to a traditional IRA without regard to income level.
2. If neither you nor your spouse participates in an employee-sponsored retirement plan, you can deduct the full amount of the traditional IRA contributions.

3. If you are covered by a retirement plan at work, there are income limits (adjusted gross income or "AGI" limits) for allowing full deductions, partial deductions, and limits above which no deductions are permitted. They are as follows:

2006 AGI Limitations for Deducting a Traditional IRA If There Is a Retirement Plan at Work

	Fully Deductible	**Partially Deductible**	**Not Deductible**
Single & Head of Household	Up to $50,000	$50,001–$59,999	$60,000+
Married Filing Jointly	Up to $75,000	$75,001–$84,999	$85,000+
Married Filing Separately	n/a	Up to $10,000	$10,001+

Note: The fully deductible amount for married individuals is scheduled to increase to $80,000 for years 2007 and after (not deductible if AGI is $100,000+).

4. A spousal contribution can also be made for a nonworking spouse when the other spouse has earned income and a joint tax return is filed. The nonworking spouse's contributions are limited when the working spouse participates in an employee-sponsored retirement plan:
   a. Fully Deductible—Up to $150,000 of AGI
   b. Partially Deductible—$150,001 to $160,000 of AGI
   c. Not Deductible—$160,000+ of AGI

If you are not eligible to deduct a traditional IRA contribution, but you are eligible and choose to make a nondeductible IRA contribution, you will still gain the advantage of tax-deferred growth, but you won't get the income tax deduction up front.

The choice between a non deductible IRA that grows tax-deferred and a Roth IRA that grows income-tax-free is a no-brainer: Choose the Roth. Neither one offers a deduction, but the Roth grows tax-free, while the nondeductible IRA only grows tax-deferred.

Contribution Limits for Both Roth and Traditional IRAs

The permitted contribution amounts are the same for both Roth IRAs and traditional IRAs. Note that the total permitted contribution amount applies both to IRAs and Roth IRAs, which means that for 2006, you can only contribute a total of $4,000 ($5,000 if you are 50 or older) to IRAs and Roth IRAs. The total IRA and/or Roth IRA contributions cannot exceed earned income, but other than that, the contribution limits for years 2006 and beyond are as follows:

Year	Annual IRA/Roth IRA Contribution Limits	Catch-up Contribution Limits for Individuals 50 and older
2006–2007	$4,000	$1,000
2008 and beyond*	$5,000	$1,000

*Beginning in 2009, the annual contribution limit will be adjusted for inflation in $500 increments.

As with traditional IRAs, a married individual filing a joint return may make a Roth IRA contribution for the nonworking spouse by treating his compensation as his spouse's.

Should I Open a Roth IRA (or Roth 401(k)) or Should I Make an IRA or a Deductible Nonmatched 401(k) Plan Contribution?

As stated earlier, a Roth versus a nondeductible IRA is a no-brainer: always go for the Roth. But for those individuals with a choice between a Roth and a nonmatched 401(k) (which conceptually is the same as a fully deductible IRA), how should you save? To simplify, I compare a fully deductible IRA to a Roth IRA.

The following analysis also applies to the question of whether it is better to open a Roth 401(k) versus a traditional 401(k).

The conclusion, in most cases: the Roth IRA and Roth 401(k) are superior to the deductible IRA and traditional 401(k).

To determine whether a Roth IRA would be better than a traditional IRA, you must take into account:

- The value of the tax-free growth of the Roth versus the tax-deferred growth of the traditional IRA including the future tax effects.
- The tax deduction you lost by contributing to a Roth IRA rather than to a fully deductible IRA.
- The growth, net of taxes, on savings from the tax deduction from choosing a deductible traditional IRA.

In most circumstances, the Roth IRA is significantly more favorable than a regular IRA. (In May 1998, I published the mathematical proof that the Roth IRA was often a more favorable investment than a regular IRA in an article I often wrote for *The Tax Adviser*, a publication of the American Institute of Certified Public Accountants.) The Jobs and Growth Tax Relief Reconciliation Act of 2003 (JGTRRA) and subsequent tax legislation changed tax rates for all brackets and reduced tax rates for dividends and capital gains to 15% for years through 2010. After these tax law changes, I incorporated these changes into the analysis of Roth versus traditional IRA. The Roth still is preferable in most situations, but admittedly, the advantage of the Roth is not quite as great as before JGTRRA. The Roth 401(k) has the same advantages.

The conclusion is, in most cases: The Roth IRA and Roth 401(k) are superior to the deductible IRA and traditional 401(k).

Figure 2.1 shows the value to the owner of contributing to a Roth IRA or Roth 401(k) versus a regular deductible IRA (or a deductible, but nonmatched, contribution to a 401(k), 403(b), or other retirement plan) measured in purchasing power:

Figure 2.1

Roth IRA Savings versus Traditional IRA Savings

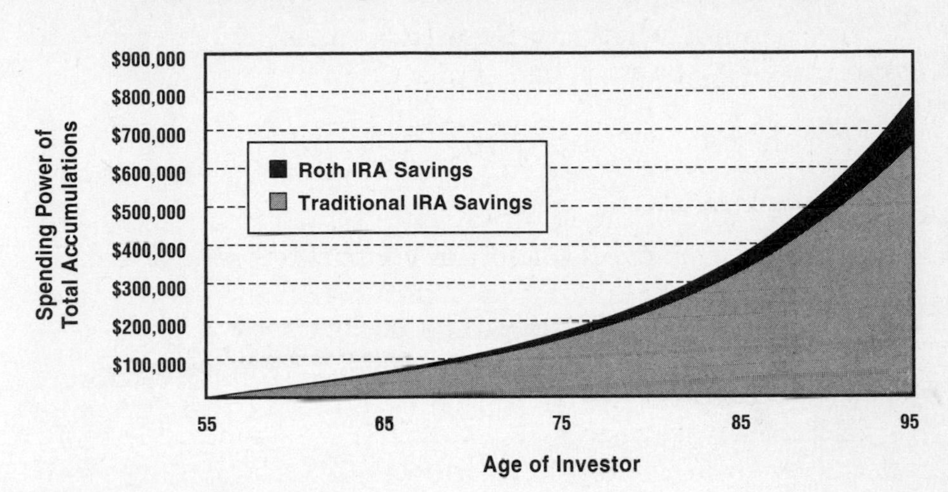

Figure 2.1 reflects the following assumptions:

1. Contributions to the Roth IRA savings are made in the amount of $4,500 per year, beginning in 2005, for a 55-year-old investor, each year for eleven years until age 65.
2. Contributions to the regular deductible IRA savings are made in the amount of $4,500 per year for the same time period, but because this creates an income tax deduction, 25% of this amount, or $1,125, is also contributed into an after-tax savings account.
3. The investment rate of return is 8% per year.
4. For the after-tax monies, the rate of return includes 70% capital appreciation, a 15% portfolio turnover rate (such that much of the appreciation is not immediately taxed), 15% dividends (taxes as capital gains from 2005 to 2008), and 15% ordinary interest income.
5. Ordinary income tax rates are 25% for all years.
6. Tax rates on realized capital gains are 15% through year 2008 and 19% thereafter.
7. Beginning at age 71, the required minimum distributions from the traditional IRA are reinvested into the after-tax savings account.

8. The balances reflected in the graphs reflect spending power, which is net of an income tax allowance of 25% on the remaining traditional IRA balance. If the full amount was actually withdrawn in one year, however, the tax bracket may be even higher and make the Roth IRA appear more favorable.

The amounts reflected in the graph always show the Roth IRA to be more favorable than the traditional IRA savings method. Because of the lower tax rates signed into law in 2003 and thereafter, the overall Roth IRA advantage appears smaller than it used to under old tax laws with higher income tax rates. Given a long enough time horizon (such as when monies are passed to succeeding generations), however, the Roth IRA advantage becomes bigger. The spending power of these methods at selected times are as follows:

Total Spending Power of Savings Methods

End of Year Age	Traditional IRA	Roth IRA
55	$ 4,677	**$ 4,680**
65	76,898	**77,901**
75	161,406	**168,182**
85	331,572	**363,093**
95	661,701	**783,890**

The analysis in this section can also be applied to employees who have a choice of making nonmatching contributions to an employer-sponsored retirement plan, such as a 401(k) or a Roth IRA.

Employees should consider prioritizing investing in retirement plans in the following order:

1. Employer-matched portion

2. Roth IRAs for employee and spouse (or Roth 401(k) or 403(b))

3. Nonmatching contributions

The Effect of Lower Tax Brackets in Retirement

The most important circumstance where I recommend the traditional IRA over a Roth IRA is when you drop to a lower tax bracket after retiring and have a relatively short investment time horizon.

Under those circumstances, the value of a deductible IRA or a nonmatched contribution to a 401(k) could exceed the benefits of the Roth IRA or Roth 401(k). You will be better off getting a high tax deduction from your contribution and withdrawing that money at a much lower rate upon distribution than you would be if you used the money to fund a Roth IRA.

The most important circumstance where I recommend the traditional IRA over a Roth IRA is when you drop to a lower tax bracket after retiring and have a relatively short investment time horizon.

For example, if you are in the 25% tax bracket, and you make a $4,500 tax-deferred contribution, you save $1,125 in taxes. Then, when you retire, your tax bracket drops to 15%. Assuming no investment growth, when you withdraw the traditional IRA of $4,500, you pay $675 in tax—you have just saved yourself $450.

$1,125	(initial tax savings)
– 675	(tax payment)
$ 450	(final tax saving)

Even with that caveat, however, my analysis shows that the Roth can become more favorable when a longer investment period is considered. The tax bracket advantage diminishes over time. So, I ran the analysis again, starting with the same assumptions as in the prior example, except that beginning in retirement, at age 66, the ordinary income tax bracket is reduced from 25% to 15%, and the capital gains tax rate is reduced from 19% to 9%.

The spending power of these methods at selected times is shown in the following table:

Total Spending Power of Savings Methods

End of Year Age	Traditional IRA		Roth IRA
55	$ 4,677		**$ 4,680**
65	76,898		**77,901**
75	**180,290**	**(lower tax**	168,182
85	**379,128**	**brackets)**	363,093
95	**784,703**	"	783,890
105	1,602,542	"	**1,692,359**

Of course, most people will not survive till age 105, but we show the analysis to point out that even facing a lowered tax bracket, the Roth IRA will become more valuable with time—an advantage for your heirs.

I usually recommend the deductible traditional IRA over the Roth IRA if you anticipate that your retirement tax bracket will always remain lower than your current tax rate, and that the IRA will be depleted during your lifetime. Unfortunately, once the minimum required distribution (MRD) rules take effect for tax-deferred IRAs at age 70½, an individual may find that the distribution rules require them to withdraw so much money that their tax rate is just as high as their preretirement tax rate or sometimes, when the MRD is added to Social Security income, a higher rate than when they were working. For these people, a Roth IRA contribution is usually preferable to a traditional IRA.

These numbers demonstrate that even with a significant tax bracket disadvantage, the Roth IRA can become preferable with a long enough time horizon. Furthermore, when you consider the additional estate planning advantages, the relative worth of the Roth IRA becomes more significant. (Please see www.PayTaxesLater.com/book/roth.htm for a free report on Roth IRAs and Roth IRA conversions that includes information on the tax law change that will eliminate the $100,000 AGI limit for converting IRAs to Roth IRAs in 2010.)

Comments on Your Actual Tax Brackets: A Subtle Point for the Advanced Reader

The above analyses reflect simple assumptions of 25% income tax savings on your deductible IRA or retirement plan contributions. This is in essence the cost of the Roth IRA in these comparisons to deductible amounts. However, the United States tax code has several complications that create actual incremental tax brackets that are much higher than the tax brackets listed on the federal tax tables based on your taxable income. These items must be considered in the context of measuring the advantages and benefits of Roth IRAs to deductible contributions.

These tax code complications can have extreme effects on the actual tax bracket for some people including retirees with Social Security income and itemized deductions that involve medical expenses. For example, consider Fred Jones, a single 65-year-old retiree who in 2005 had pension income of $32,000, Social Security income of $25,000 and part-time wage income of $4,500. He also has itemized deductions of $15,000 including $10,000 of medical expenses. After seeing the above graphs, Fred is considering the potential advantages of making a $4,500 Roth IRA contribution rather than a deductible IRA contribution of $4,500. If he makes the traditional deductible IRA contribution, he pays $4,196 of tax. If he chooses the Roth IRA, his tax is $6,421, or $2,225 more. This is 50% of the IRA contribution amount. This means his actual tax bracket is almost 50% even though the IRS tables indicate he is in the 25% tax bracket! The reasons, in Fred's situation, are that the additional income from losing the IRA deduction also caused much more of his Social Security income to be taxable as well as losing out on some of the medical expense deduction, due to its 7.5% of AGI limitation. Thus, Fred felt the cost of choosing the Roth IRA was too high that year and wisely chose the deductible IRA.

Although Fred's future situation may not always be so extreme, his numbers did not appear to be that unusual. Fred's example is an illustration of why careful tax planning is so important. There are many things in the tax code that result in a different actual tax bracket than the IRS tables would indicate. Before finalizing Roth contribution or conversion decisions, it is best to run the numbers or see a competent tax advisor to determine the actual effects.

In our analyses of Roth IRA advantages and disadvantages when compared to deductible contributions, we keep referring to the marginal tax rates to help us decide if the conversion makes sense in the long-term. For most people, the current actual marginal tax rate is not hard to determine, and similar to what the IRS tables would indicate. Therefore, we will continue to use these references to a simply calculated tax bracket rate in our analyses of Roth accounts. But please keep in mind that it is prudent to calculate the actual current year tax cost of the Roth.

In addition, our analyses do not reflect any additional advantages of the Roth accounts when held in retirement due to these actual tax bracket variances. For example, Fred's situation can be turned around to result in an extreme advantage if instead of considering a Roth IRA contribution, Fred is in need of an additional $4,500 in income for December and he is comparing the effects of a withdrawal from either a taxable traditional IRA account or a Roth IRA account. Being able to get his money tax-free will then save him from paying an additional 50% tax when he files his return. This kind of situation gives the Roth IRA a potential advantage that our analyses in this book do not reflect. Instead we refer to a simple measure of the tax bracket, both when the Roth account is established and during retirement.

Distribution Rules for Roth IRAs

1. To make completely tax-free withdrawals from a Roth IRA that has grown in value, five years must have elapsed since opening the account.
2. This restriction also applies to the beneficiary of a Roth IRA whose owner dies before the five-year period has ended. The beneficiary may withdraw funds tax-free as long as they do

not exceed the contribution amount, but he or she must wait until the five-year period has passed before being able to enjoy tax-free withdrawal of the Roth IRA's earnings.

3. Withdrawals prior to age 59½ may be taken without tax or penalties to the extent of previous annual contributions.
4. All withdrawals after the five-year holding period is met, including those in excess of previous contributions, are tax-free in the following circumstances:
   - Made to a beneficiary (or the individual's estate) on or after the individual's death
   - Attributable to the individual's being disabled
   - For qualified first-time home purchase expenses
5. Withdrawals in excess of previous contributions made before the five-year holding period is met are taxable, but penalty-free in the following circumstances:
   - For qualified college expenses
   - For qualified medical expenses that exceed 7.5% of adjusted gross income
   - For health insurance premiums paid for certain unemployed individuals
   - If withdrawals are part of substantially equal periodic payments over the life of the participant
   - If the distribution is part of an IRS levy
6. All other withdrawals prior to age 59½ that are in excess of previous contributions are taxable and subject to a 10% penalty.
7. Roth IRA amounts are not subject to minimum required distributions during the original owner's lifetime.

Furthermore, a Roth IRA owner can designate his or her spouse as the beneficiary who, upon the Roth IRA owner's death, would have the option of postponing minimum distributions until death. After the second spouse's death, the subsequent beneficiary (usually a child) would be required to make nontaxable minimum distributions based on her own long life expectancy. (Please see Chapter 10 for distribution rules for inherited IRAs and inherited Roth IRAs.)

The five-year "holding" requirement for Roth IRAs is to promote long-term savings. The five-year clock starts ticking on January 1 of the tax year associated with the first contribution or conversion, which results in making the five-year period actually less than five years. The period begins on the first day of the tax year for which a contribution is made. If you open a Roth IRA account for the 2005 tax year by making a contribution on April 15, 2006 (the last day you can make your Roth IRA contributions for 2005), the five-year period is from January 1, 2005, to December 31, 2009. To achieve the same five-year period start date when opening a Roth IRA account using a Roth IRA conversion, you must make the conversion by December 31, 2005 (the last day you can make your Roth IRA conversions for 2005). Pursuant to these Roth IRA rules, if you suddenly need the money the day after or at any time after you make the contribution, you can take the contributed amount out free of tax.

Wealthy clients and readers raise a lot of questions about the five-year holding period. What I really want to do when I hear that question is yell, "Why do you care?"

Wealthy clients and readers raise a lot of questions about the five-year holding period. What I really want to do when I hear that question is yell, "Why do you care?"

I have never met anyone who has all their money in a Roth IRA. Virtually everyone who has a Roth IRA has at least some after-tax money and some traditional IRA funds. Because the Roth IRA is the last money I want people to spend, it should not matter that there is a five-year waiting period to achieve tax-free growth. The important features described below almost always more than make up for any lack of liquidity resulting from the five-year rule.

The fact that individuals can continue to contribute to a Roth IRA if they continue working past age 70½ is a great opportunity to continue saving, especially since more and more people continue to earn income well after the traditional age of retirement.

The no-minimum distributions rule gives rise to significant estate planning opportunities to stretch savings for those willing to leave the money in the tax-free account for a long time. As with traditional IRAs, heirs must take minimum required distributions, but they generally are extended over a lifetime. Depending on the lifespan of the beneficiary, the funds can grow tax-free to great advantage.

Advanced Distribution Rules for Traditional IRAs

1. Traditional IRA withdrawals are generally taxable. For traditional IRAs with basis (after-tax amounts in an IRA are referred to as its "basis"), the basis comes out tax-free but is determined in pro rata amounts based on the ratio of the basis to total value. Basis is created by making nondeductible contributions to the account. In other words, if you received a tax deduction for your retirement plan contribution, you have no basis. If, for some reason, you made an IRA or a retirement plan contribution for which you did not receive an income tax deduction, to the extent of your nondeductible contribution, you have basis. I hope you filed a Form 8606 to keep track of the basis of the IRA. My companion book on Roth Retirement Plans and IRAs, including conversions, will reveal how to convert after-tax IRAs or retirement plans to Roth IRAs without paying any tax.
2. All traditional IRA withdrawals prior to age 59½ are subject to a 10% penalty and are taxable (for amounts exceeding basis) unless the withdrawal falls under one of the following exemptions:
    - Made to a beneficiary (or the individual's estate) on or after the individual's death

- Attributable to the individual's being disabled
- Qualified first-time home purchase expenses
- Qualified college expenses
- Qualified medical expenses that exceed 7.5% of adjusted gross income
- Health insurance premiums paid for certain unemployed individuals
- Part of substantially equal periodic payments over the life of the participant—that is, distributions qualifying under Section 72(t) (which we do not cover in this book) for exemption from the premature distribution penalty
- Due to an IRS levy

3. All traditional IRAs are subject to minimum required distributions for years after age 70½.

A Key Lesson from This Chapter

Most employees should invest in retirement plans in the following order:

1. Employer-matching plans
2. Roth IRAs and Roth 401(k)s
3. Nonmatching plans

Part Two

THE DISTRIBUTION YEARS

Spend the Right Funds First

Approaching Retirement and During Retirement

I am having an out-of-money experience.

— author unknown

Main Topics

- The optimal order for spending assets
- Four mini case studies:
  - 3.1 Spend Your After-Tax Money First
  - 3.2 A Note for Those Who Fear Capital Gains Tax
  - 3.3 The Optimal Order for Spending Classes of Assets
  - 3.4 Figuring Your Tax Bracket Advantage into the Spending Order

KEY IDEA

Spend after-tax dollars first and tax-deferred dollars second.

Which Assets Should I Spend First?

With retirement an individual moves into distribution mode—that is, beginning to spend one's retirement savings. This is not to say that accumulation stops. Income and appreciation on the investments, Social Security funds, and any pension plan proceeds might still be exceeding your expenses.

You may be fortunate enough to find that your Social Security, pension, required distributions from your IRA (if any), and dividends and interest on your after-tax investments produce enough funds for your living expenses. Let's assume, however, that isn't the case, and you are required to either invade your after-tax funds (your nest egg) or make (additional) taxable withdrawals from your IRA or retirement account to make ends meet.

In general, it is preferable to spend principal from your after tax investments rather than taking taxable distributions from your IRA and/or retirement plan.

I've been in business for 27 years and most of my clients actually listen to me; but I've had quite a few who don't. Instead of following my recommendations, some prefer to spend their IRAs first. It drives me crazy. When I review their tax return, I see it. You can't hide it because it's an IRA distribution and you have to pay taxes on it. With this one particular client, every year, when I delivered his tax return, I would include a personal note saying, "I really hate to see you pay income taxes on this." I would also call him. He said his stockbroker wanted to maintain a balance between IRA and after-tax dollars. Now, I'm all for an appropriate and well-balanced portfolio. I agree that you don't want to have all your eggs in one basket. But I'm not into this allocation between IRA and non-IRA dollars. Particularly if you're past 59½, you don't have to worry about having after-tax dollars because you can take money out of an IRA whenever you want without a penalty. I would much rather follow the "pay taxes later" rule.

In general, it is preferable to spend principal from your after-tax investments rather than taking taxable distributions from your IRA and/or retirement plan.

Mini Case Study 3.1 and Figure 3.1 provide a graphic comparison of the benefits of spending after-tax savings before pretax accumulations.

MINI CASE STUDY 3.1
Spend Your After-Tax Money First

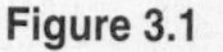

Figure 3.1

Benefits of Spending After-Tax Savings Before Tax-Deferred Retirement Accounts

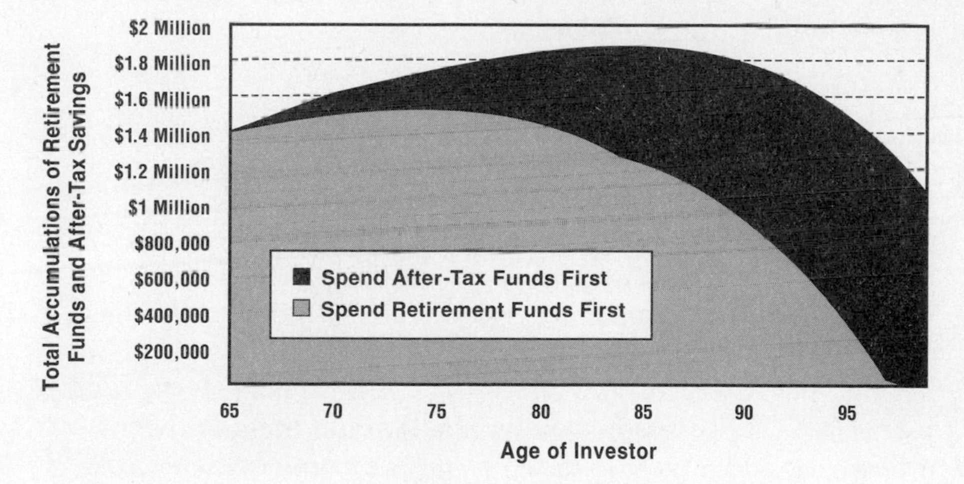

Both Mr. Pay Taxes Now and Mr. Pay Taxes Later start from an identical position. They are both 66 years old and both have $300,000 in after-tax funds, with a cost basis of $255,000, and $1,100,000 in retirement funds. They both receive $25,000 per year in Social Security income. They want to spend $8,000 per month, or $96,000 per year after paying income taxes. Their investment return is 8%, consisting of 70% capital appreciation with a 15% portfolio turnover rate, 15% dividend income, and 15% interest income. Income-tax assumptions include the new lower rates on ordinary income and capital gains established by JGTRRA and subsequent tax laws. State income taxes are ignored.

The Big Picture

Mr. Pay Taxes Now does not spend any of his after-tax funds until all the retirement funds are depleted. By spending his retirement funds first, he triggers income taxes on the withdrawals, reducing the tax-deferral period, and his balance goes down. He also subjects a larger share of his after-tax funds to income taxes on the dividends, interest and potential capital gains. All income taxes due on the retirement funds and the after-tax funds cause a greater amount to be withdrawn from his retirement account. In 32 years, by paying taxes prematurely, he has sacrificed a fortune in tax-deferred growth. When he is 98 years old, Mr. Pay Tax Now is out of funds.

Mr. Pay Taxes Later first uses his after-tax funds to meet expenses. Only when the after-tax funds are depleted are withdrawals made from the retirement accounts. He fully uses the tax deferred features of the IRA. Mr. Pay Tax Later has over $1,200,000, when he is 98. Both he and Mr. Pay Taxes Now enjoyed an identical lifestyle, investments, etc., but there was a $1,200,000 difference in the remaining amounts. In states like Pennsylvania that do not tax retirement income but do tax after-tax investment income, the benefits of spending the after-tax money first is even greater. The principle stands: don't pay taxes now—pay taxes later!

Please note that the conclusion would most likely be the same for any reasonable set of assumptions in terms of how much money there is and what interest rate you assume.

MINI CASE STUDY 3.2

A Note to Those Who Fear Capital Gains Tax

One of the primary reasons people think it may be better not to spend the after-tax money first is because of capital gains. For example, if instead of having a basis of $255,000 on the $300,000 of after-tax funds, let us assume the basis is zero. All spending of these after-tax funds will be taxed as capital gains. If we use the same assumptions as above, the graph now looks like: Figure 3.2.

Figure 3.2

Benefits of Spending After-Tax Savings With No Tax Cost Basis Before Tax-Deferred Accounts

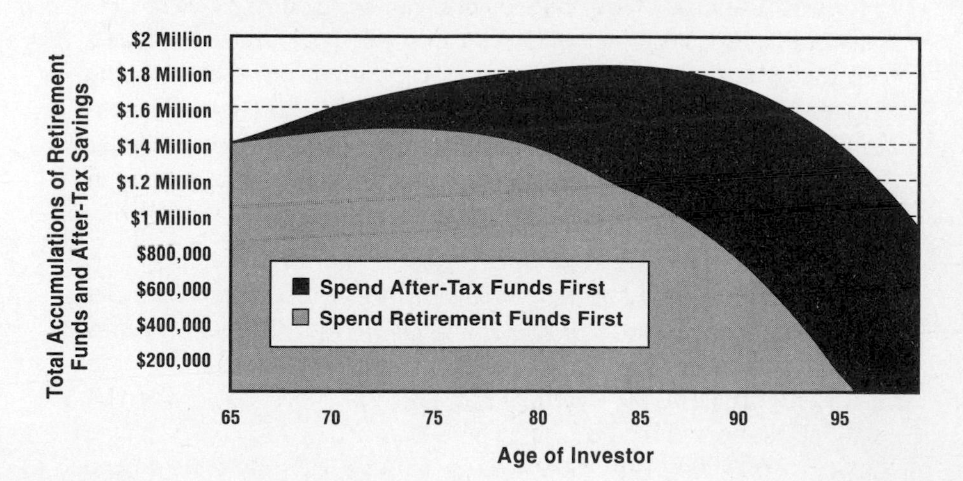

You may have a hard time telling the difference. These results show that Mr. Pay Tax Now is out of funds at age 96 rather than age 98 as in Mini Case Study 3.1, while Mr. Pay Tax Later still has over $1,300,000 left, which will last him another nine years. The bottom line is that spending after-tax money first is still wise, even when capital gains are involved. The step-up in basis rules, however, may provide planning scenarios that contradict this conclusion. The step-up in basis rule states that inherited property assumes a basis equivalent to its fair market value at the date of the decedent's death. It is referred to as a "step-up" because frequently the fair market value of the property at the date of death is greater than the decedent's basis—that is, its cost when it was first acquired.

For example, in estate situations where only a short remaining lifetime is anticipated or where the plan is to pass on the funds inside the estate, it may be advantageous to not spend highly appreciated investments. If you anticipate being in a situation like this, consult with a qualified advisor who will run some numbers for you. Most of the numbers we have run indicate that unless you are going to die in a few years, you are usually better off spending your after-tax dollars first, even if you will incur capital gains tax and give up your step-up in basis.

MINI CASE STUDY 3.3

The Optimal Order for Spending Classes of Assets

Phyllis Planner is 65 years old and widowed (though the conclusion would be basically the same for a married taxpayer). She is thinking ahead. She wants her money to provide her with a comfortable standard of living, and she also wants to leave some money to her three children. How should Phyllis evaluate which pool of money to spend first and which to save for as long as possible?

There are four general categories of money to support her retirement. They are ranked in order of how I recommend Phyllis spend her money, exhausting each asset category before breaking into the next asset category.

1. After-Tax Assets Generated by Income Sources

- Pension distributions

Determining a strategy for the distribution years is where the rubber meets the road. I've had clients who, while beginning their planning, get upset because they haven't accumulated as much as they could have, or for mistakes made along the way. That's water over the dam. If that's you, that's okay. Properly planning a strategy for the distribution years will help you make up for mistakes made during the accumulation years!

- Dividends, interest, and capital gains
- Earned income, not reinvested
- Social Security

Of course when Phyllis is 70½, she will be required to take minimum distributions from her IRA. Since she will have to pay income taxes on the distributions, the proceeds that remain after she pays taxes on the IRA distributions could also be spent before any of the following assets or sources of income.

2. *After-Tax Assets* *(Investments that are not part of a qualified pretax retirement plan that would generate income subject to taxes annually):*

- Investments that will either sell at a loss or break even
- Then, more highly appreciated investments

3. *IRA and Retirement Plan Assets* *(Assets subject to ordinary income tax):*

- IRA, 403(b), 401(k), etc., dollars over and above minimum required distributions

4. *Roth IRA*

- Roth IRA dollars

The assets in the income category should be spent first, since she has to pay tax on that money anyway. But let's assume that Phyllis's Social Security and the pension, dividends, and interest are not sufficient to meet her spending needs. Then the question becomes, "Which pool of money should be spent next?" If we keep in mind the premise of "don't pay taxes now—pay taxes later," the answer is obvious: the after-tax dollars. If we spend our after-tax dollars, except to the extent that a capital gain is triggered on a sale, those dollars will not be subject to income taxes and the money in the IRA can keep growing tax-deferred. Then, when Phyllis has exhausted her "after-tax" funds, then she delves into her IRA or pre-tax funds.

Whenever you make a withdrawal from the IRA, you are going to have to pay income taxes. To get an equivalent amount of spending money from the IRA assets and the after-tax assets, you have to take the taxes into consideration. Assuming a 25% tax bracket, you need $1.33 from the IRA assets to get $1.00 of spending money ($1.00 cash + $0.33 to pay the taxes). We get .33 cents because $1.33 times 25% = .33. On the other hand, the after-tax money is withdrawn tax-free, so to get $1.00, you withdraw $1.00 (with the exception of capital gains tax at 15% on the appreciation when you withdraw the money).

Finally, when she exhausts her IRA and pre-tax funds, she spends her Roth IRA. Why should she spend her traditional IRA before her Roth IRA? If tax-deferred growth is a good thing, then tax-free growth is even better. By spending taxable IRA money before Roth IRA money, she increases the time that the Roth IRA will provide income-tax-free growth.

If your plan is to leave money to your heirs, their tax situations should be considered as well. If the heirs to the Roth have tax deferral/avoidance as a goal, and their tax bracket is the same as yours or higher, then the Roth assets are the best to inherit. The opposite conclusion may be reached if the heirs plan on spending the money soon after they inherit it and are in a lower tax bracket. If that is the case, you could be better off spending the Roth IRA yourself. The facts of each case should be considered. In general, however, I would stick to what I recommended for Phyllis.

I had a client who came in to see me six or seven years ago, and at the time we thought this was going to be his last chance to make a Roth IRA conversion. I recommended that he make a $500,000 Roth IRA conversion, which is much higher than I would normally recommend for anyone. When we were done with the conversion, he had three "pots" of money. He had after tax dollars, his traditional IRA, and the $500,000 Roth IRA.

The plan that we worked out for him (and by the way he has stuck to that plan) was for him to start out by using only his after tax dollars for spending purposes and for gifts to his children and grandchildren. He was planning to spend and give away all of his after tax dollars, so that within a couple of years he would have no after tax dollars left.

The next step of the plan was to eat up his IRA based on his spending pattern; it was going to take till he was 90 to exhaust his IRA. If he and his wife were still alive at age 90, then they would have the Roth IRA that, if it earned 7% interest, would be worth $2,000,000 dollars. So, he wasn't likely to run out of money. More likely what is going to happen is that he is going to die, leaving the entire Roth IRA to his heirs.

That was a terrific plan. We calculated that this plan will literally save his family millions of dollars. Maybe your numbers aren't quite so high, but the concept is the same. The spending order is critical to both your financial good as well as your family's.

MINI CASE STUDY 3.4

Figuring the Tax Bracket Advantage into the Spending Order

One possible exception to spending after-tax dollars first is to "prematurely" make small IRA withdrawals if you are in a lower tax bracket now than you will be in the future when you have to start taking minimum required distributions. If you withdraw just enough to take you to the top of your current (low) tax bracket, then you get that money out at a lower tax rate than if you were to take the money out after you retire. But first, let me clarify a common misunderstanding about taxes and tax brackets.

What many people don't understand is that the first sliver of income is taxed at a lower bracket (income up to $14,600 in 2005 is taxed at 10% for married filing jointly). Then the next layer of income is taxed at the next bracket (income from $14,601 to $59,400 is taxed at 15% for married filing jointly), then the next layer is taxed at the next bracket (income from $59,401 to $119,950 is taxed at

25%). (Rates are married filing jointly for 2005.) Some people are deathly afraid of getting one more dollar. They think, "Oh no! If I get one more dollar I'm going to be thrown into the 25% tax bracket and my taxes are going to explode." But that's not right. What happens is that just the one additional dollar would be at the 25% bracket.

Though Joe and Sally Retiree, aged 65, have an estate of $1.5 million, their taxable income is only $30,000. (Taxable income is arrived at after subtracting itemized deductions and personal exemptions and dependents.) When Joe reaches age 70½, his minimum distribution will push his income well into the 25% tax bracket. Joe decides to make voluntary withdrawals from his IRA every year until he reaches his minimum required distribution date as follows:

One possible exception to spending after-tax dollars first is to "prematurely" make small IRA withdrawals to stay in a low tax bracket.

The top of the 15% bracket for married filing jointly (using 2005 tables) is $59,400. Joe and Sally already have $30,000 in taxable income before any IRA withdrawal. If Joe then makes an additional $29,400 IRA withdrawal, he still pays tax at the 15% rate. If he waits, much of the later distributions will be taxed at 25%. Depending on the circumstances, this might be a reasonable strategy. Calculations reveal the higher distribution yields a slight long-term advantage, although not as much as you might think because of the simultaneous loss of some tax deferral.

For many clients, particularly frugal clients, I would prefer a variation of this strategy that provides better long-term benefits. Instead of making an IRA withdrawal of $29,400, paying tax on the funds, and then being left with "after-tax" dollars that will generate taxable income, I would recommend Joe make a $29,400 Roth IRA conversion. Many clients will resist this advice, but I urge you to at least consider it. This advice is perfectly consistent with Jonathan Clements's article in The *Wall Street Journal* dated February 23, 2005, in which Jonathan quoted me giving this identical analysis.

It is beyond the scope of this book to assess all the implications of Roth IRA conversions. Suffice it to say that I am a big fan of Roth IRA conversions and my wife and I have made a Roth IRA conversion well into the six figures.

If Joe doesn't want to make a Roth IRA conversion, he should at least consider making "premature" IRA distributions based on tax brackets. Please note that adding income in the form of extra IRA distributions and/or Roth IRA conversions may have an impact on the taxability of Social Security benefits and other items as discussed in the previous chapter, which should be worked into the numbers for the amount to withdraw or convert.

A Key Lesson from This Chapter

Leaving money in the tax-deferred environment for as long as possible confers advantages that almost always outweigh concerns over paying capital gains on your after-tax assets.

Minimum Required Distribution Rules

There was a time when a fool and his money were soon parted,
but now it happens to everybody.

— Adlai Stevenson

Main Topics

- An overview of the minimum required distribution rules
- How to calculate your MRD
- An explanation of the new IRS tables

KEY IDEA

If you can afford it, take only the minimum the government requires you to withdraw from your retirement plan or IRA. This distribution pattern retains more money in the tax-deferred account and is consistent with our motto, **don't pay taxes now—pay taxes later**. Please note taking only the minimum required distribution (MRD) does not prevent you from withdrawing more money should the need arise.

Eventually Everyone Must Draw from Retirement Savings

Even if you stick to the game plan to spend your income and after-tax dollars first, eventually, by law, you will have to withdraw funds from your IRA (not your Roth IRA) or qualified retirement plan. You will usually be required to take annual minimum distributions by April 1 of the year following the year that you reach age 70½. The key word here is "minimum." Keeping in mind the "don't pay taxes now—pay taxes later" rule of thumb, I want you to continue to maintain the highest balance possible in the tax-deferred environment. Take a minimum distribution the year that you turn 70½ and a distribution the following year; you may remain in a lower tax bracket, which would be advantageous. You can always take out more if you need it.

… eventually, by law, you will have to withdraw funds from your IRA (not your Roth IRA)or qualified retirement plan.

Calculating Your MRD after Age 70½

Calculating minimum required distributions used to be a nightmare. Prior regulations were full of traps with far-reaching consequences in terms of designated beneficiaries and minimum required distributions. Fortunately, regulations completed in April 2002 dramatically simplified the process.

Under prior law there were also a number of options in terms of calculating minimum distributions. Before we get technical about it, please recognize that if you don't care how the calculation is made, the new tables are in the IRS's Supplement to the 590 Publication printed in June 2002. Alternatively, you could go to www.PayTaxesLater.com/calculator, select the minimum required distribution calculator, enter your birth date and the balance of your IRA, and your minimum required distribution will appear. There are also tables in the appendix of this book.

Currently, minimum required distributions (MRD) are calculated by taking your projected distribution period, based on your age and the age of a beneficiary deemed to be 10 years younger than you, and dividing that factor into the balance of your IRA or qualified plan as of December 31 of the prior year. Bear in mind that your projected life expectancy factor or the projected distribution period is not based on your eating and exercise habits or even your genetic history! It is an actuarial calculation from the IRS.

The following explanation will help you understand how the minimum distribution figures are derived.

The IRS provides three life expectancy tables. (In keeping with the IRS's contrary nature, the most frequently used table is Table III, not Table I. I present them here in the reverse order.)

Table III: Uniform Lifetime Table (*for use by unmarried IRA owners and married owners whose spouses are not more than 10 years younger*). The table is available at www.PayTaxesLater.com/mrd_table.htm, or from a link on the page www.PayTaxesLater.com/calculator or in the appendix.

Table II: Joint Life and Last Survivor Expectancy Table (*for IRA owners with spouses 10 or more years younger*). Not covered on our Web site, nor in the appendix because it is too long. See IRS publication 590.

Table I: Single Life Expectancy Table (*for IRA beneficiaries*). The table is available on the web page with the IRA Beneficiary Calculator at www.PayTaxesLater.com/calculator and the appendix.

Table III: Uniform Lifetime Table for IRA Owners

Generally speaking, most IRA owners will use Table III. In effect, the age-dependent projected distribution periods in Table III are based on joint life expectancy projections of an IRA owner and a hypothetical beneficiary 10 years younger. Using a joint life expectancy is advantageous because the longer joint-life expectancy factor reduces the annual minimum required distribution. But rather than using the actual life expectancy of the beneficiary for the calculations, the IRS simplified the terms. Table III deems all beneficiaries—from children to grandmothers—to have a life expectancy 10 years longer than that of the owner. At age 71, the projected distribution period is 26.5 years (roughly the single life expectancy from Table I plus 10 years, although you must refer to the tables for the precise factor).

MINI CASE STUDY 4.1
MRD Calculation for IRA Owners

Bob turns 75 in 2006; his beneficiary is his son Phillip, age 48. The balance in Bob's IRA on December 31, 2005, is $500,000. To calculate his minimum required distribution for 2006, he takes the life expectancy from Table III, 22.9, and divides that into his balance, $500,000, to arrive at $21,834.

When Bob dies, his son Phillip will inherit what is left of the IRA, and Phillip will then have to take minimum distributions on the inherited IRA. The minimum distribution of the inherited IRA is based on Phillip's life expectancy as determined under Table I.

Table II: Joint Life and Last Survivor Expectancy Table for IRA Owners with Spouses 10 or More Years Younger

Because nothing is ever without complications, there is an exception for married individuals when the IRA owner is 10 or more years older than the spouse beneficiary. Those individuals are permitted to use their actual joint life expectancy factor, which will be greater and result in smaller minimum required distributions.

MINI CASE STUDY 4.2

MRD Calculation with IRA Owner and Spouse More Than 10 Years Younger

Mark is 75; his beneficiary is his wife Mary, who is 63. According to Table II, their joint life expectancy factor is 24.3. Mark calculates his MRD by dividing 24.3 into his balance of $500,000 to arrive at $20,576. Mark's MRD is lower than Bob's as shown in the previous example because Mark and his wife were permitted to use their actual joint life expectancy factor for his calculation.

Table I: Single Life Expectancy Table for IRA Beneficiaries

Nonspouse beneficiaries of inherited IRAs must take distributions based on their actual life expectancies as projected in Table I. The beneficiary finds his life expectancy factor in Table I as of the year following the year of the IRA owner's death. A spousal beneficiary of an IRA owner who dies before 70½ who does not wish to treat the IRA as his or her own can choose to defer distributions until the year that the IRA owner would have attained 70½ and then find his or her life expectancy factor in Table I as of that year. That is his divisor. For each subsequent year, the nonspouse beneficiary subtracts one from the original number, because his life expectancy is diminished by one year for every year he survives.

Calculating Your Life Expectancy after the Initial Year

Notice in Table I that the life expectancy of the beneficiary is reduced by one full year as each year passes. Tables II and III, however, reduce the life expectancy of the IRA owner by less than one each year. This is analogous to the old double recalculation method. The idea is that as we age, our life expectancy declines, but it does not decline by an entire year.

There is a unique exception for a surviving spouse who inherits an IRA but does not roll over the IRA to treat it as his or her own IRA. During the surviving spouse's lifetime, the life expectancy is recalculated each year based on his or her life expectancy under Table I. When the surviving spouse dies, the non-spouse heirs must use the life expectancy of the surviving spouse at the time of death reduced by one for each subsequent year. For a discussion on whether a spouse should treat an IRA as his or her own IRA, please refer to Chapter 10.

Timing Your First Required Distribution

Participants born between January 1, 1936, and June 30, 1936, will have to take one distribution in 2006 and one in 2007, or two distributions in 2007 if he or she failed to take a distribution in 2006. If the participant failed to take a distribution in 2006, the first distribution in the year 2007 would have to be taken prior to April 1, 2007 (in effect for what should have taken in the year 2006), and the second distribution will have to be taken by December 31, 2007.

A participant born between July 1, 1936 and June 30, 1937, will reach 70½ during 2007. Technically, he or she could delay taking the first required minimum distribution until April 1, 2007. The rule was and remains that the required beginning date for taking minimum required distributions is April 1 of the year following the year the participant turns 70½. If, however, a participant was born between July 1, 1936, and June 30, 1937, and waits until 2008 for the first distribution, then that person must take two distributions in 2008. The first distribution would be due before April 1, 2008, and the second distribution would be due by December 31, 2007. Annual minimum distributions would continue for the rest of the participant's life.

For participants born July 1, 1937, or afterwards, there is no minimum required distribution for 2007. Unless the participant needs the money or is pursuing the early distributions of an IRA based on lower income tax brackets or estate plan strategies, he or she is better off leaving the money in the IRA and taking the first minimum required distribution when required in 2008 or later.

So, if you have a choice, should you limit your distributions to one per year, or should you wait and then take two the following year? If you take a minimum distribution the year that you turn 70½ and only one distribution the following year, you may remain in a lower tax bracket, which would be advantageous. Taking two distributions in one year could push you into a higher tax bracket and possibly accelerate the phase-out of certain tax credits or deductions. If that is the case, you will likely be better off violating our "pay taxes later" rule by taking one distribution and paying some tax before you have to. On the other hand, if it will not make a difference "that is, if you will remain in the same tax bracket even with two distributions" then wait until you are required to begin distributions, and take advantage of the additional period of tax-deferred growth.

Special Rule for Qualified Plan Owners Who Are Still Working Past Age 70½

Minimum required distribution rules apply to traditional IRAs (not Roth IRAs) and qualified plans (401(k)s, 403(b)s, Roth 401(k)s and Roth 403(b)s, etc.). The rules, however, governing 401(k)s and 403(b)s are slightly different than for IRAs.

- If you are still working after age 70½, you do not have to take a distribution from the retirement plan connected to your current job as long as you do not own more than 5% of the company.
- If you have a plan such as a 401(k) plan associated with a job from which you have retired, you will have to take your initial minimum required distribution by April 1 of the year following the year in which you reached 70½.
- If you had a 401(k) plan from a former job and rolled that 401(k) plan into a plan associated with the job

at which you are still working, then you will have to check with the plan administrator of your current plan to see whether you will be forced to take MRDs from the portion of that 401(k) plan that is attributable to your former employment upon attaining age 70½. PLR 200453015 published in January 2005 states that the IRS permits deferral of the MRDs on all of the funds in the new employer's account including the rollover contributions from the former employer until April 1 of the year after the employee retires from the new employer. You must, however, make sure that the employer's plan will allow you to do what the IRS will allow you to do.

MINI CASE STUDY 4.3

MRDs If Still Working Past Age 70½

Joan continues to work although she is older than 70½. She has a total of $1 million in her 401(k) plans: $500,000 associated with her current job and $500,000 from a former job. She has never consolidated the two plans. Her new plan has her and her employer's most recent contributions.

By April 1 of the year after she turns age 70½, she will be required to take minimum distributions from the $500,000 associated with the job she left but not from the account that is still active due to her employment. Whether she could take the money from the 401(k) from the job she retired from, roll it into her current plan (by trustee-to-trustee transfer), and avoid an MRD is not clear. The IRS will allow it, but her current employer may not.

There may be an incentive for someone still working after age 70½ to consider rolling money out of their IRA and into a retirement plan at work. Usually, I prefer money going the other way, which is from 401(k) to IRA.

I have a client who became really excited about the prospect of avoiding his minimum distribution. He wanted to start his own retirement plan (actually a SIMPLE) based on his small

Schedule your IRA distribution
for Thanksgiving

self-employment income. Then he wanted to roll his IRA into the SIMPLE and suspend his minimum required distributions on his IRA. It was a good thought, but with a fatal flaw. He is more than a 5% owner of his consulting business, and the rule about deferring the MRD distribution after 70½ does not apply to individuals with a 5% or greater ownership in the company.

Special Rule for 403(b) Participants

Both employee and employer contributions to a 403(b) plan made before January 1, 1987, are not subject to minimum required distributions until age 75. As a result, the balance in your 403(b) as of December 31, 1986, is not subject to MRDs until you reach 75, not 70½, even if you have retired. If you fall into this special category of 403(b) account holders, you should consult with your organization's benefits office to determine the balance of the account as of December 31, 1986. Surprisingly, many institutions, including TIAA-CREF, do a good job of tracking that balance.

On the other hand, when you actually calculate the tax advantage of keeping the funds in the 403(b) to defer a portion of the minimum distribution, it is relatively small. If you think you could get even a slight investment advantage by doing a trustee-to-trustee transfer from your 403(b) to an IRA, it would still be worthwhile.

Would you like more cutting edge information on distribution planning for TIAA-CREF participants? Please go to www.paytaxeslater.com/book/tiaa-cref.htm or go to the back of the book and fill out the order form. Please sign up now while it's fresh on your mind!

When Should You Schedule Taking Your MRD?

Ideally, you should take your MRD on December 31 to accrue the full year's deferral. By taking the MRD in December and having federal income tax withheld, the tax withheld is treated as if it was withheld throughout the year. In the real world, however, it is difficult to get any work done in December, and trying to comply with a deadline between Christmas and the last day of the year is a nightmare. Remember, *if you miss taking a withdrawal by year-end, you face the 50% penalty for failing to take your required minimum distribution: an expensive penalty*. If you don't need the cash, I recommend scheduling your distribution for Thanksgiving or early December. If you need the MRD distribution for your spending needs, it may be best to schedule 12 equal monthly distributions throughout the year.

If you don't need the cash, I recommend scheduling your distribution for Thanksgiving or early December.

A Key Lesson from This Chapter

Keep your MRD to a minimum. Do not take out more money than you need so that you keep the balance in your tax-deferred accounts as great as possible.

Critical Decisions You Face at Retirement: Rollovers versus Trustee-to-Trustee Transfers and Other Strategies

They say it is better to be poor and happy than rich and miserable, but how about a compromise like moderately rich and just moody?

— Diana, Princess of Wales

Main Topics

- Assessing the flexibility of your retirement plan
- Advantages of IRA investment options
- Advantages of trustee-to-trustee transfers
- Disadvantages of trustee-to-trustee transfers
- The mechanics of initiating the transfer or rollover

> **KEY IDEA**
>
> Transferring a retirement plan into an IRA is generally a good idea, and even more important if the rules governing your retirement plan do not allow your beneficiary to "stretch" distributions over his or her lifetime.

When someone retires or is "service terminated," the big question is, "What should I do now?"

Without getting into specific investment ideas, first let's consider whether it makes sense for you to keep your money in your existing retirement plan, transfer it to an IRA, or take a lump-sum distribution.

Contingent on the specifics of any given retirement plan, the basic options are as follows:

1. Transfer the money into a separate IRA.
2. Leave the money in the plan where it already is.
3. Annuitize the balance.
4. Some combination of options 1, 2, and 3 (often my favorite choice).
5. Take a lump-sum distribution.

Lump-Sum Distribution

First, let's get the terminology straight. When I refer to the "lump-sum distribution," I am referring to the special tax treatment afforded retirees when they withdraw their entire account and pay income tax on the entire amount. Ouch!

Many retirees say they "took the lump-sum," but what they really mean is that they chose *not* to annuitize their retirement plan accumulations—that is, not to accept regular monthly payments for the rest of their lives. (For more information on annuitizing, see Chapter 6.) What actually happened was that they rolled or transferred the money into an IRA or left the money in the existing retirement plan. Few retirees actually elect the special tax treatment per Internal Revenue Code (IRC) Section 402(d), which is the proper meaning of "taking a lump-sum distribution."

The advantage of a lump-sum distribution is the special tax calculation applied to the entire lump-sum. The tax calculation is called 10-year averaging, and it is available only to individuals born before 1936. The essence of 10-year averaging is that you may take your entire retirement plan and pay income taxes on it immediately but at a reduced income tax rate. In addition, a 20% capital gains tax rate is available for the amount attributable to pre-1974 contributions to the plan. This amount will often be less than the ordinary income tax that would otherwise be due.

Only participants in Section 401(a) qualified retirement plans (i.e., Section 401(k), pension, or other profit sharing plans but not Section 403(b), IRA, or SEP-IRA plans) can qualify for lump-sum distribution treatment. A lump-sum distribution is only permitted when the participant reaches 59½, or if the participant is separated from service, or if the participant dies. Finally, a lump sum distribution must be made within a 12-month period from the triggering event for the distribution (i.e., death, attainment of age 59½, separation from service), subject to certain exceptions, to qualify as a lump-sum distribution.

Ten-Year Averaging Is a Hellish Calculation

Do you qualify? Should you do it?

The answer in both cases is usually no. I will spare you the details. Even assuming you are willing to jump through enough hoops to qualify, for most employees it will result in a needless acceleration of income taxes, though admittedly at a lower-than-normal rate.

In practice, I have never recommended a 10-year averaging plan but have preferred to take advantage of the net unrealized appreciation (NUA) provisions when available (described in more detail later in this chapter) and roll the rest into an IRA. My reason for not getting too excited about the 10-year averaging is not the restrictions, but the fact that you must come up with taxes now. Remember: *pay taxes later*. Nonetheless, running the numbers is a prudent approach.

The general idea behind the lump-sum distribution is that if you successfully jump through a series of hoops, the IRS will discount your taxes. That said, even at a reduced tax rate it would require some very compelling arguments to persuade me that accelerating taxes is a good idea—especially if large sums of money are involved, which is often the case.

In theory, I can picture the lump-sum distribution (LSD) being useful in two situations.

1. You have a phenomenal use for the money. Some physicians, who have pensions in addition to a 401(k), have taken an LSD and used the money to speculate in real estate. They paid the reduced tax on the LSD and used the remaining proceeds as a down payment on commercial real estate. If the rent covered the mortgage, the idea was that the building appreciation

would be on the entire purchase price of the real estate and not the amount invested (the down payment). With the boom real estate market of the past decade that strategy worked for a number of taxpayers, leading invariably to unrealistic expectations for the next generation of would-be landlords. During the best of times that strategy was too aggressive for me, and in today's environment I would not even think about it.

2. I could picture considering the LSD if the retirement-plan owner was rich and either terminally ill or extremely old and if the value of the total estate was worth well more than the exemption equivalent amount ($2 million in 2006). In that case, he or she might want to consider the LSD to avoid the combined income and estate taxes on the IRA after death.

Other professionals certainly disagree with me. My natural bias is toward keeping retirement assets in IRAs or retirement plans rather than withdrawing the money and paying the tax earlier than necessary. If there were a good reason to make early IRA or retirement plan withdrawals, then the LSD becomes attractive. I just hate paying tax up-front.

Deciding on a good strategy for handling your retirement assets is an area where the appropriate financial advisor can be worth his or her weight in gold.

You may find a situation where the LSD may be a good choice, but approach LSDs with a predisposition against the LSD and make a qualified financial professional prove to you, with hard numbers, that it would be a good thing. If you take that approach, you will likely be safe from making a bad decision.

Of much greater benefit is the discussion about NUA (later in this chapter), which often is found with the discussion of LSDs.

Deciding on a good strategy for handling your retirement assets is an area where the appropriate financial advisor can be worth his or her weight in gold, particularly if they are number runners. Getting good advice at this point can have a significant impact on your future.

Rolling Over to an IRA

Retirees often talk about "rolling over to an IRA" or "rolling money out of a retirement plan and into an IRA." Technically we should to use the term "transfer," simply because the IRS makes a significant distinction between the mechanics and regulations of a rollover versus a trustee-to-trustee transfer. The trustee-to-trustee transfer is simpler, and what I usually recommend. I talk further about the distinctions between rollovers and transfers at the end of this chapter. (In keeping with common usage, when referring to a transfer, I will use the terms "rollover" and "transfer" interchangeably throughout this book.)

Retirees often talk about "rolling over to an IRA" or "rolling money out of a retirement plan and into an IRA." Technically we should use the term "transfer," simply because the IRS makes a significant distinction between the mechanics and regulations of a rollover versus a trustee-to-trustee transfer.

Though there are a few downsides, transferring retirement plan accumulations into an IRA via a trustee-to-trustee transfer is usually the best option. As with most decisions, there are advantages and disadvantages.

Tax Advantages of Transferring a 401(k) (or Other Retirement Plan) into an IRA

The "stretch IRA" concept—limiting distributions from an inherited IRA to the minimum to maintain money in the tax-deferred environment for as long as possible after the death of the IRA owner—is sound. I discuss more about the stretch IRA in Chapter 10.

With proper planning you can put in place the mechanisms to stretch taxable distributions from an inherited IRA and certain retirement plans for decades, sometimes as long as 80 years after the original owner dies. If, however, the employer's retirement plan document stipulates the wrong provisions, the stretch may be replaced by a screaming income tax disaster. The heirs could be in for a tax nightmare if Dad never transferred his retirement plan into an IRA.

Many investors fail to realize that the specific plan rules that govern their individual 401(k) or other retirement plan take precedence over the IRS distribution rules for inherited IRAs or retirement plans. The distribution rules that come into play at the death of the retirement plan owner are usually found in a plan document that few employees or advisors ever read. Many, if not most plan documents say that in the event of death, a nonspouse beneficiary must receive (and pay tax on) the entire balance of the retirement plan the year after the death of the retirement plan owner. These retirement plans don't allow a nonspouse beneficiary to stretch distributions.

For example, in Pittsburgh there are a lot of retired Westinghouse 401(k) plan owners who still maintain the balance of their retirement plans in the Westinghouse 401(k). If they die with a balance in the Westinghouse 401(k) plan and have named someone other than a spouse as a beneficiary, the entire balance must be withdrawn by the beneficiary in the year following the 401(k) plan owner's death. This enormous distribution results in a huge acceleration of fully taxable income. If there is a $1 million balance, the nonspouse heir or heirs will have to pay income taxes on $1 million. Then, the remaining balance, roughly $650,000 ($1 million minus the $350,000 immediate income tax hit) would be outside of the tax-deferred protection of an inherited IRA.

Had the Westinghouse 401(k) participant taken that money and transferred it into an IRA before he died, the nonspouse beneficiary would have been able to stretch the distributions based on his or her life expectancy. Failing to make the IRA transfer will result in an unnecessary massive income tax burden for the nonspouse beneficiary. I know of many real-life examples where that acceleration of taxes on an inherited 401(k) resulted in an income tax nightmare for the beneficiaries. Please don't compound the tragedy of your death by creating a tax nightmare for your heirs.

If I compare the results of inheriting a retirement plan that makes no allowances for a nonspouse to "stretch" distributions versus an inherited IRA where the beneficiary can stretch the distributions (and defer taxes), I can chart the result for the beneficiary as in Figure 5.1.

Figure 5.1

Stretched IRA or Retirement Plan Balance versus Accelerated Lump-Sum Distribution

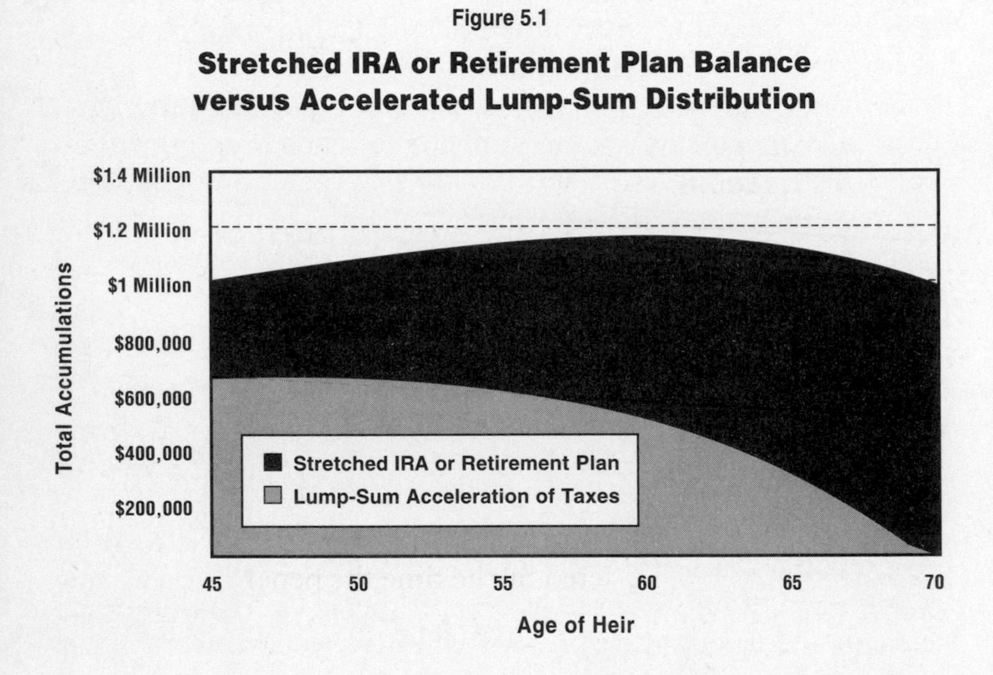

The following assumptions are reflected in Figure 5.1.

1. The inheritances begin with a beneficiary IRA of $1 million versus $650,000 of after-tax funds, assuming 35% tax would be paid on a $1 million taxable withdrawal in one year.
2. Annual spending needs of $40,000 after taxes are deducted annually from each inheritance, indexed for 3% inflation.
3. Assumptions for the $650,000 of after-tax funds are as follows:
   - Investment returns are 7% annually, 70% of which is capital appreciation and 30% of which is ordinary interest income.

- Capital gains are realized on 15% of the prior year's cumulative unrealized capital appreciation (a 15% portfolio turnover rate).
- Capital gains are also realized on the withdrawals for expenses and to pay income taxes.
- A small capital gains tax rate of 9% is used for the realized capital gains on after-tax funds.
- Ordinary interest income is taxed at a rate of only 15%, a lower rate than for the tax rate on the retirement plan distributions.

4. Annual withdrawals from the inherited IRA are taxed at a higher rate of 25% and are equal to the spending amount plus taxes.

These assumptions actually favor the after-tax inheritance by using lower capital gains tax rates in the future, but this treatment is nowhere near enough to compensate for the large initial tax hit of 35%. The dramatic difference noted in the two inheritances show the value of continuing tax deferral on a large amount of money. The accelerated lump-sum distribution scenario shows that all the funds are depleted by the time the beneficiary reaches age 70, when the IRA or retirement account's value of the inherited IRA is nearly $1 million.

If your nonspouse beneficiary must take the money all at once—thus ending the deferral—the large amount of ordinary income will likely move him or her into a higher tax bracket. This accounts for the significantly lower starting amount for the "accelerated 401(k) fund," which must be converted into after-tax funds.

Rolling the 401(k) into an IRA

Are you considering navigating these potentially rocky waters **without** a professional who is qualified and experienced in distribution and estate planning for IRAs and retirement plans?

Please read this next tragic story. This happens all the time. You can avoid it with the right professional and proper planning.

MINI CASE STUDY 5.1

True Story of the Disastrous Consequences of Not Making a 401(k) Rollover to an IRA (details adapted)

Even before the divorce papers were final, the mother of a young son had her divorce attorney draft a new will and retirement plan beneficiary designation. In her will and in her retirement plan from her old job, she left everything to her son via a trust that provided for his education, among other things. Making provisions for her son was particularly important because she was in poor health and was no longer able to work.

She saw a financial planner about the possibility of rolling her retirement plan into an IRA. She hated to pay fees and found it particularly distasteful because she liked the fixed account of her employer's plan. She was not aware that the rules of her retirement plan, as stated in the plan document, stipulated that the entire plan balance must be withdrawn within a year of her death. Her retirement plan would not permit her son to use his own life expectancy for minimum required distribution purposes.

... retirees who still have their money in a retirement plan that doesn't allow the stretch should strongly consider rolling their retirement plan, or at least a major part of their retirement plan, into an IRA ...

The financial planner, using only investment-related advice, could not convince her to roll over her 401(k) into an IRA. The attorney preparing the will and the beneficiary designation of the 401(k) never recommended an IRA rollover.

The mother died with over $250,000 held in her former employer's retirement plan. Because of the mandatory withdrawal, the trust for her son had to pay massive income taxes on the balance of the entire 401(k) in the year after she died. Also, the trust for her son had an even higher income-tax rate than he would have had individually, which meant that the effective income-tax rate on those retirement monies was the highest (35%) bracket. Additionally, the remaining funds in the trust after paying the income taxes on the inherited IRA were "after-tax funds" that generated income. As a result, the trust for her son would have to pay income tax on the earnings every year.

Had the mother taken her retirement plan and rolled it into an IRA the day before she died, and used the appropriate beneficiary designation, the money would have remained as an inherited IRA in a tax-deferred environment. Distributions and thus taxation could have been spread over the son's life expectancy. For at least a portion of that money, income tax could have been deferred for over 80 years.

If they had read *Retire Secure!* they would have foreseen the problem of the accelerated income tax rules in the employer's plan. The advisor could have pointed to compelling reasons to transfer the money into an IRA that went beyond investment issues. They might have considered rolling everything but the fixed income fund into an IRA, but they didn't. The result of the lack of planning and the lack of a knowledgeable advisor left the son financially handicapped, on top of losing his mother.

Moral of the story: Retirees who still have their money in a retirement plan that doesn't allow the stretch should strongly consider rolling their retirement plan, or at least a major part of their retirement plan, into an IRA to protect the next generation from an unnecessary massive acceleration of income tax. If you are unaware of your plan's death distribution rules, please learn them right away. It could save your family a bundle in the long run.

Investment Reasons to Transfer to an IRA

Perhaps even more compelling than the tax reason to transfer the money out of the retirement plan and into an IRA is the opportunity to take advantage of the universe of investment choices offered by IRAs. In the IRA world, the big challenge is choosing among the thousands of funds, stocks, bonds, etc., that are available for investments in an IRA. Leaving the money in the company plan will limit your options. The argument for greater investment choices becomes even more critical if your plan does not offer good investment choices. Though the trend is to give employees more choices and more advice than in the past, transferring the money into an IRA will always give the retiree more and often better choices.

Advantages of Leaving the Money Where It Is

Let's assume for a moment that you are retired and have the option of transferring your retirement plan into an IRA. Are there good reasons to leave the money where it is and not make the trustee-to-trustee transfer? There sure are. Don't skip this part.

The best reason for leaving the money in the plan is that your current retirement plan may have an excellent fixed income fund, often guaranteed in the form of a GIC (guaranteed income contract). Many of the fixed funds that purchased long-term bonds, mortgages, and commercial paper a number of years ago when interest rates were higher are still holding those investments. As a result, many of these fixed-income accounts are paying out higher returns than those available for comparable current investments with the same degree of safety.

But, in general, if you hold stocks or alternate investments—other than a much-better-than-average type of fund that you could not replicate outside of your retirement plan—I would like to see you make a trustee-to-trustee transfer out of the retirement plan and into an IRA (subject to other exceptions coming up). Even with that good investment, in general, I still prefer the trustee-to-trustee transfer.

On the other hand, some commentators feel that naive retirement plan owners are likely to be the victims of unscrupulous financial advisors. The argument goes that if you stay in your 401(k) plan then you will avoid some of these unscrupulous advisors. Though I hate to admit it, for at least some 401(k) participants, and for some advisors, the concern has merit.

Weighing the Investment Advantages versus the Threat of Income Tax Acceleration

My Westinghouse clients and similarly situated retirees often tell me they understand about the stretch IRA and the acceleration of income taxes for their heirs, but they don't want to give up the security of their fixed-income account that is paying higher-than-current interest rates on comparable investments. At least to some extent, they are right. What should you do if you are in that situation? For one thing, just because a GIC (guaranteed income contract) is paying a higher rate now, please don't assume that will be an indefinite arrangement. As the old bonds and paper mature, the GIC will be forced to lower its return in keeping with the lower current rates. Therefore, the investment advantage, while real, will likely only be temporary. Beyond the investment issue, I would like to revisit the distinction between spousal and nonspousal beneficiaries.

Let's assume you have named your surviving spouse as the primary beneficiary. Your plan is that after your death, your spouse will choose to retain the retirement plan as his or her own rather than "disclaiming" to the children. In that case, under the rules of most retirement plans, the surviving spouse will be allowed to inherit the retirement plan with no obligation to withdraw it all and pay the income taxes. By naming your spouse as beneficiary, he or she will get the lifetime stretch even if the money remains in the 401(k) and you avoid the income tax acceleration at the first death.

The problem arises upon the death of the second spouse, when the money is left to the children or any nonspouse beneficiary. The income tax will be accelerated at the death of the second spouse. Over time, as shown in Figure 5.1, this income tax acceleration could cost the children $1 million. The only rational justification for risking the $1 million is that you prefer the fixed income account and the projected time frame for the problem seems very far removed; both you and your spouse have to die before the income tax is accelerated.

In trying to prepare for the death of the second spouse, the general strategy might include having the surviving spouse transfer the 401(k) into an IRA when the first spouse dies. The reason for thinking ahead in this way is that you never want to be in a situation where there is only one life separating the family from accelerated income taxation. The strategy might even include the idea that if the 401(k) owner gets sick, he or she would abandon taking advantage of the fixed contract, guaranteed investment advantage. The plan would be to transfer the money into an IRA to avoid the massive income tax hit in the event of the employee's death and the subsequent death of the employee's spouse.

If we use this straddle plan, that is, leave the money in the 401(k) but be prepared to roll it over into an IRA on short notice, you could argue that you are getting the best of both worlds. You and your spouse get the higher fixed-income-fund interest during your life and the stretch afterwards for children. This solution is comfortable.

Is it, though, a reasonable strategy? Not really. Too many things could go wrong. Failing health and advanced age seriously complicate the picture. In addition, my experience has been that people don't like to acknowledge how sick they are, and putting decisions off until you reach that state is not wise. A person who gets sick often pushes financial matters aside. I have often seen sick clients who just were not up for dealing with money. Justifiably, they want to devote all their remaining time and energy on their health and their family.

The strategy above would fail if upon the first death (it could be either spouse), the surviving spouse fails to make the transfer from the retirement plan to the IRA. After a death, I have seen surviving spouses freeze, that is, be afraid to do anything. If this happens and the surviving spouse dies before the transfer to an IRA is made, then we have the income tax acceleration disaster. If there is a sudden or unexpected death, the trauma can be even more paralyzing.

If you are currently a participant in a plan that accelerates income at your death for nonspousal beneficiaries, in order to avoid the acceleration, you must transfer this money to an IRA before the nonspouse beneficiary inherits the funds or the nonspouse beneficiary will face massive taxation. I recommend moving the money out of the 401(k) while everyone is healthy and choosing the appropriate investments, perhaps with the help of a qualified and reputable investment advisor or money manager to compensate for the loss of the fixed income fund.

One compromise might be to leave in the 401(k) the fixed asset portion of your portfolio that is currently invested at higher-than-current market rates and transfer the rest into an IRA that will allow the stretch. I would consider this approach the minimum that you should do to avoid the income tax acceleration.

Additional Advantages of Retaining a 401(k) Rather Than Rolling Into an IRA

1. *Superior credit protection*: Many ERISA-(Employee Retirement Income Security Act of 1974) type plans enjoy the federal protection against creditors and bankruptcy that IRAs do not enjoy. It should be noted, however, that the Bankruptcy Abuse Prevention Act of 2005, signed in April 2005 by President Bush includes a $1 million exemption for contributory IRAs and Roth IRAs. It further exempts all rollovers from retirement plans to IRAs. Because there are two different types of creditor protection, owners of large IRAs are advised to keep their rollover IRA in a separate account as their contributory IRA. IRAs usually have state law protections, but over time, even these state law protections have diminished. For the vast majority of participants, a good umbrella insurance policy providing coverage of at least $1 million or possibly $2 million or more (to protect against unexpected liabilities) is the best solution. For participants with serious liability issues, such as emergency room doctors or surgeons, the superior credit protection may be more important than the investment and estate planning advantages of the IRA. For example, I recently worked with a physician who decided not to terminate his qualified retirement plan for these reasons when it would have been easier to terminate the plan and roll the plan balance into an IRA. For the physician, the additional asset protection feature of an ERISA plan was more important than the simplicity and reduced fees of an IRA.
2. *Special rules allow employees of companies whose ownership interest is 5% or less, to defer taking their minimum required distributions until they retire,* even after they turn age 70½. For example, let's assume you are such an employee, aged 72, and

still working. Half of your retirement assets are in a 401(k) where you currently work. The other half is in an IRA, which came from a rollover from a previous employer. Regarding the 401(k) where you are still working, there is no required minimum distribution as long as you continue to work. You must take your annual minimum distribution from your traditional IRA. Even if the company allows you to transfer a portion of the 401(k) into an IRA, there is at least an argument for leaving it in the 401(k) to continue deferring taxes until the time arrives for minimum required distributions.

3. *Borrowing privileges:* The 401(k) plan may have provisions that allow you to borrow against the plan. Though I normally prefer borrowing by using a mortgage or home equity loan or line of credit when the interest expense can be deducted on your tax return, there are situations when it may be handy to borrow money from a 401(k) plan. Borrowing from an IRA is not permitted.
4. Before you initiate a trustee-to-trustee transfer out of a 401(k) into an IRA you might be giving up an enormous opportunity if you do not check to see if there is any net unrealized appreciated (NUA) stock and any after-tax money in the 401(k) or other qualified plan. *If there is any NUA or after-tax money in the retirement plan, then special treatment is highly recommended.* (Please see Chapter 7 for more on NUA.) Checking for NUA is even more important since recent tax law changes have temporarily reduced capital gains tax rates.

Music to the Ears of a CD Investor

I bet you are tired of hearing everyone talk about the benefits of a well-balanced portfolio, aren't you? You don't want to hear that inflation will eat at the purchasing power of your CD investments. You just want some good advice on how to manage your CDs. OK Fair enough. This is for you.

With interest rates increasing as this is written, 5- to 10-year CDs, appropriate for an IRA, can be obtained with annual rates approaching 5%. Perhaps even more attractive to conservative retirees are the offers by some banks to allow seniors to upgrade their CDs annually to a higher interest rate and longer term. When the maximum term, typically 10 years, is reached, the annual upgrade in rates is still permissible, but you have to ask for it. Choosing CDs with a term of 5 to 10 years should alleviate some of the worry about market ups and downs. Also many retirees are unaware that many banks permit annual MRDs to be taken from CDs without breaking the CD or incurring any penalty or loss of earnings. Virtually all institutions follow this rule when taking MRDs from IRA CDs. But, don't just arbitrarily roll over a sizeable portion of your 401(k) to your current bank; get quotes from three or four banks. Share the quotes with the bank manager you really want to do business with, and ask her or him for their best and final rates.

The Mechanics of IRA Rollovers and Trustee-to-Trustee Transfers

Let's assume the goal is to move your retirement plan funds from one retirement plan to either another retirement plan or an IRA (what I generally recommend). The lay public usually calls this kind of transfer a "rollover." But you need to be aware that according to the proper terminology, there are:

- Rollovers
- Trustee-to-trustee transfers

Individuals planning to move money from a 401(k) retirement plan (or similar plan) to an IRA generally will want to conduct a trustee-to-trustee transfer.

A rollover from a 401(k) or other type of qualified retirement plan into an IRA is tax-free, provided you comply with the rules. IRC Section 402 states that retirement plan distributions are not taxed if rolled over to a retirement plan or an IRA. Technically, a rollover is a distribution from one retirement plan or an IRA to the owner, and then taken by the owner to the new retirement plan. If you effect a transfer of funds through a rollover, you have to worry about the following rules:

- The 60-day rule
- The 20% withholding-tax rule
- The one-rollover-every-12-months rule

The best way to avoid the problems of the 60-day-rule, the 20% withholding-tax rule, and the one-rollover-per-12 months rule is via a trustee-to-trustee transfer of a retirement plan to an IRA. In a trustee-to-trustee transfer, no participant or IRA owner ever touches the actual money. It is an electronic blip; a few pieces of paper (not green) pass from one financial institution to another. Alternatively, some institutions make the check payable to the new trustee but send it to the participant who is then responsible for forwarding the check to the new trustee. Although this is a permissible method of completing a trustee-to-trustee transfer, please speak to a qualified advisor and the plan administrator before completing a trustee-to-trustee transfer under these circumstances.

The following three sections provide a short description of the problems you may encounter if you do not do a trustee-to-trustee transfer. If the merit of doing the trustee-to-trustee transfer rather than a rollover is established, you may safely skip the next three sections and jump to "What You May Rollover and What You May Not."

Avoiding the 20% Withholding-Tax Rule

When someone elects to roll over a 401(k) or other retirement plan to an IRA without using a trustee-to-trustee transfer, the transferring company must withhold 20% of the amount rolled over. This can be a nightmare if the objective is to roll over the entire amount. Obviously, we want to keep this transaction income-tax-free. By not doing a trustee-to-trustee transfer, however, you create an unnecessary 20% withholding of income taxes. This withholding trap has caught many unwary 401(k) owners off guard. If your former employer must withhold 20%, the only way you will not have to pay any income taxes on the rollover is for you to come up with the 20% amount yourself, from other sources. If you don't have the 20% amount to restore to your retirement plan, you have even more headaches because you will have to pay income taxes on the rollover to the extent that the 20% withholding is insufficient to cover the taxes. The best way to avoid the 20% withholding rule is by simply doing a trustee-to-trustee transfer.

Note that the 20% withholding-tax rules do not apply when rolling over one IRA to another.

The 60-Day Rule

Let's assume you can get around the 20% withholding problem. Another problem remains. You must comply with the 60-day rule. You must restore the funds to another retirement plan or an IRA within 60 days of receiving the distribution. Otherwise, income taxes must be paid on the entire amount; furthermore, if you are age 59½ or younger, you have the added 10% premature distribution penalty—a nightmare.

Are there exceptions? A few—but basically, you don't want to go there. If you are planning to do a rollover as opposed to a trustee-to-trustee transfer, get the money back in a retirement plan or IRA within 60 days. Most of the reasons the IRS will accept as an excuse are so terrible that you would never want to plan for any of them to happen. If you do miss the 60-day rule accidentally, then you can start looking at the reasons the IRS will waive the rule, but don't expect to obtain relief.

In practice, people who want to do a rollover versus a trustee-to-trustee transfer may be looking for a short-term loan, and the only source of money is the IRA or a qualified plan. If the money was in an IRA that didn't allow a loan or the loan allowed by the qualified plan wasn't enough or had some undesirable restriction, some people who think they are clever might choose to withdraw their IRA or retirement plan and attempt to restore the account within the 60 days. That might work, but it is risky at best.

The classic reason for trying to finesse the system is to use the money for some type of real estate transaction. That is, however, what bridge loans at the bank are for. If avoiding those fees is so critical, and you are certain that there will be no hang-ups with either the sale or purchase of whatever the money is needed for, good luck. But if the deal goes sour because of some unforeseeable event, don't expect the IRS to have any sympathy.

Perhaps the Horse's Ass Award goes to the guy who wants to take advantage of some type of financial tip on an investment that isn't listed on one of the popular exchanges. He is told he can double his money in a month. The horse's ass has no other funds to invest except his IRA or retirement plan. He goes to his retirement plan, withdraws funds as a loan, invests in his "sure winner," and plans to restore the retirement plan before 60 days pass. The "sure winner" implodes, and the horse's ass not only lost money on his investment, but he will have to pay income taxes on money he doesn't have anymore. The $3,000-per-year loss limitation on deducting the capital loss will virtually make the tax benefits of the loss meaningless, and the income tax he must pay on the retirement plan withdrawal will be draconian.

If the hot tip were a stock or mutual fund that is traded over any of the recognized stock exchanges, he would have been better off rolling the money into an IRA and purchasing the security in his IRA. That way, when the account gets clobbered, at least he will not face the tax liability in addition to the loss.

The One-Rollover-Every-12-Months Rule

An individual is allowed only one rollover every 12 months, but the number of trustee-to-trustee transfers anyone can make is unlimited. If you have different IRAs or different retirement plans, you may have one rollover per separate IRA or separate retirement plan.

Also, the one-rollover-every-12-months rule applies only to IRAs. For example, a reader who initiates a direct rollover from a 401(k) to an IRA on January 2, 2005, can roll over to another IRA on January 15, 2005, if he or she so desires. This move is permissible because the first distribution was not from an IRA.

Again, life is complicated enough. Do a trustee-to-trustee transfer, and don't worry about this rule, the 60-day rule, or the 20% withholding rule.

What You May Roll Over and What You May Not

The general rule of thumb under the new expanded portability rules is that an individual can roll anything into anything. Of course, that is a slight exaggeration, but the general idea now is that funds can go from one qualified plan to another without taxation, though some restrictions may apply.

... the general idea now is that funds can go from one qualified plan to another without taxation, though some restrictions may apply.

Most of the recommended rollovers—or to be more technically correct, trustee-to-trustee transfers—will be from taxable retirement plans to IRAs. For example, a retired or service-terminated employee owning a fully taxable account, such as a 401(k), a 403(b), a 457 plan, an SEP, a Keogh, and so on, will usually be well served to institute a trustee-to-trustee transfer to an IRA. The employee is allowed to transfer from account to account if he or she likes. For example, if you leave your university job and go into the private sector, you might think it's a good idea to consolidate your old 403(b) with your new company's 401(k). You can, but I don't think it would be in your best interests. I would prefer you transfer the old 403(b) into a separate IRA and then start new contributions in the 401(k), which will eventually leave you with balances in an IRA and a 401(k).

Now, there will be times when it might be advisable to go backwards. For instance, if a working or self-employed IRA owner wanted to use retirement funds to purchase life insurance, he or she might take his or her IRA (through which he or she is not allowed to purchase life insurance), transfer it into a different qualified plan, and then purchase his or her insurance inside the qualified plan. Caution is advised, however, for retirement plan owners who want to purchase life insurance inside a retirement plan. We do not cover that risky strategy.

You can't, however,

- Transfer or roll over minimum required distributions from a retirement plan or an IRA into another retirement plan. You must pay tax on that MRD money.
- Make a Roth IRA conversion from your MRD.
- Open a Roth IRA with your MRD distributions.
- Transfer or roll over inherited IRA distributions.
- Transfer or rollover Section 72(t) payments (a series of substantially equal payments distributed from a qualified plan for the life of the employee or the joint lives of the employee and his designated beneficiary that qualifies for an exception from the 10% penalty otherwise imposed on 72(t) payments).

Special Exception for 403(b) Owners with Pre-1987 Balances

Even if retired, a 403(b) owner's pre-1987 balance is not subject to minimum distribution until he or she is age 75, not age 70½. If he takes the 403(b) money and rolls it into an IRA, he will be required to take his minimum required distribution on the entire balance in the account (including his pre-1987 dollars).

If the terms of the 403(b) retirement plan allow the stretch for the nonspouse beneficiary, then there is no tax motivation to do the rollover (assuming the retiree is happy with the investment accounts offered). In fact, there is a tax disincentive because of the acceleration of the minimum required distribution. The tax disincentive ends up being so minor, however, that if you think you can do even a tiny bit better by investing outside of the 403(b) with an IRA, then don't worry about the minor acceleration of income you will make by losing the option to defer the pre-1987 MRDs until you would have reached age 75.

Would you like more cutting edge information on distribution planning for TIAA-CREF participants? Please go to www.paytaxeslater.com/book/tiaa-cref.htm or go to the back of the book and fill out the order form. Please sign up now while it's fresh on your mind!

Inexact Language on a Beneficiary Form Spells Disaster

Sloppy titling could ruin the entire stretch IRA concept for nonspouse beneficiaries of an IRA. It is imperative that the deceased IRA owner's name remain on the account.

MINI CASE STUDY 5.2

The Difference between Proper and Sloppy Language on a Beneficiary Form

Grandpa and Grandma both name a well-drafted trust for their grandchild, Junior, in the beneficiary designations of their respective IRAs.

They both die during the same year. Due to a quirk in estate administration, Detailed Danny becomes the administrator for Grandpa's IRA, and Sloppy Susan becomes the administrator for Grandma's IRA. Detailed Danny, when transferring the inherited IRA to the trust for Junior, follows the advice of his grandfather's financial planner and titles the account "Grandpa's IRA (deceased, December 2004) Trust for Benefit of Junior." Junior, being only 10 years old at Grandpa's death, ends up stretching Grandpa's IRA for his entire lifetime. Even when Junior is 70 years old, the account continues to have Grandpa's name. Because the inherited IRA makes a tremendous difference in Junior's life and his financial security is assured, he often thinks of Grandpa's thoughtfulness and also appreciates Detailed Danny's care in handling the inherited IRA.

Sloppy titling could ruin the entire stretch IRA concept for nonspouse beneficiaries of an IRA. It is imperative that the deceased IRA owner's name remain on the account.

Sloppy Susan, when doing similar work for Grandma's IRA, titles the account "Trust for Junior." The trust is audited, and the IRS requires the trust to pay income tax on the entire balance. If the titling of the account does not make it clear that the IRA is inherited from the deceased IRA owner, the income tax on the inherited IRA is accelerated. The trust is then required to pay income tax on the entire balance and, to make it worse, at the higher trust income tax rates. When Junior turns 21, he finds out what happened and his attorney suggests he sue Sloppy Susan for negligence in the handling of his IRA.

Junior decides not to sue Sloppy Susan because it isn't nice to sue your mother. His mother, Sloppy Susan, did, however, deprive Junior of the stretch for Grandma's IRA, which will end up costing him over $1 milllion. His only consolation is that he will still receive inherited IRA benefits from Grandpa's IRA for the next 60 years. When Junior is age 70, he shakes his head while thinking of his grandmother. Grandma's legacy, of course, has long since vanished—ravaged by taxes due to sloppy titling.

Do you have a trusted advisor to help you with your retirement plan? Do you feel confident he or she is qualified and experienced in distribution and estate planning for IRAs and retirement plans? If you do, great. Please, finish reading this book, list your comments and concerns, and set up an appointment as soon as possible.

If, however, you don't have a trusted advisor and can't find anyone that you feel has the appropriate expertise in retirement plans and IRAs, there is another option for some readers. I am offering a number of free consultations and taking on a very limited number of private clients who will work with me directly. If you are interested in working with me one on one and you are a resident of PA, CA, FL, OH, NY, or VA, please visit www.PayTaxesLater.com/book/freeconsultation .htm or refer to the end of the book for contact information.

Make sure that your executor or administrator knows how to title the inherited IRA correctly. If you are a financial planner, I hope I have made a compelling case for correct titling of an inherited IRA. If you are in charge of internal office procedures at a financial institution, create a policy which ensures that all inherited IRAs retain the name of the deceased IRA owner; you will do a lot of beneficiaries much good.

Also, please don't assume that your financial professional, whether a CPA, financial planner, or (with all due respect) an attorney, will know about proper titling and act accordingly. Recently I received a call from a planner in California. This is a true story. He said "Jim, my client died, with more than a million dollars in an IRA. He left it to his son. When my secretary saw that the son was the beneficiary, she took the money and transferred it to his son's account. Is that okay?" Oh no! She just accelerated the income tax on one million dollars. He said to me, "Oh Jim, I'm sure the IRS will understand that it was just my secretary and she didn't mean to do it." No. The IRS won't. The client's son had to pay tax on $1 million instead of stretching that million out over the course of his life. Boom! Income tax on the whole thing. So instead of having a million the son now has only $600,000 (application of IRC 408[d][3][C] "Denial of Rollover Treatment for Inherited Accounts"). I hope his malpractice premiums were paid up. Whether he actually gets sued or not, the planner has to live the rest of his life knowing that mistake cost his client a bundle.

Other Titling Notes

If there are multiple beneficiaries (as is typical with accounts left to "children equally"), the accounts should be split after death and the inherited IRAs should then be kept separate. Please note that under the new rules, each child will be able to take MRDs from the inherited IRA based on his or her own life expectancy. In addition, though the deceased IRA owner's name will remain on the account, the Social Security number of the beneficiary should be used.

Choosing an Investment Institution after the Death of the IRA Owner

Let's assume that Detailed Danny knows all about the titling and takes equal care in looking at Grandpa's portfolio. As a result of his analysis, he determines that he wants to replace the financial institution where the money currently resides—the High Fee, Low Service Bank—to the firm where he invests his own money with his own trusted financial advisor who was actually the person who told him about the titling problem.

He requests the appropriate paperwork for transferring to his firm the account from the High Fee-Low Service Bank where Grandpa invested. He is informed that Grandpa's bank will not allow a trustee-to-trustee transfer of the inherited IRA. He objects but soon realizes that it is well within the power of the bank not to accommodate him on a trustee-to-trustee tax-free transfer. Sure, he can demand the bank be forced to distribute the money, but the bank cannot be forced to do a trustee-to-trustee transfer. Also, *the 60-day rule does not apply to inherited IRAs!* The High Fee, Low Service Bank could make Detailed Danny choose between leaving the money with them or suffer the income tax acceleration if the bank makes the transfer.

My approach to these problems is to try to be nice at first. That failing, I would apply relentless pressure and use whatever leverage I have to make the bank accommodate my wishes. The best way to approach the problem is for the IRA owner to know in advance the financial institution's policy with respect to this type of transfer. Don't work with one that imposes these types of limitations.

A Key Lesson from This Chapter

For most individuals approaching or at retirement, initiating a trustee-to-trustee transfer of a qualified retirement plan to an IRA is a good decision. With proper titling, you can preserve the stretch, and you can offer your heirs the continued advantage of tax-deferred growth and take advantage of a wider variety of investment choices during your lifetime. That said, you still have to weigh the decision carefully and look at the particular circumstances of your situation. Deciding how to manage your retirement assets at the time you retire is important and deserves your full attention.

Annuitizing Your Financial Accumulations: Does It Make Sense for You?

I advise you to go on living solely to enrage those who are paying your annuities.

— Voltaire

Main Topics

- Defining annuitizing
- Types of annuities
- Determining your "life expectancy"
- Picking among survivorship options
- Drawbacks of annuitizing

KEY IDEA

Annuitizing your retirement plan or "after-tax" accumulations can be a method of making sure you don't outlive your money. For some individuals, annuitizing part of their financial assets is a reasonable choice.

What Is "Annuitizing"?

An annuity refers to receiving a specified income payable at stated intervals for a fixed or contingent period. The counterpoint to an annuity is a lump-sum.

Annuitizing your retirement plan accumulations or after-tax money means purchasing an immediate annuity. Purchasing an immediate annuity ("annuitizing") involves surrendering all or a portion of your money in exchange for receiving regular, recurring payments.

There are other annuities, such as nonqualified tax-deferred annuities, which allow you to accumulate after-tax funds in an annuity vehicle prior to the time it is annuitized. That is often referred to as a commercial annuity. We do not examine commercial annuities in this book.

Choosing to annuitize your retirement plan is essentially the same as what a retirement plan participant is forced to do in a defined-benefit plan. That is, you get regular payments for the rest of your life as opposed to having access to a large chunk of money.

Choosing to annuitize your retirement plan is essentially the same as what a retirement plan participant is forced to do in a defined-benefit plan. That is, you get regular payments for the rest of your life as opposed to having access to a large chunk of money. The total of the monthly annuity payments is usually going to be more than the lump-sum amount, provided the owner does not die prematurely.

We combine the discussion of annuitizing your retirement plan and purchasing an immediate annuity because they are conceptually quite similar.

The basic concepts of annuitizing apply to both retirement funds and after-tax funds. The major difference is the income tax treatment of the annuity payments.

- Payments from an after-tax annuity are partially taxable in the early part of the payment stream, *partially taxable* because one portion of the payment is considered a return of the original capital and is not taxable until the entire original cost is recovered. The other portion of the payment is considered ordinary taxable income, such as interest income. After the initial period of cost recovery, which can last for many years, the payments become fully taxable.

- Distributions from annuities purchased with retirement funds, on the other hand, are fully taxable like pension income.

Payment Schedules

The terms and the duration of the annuity payments depend on what is offered and the choices made. Usually, the choices include receiving payments for:

- The remainder of your life
- The remainder of your and your spouse's life
- A fixed number of years
- One of the above plans with an extra provision to extend benefits to your heirs

There are many variations in payment schedules, including various guaranteed periods such as payments for life with 10 years of payments guaranteed. If the owner dies within 10 years of annuitizing the remaining payments within the 10 year period are paid to their heirs. Sometimes you can choose a higher payment while both the owner and his or her spouse are alive and a lower payment after the first death, such as a 100% benefit initially and a 50% or 66% benefit for the surviving spouse. *Remember, unless you pick one of the survivorship or guarantee options, there will be no money left to pass on to your heirs.*

Remember, unless you pick one of the survivorship or guarantee options, there will be no money to pass on to your heirs.

Which is the better deal? It depends. An ideal candidate for an annuity is a healthy single person with a long life expectancy who doesn't care about leaving any money behind. If the person is married, then a joint life annuity to last through both lifetimes could work equally well. Annuitizing a portion of a retirement plan is also a reasonable choice in many situations.

Most insurance companies and retirement plans will calculate your annuity payment according to your actuarial life expectancy based on age and sex. Your actual physical condition does not enter into the calculation unless you ask the insurance company to rate you. This is the opposite of life insurance. When purchasing life insurance, you want to show the life insurance company how healthy you are. The sooner you die, the better the decision to buy life insurance. With an immediate annuity you want to show the life insurance company that you have a much-reduced life expectancy. The longer you live after purchasing the annuity, the better it will work out for you and your family. Please note, annuitizing a portion of your assets is a method that insures your money lasts at least as long as you do.

Annuitizing would not be a good choice if you have a reduced life expectancy. Usually the annuity company or retirement plan does not give sufficient weight to the health of the applicant for me to recommend an annuity for someone with a reduced life expectancy. Occasionally, a company considers these factors, but not always. For example, I had a client with multiple sclerosis who was denied a favorable annuity rate in spite of her health condition.

Annuitizing: A Conservative Strategy?

One view holds that annuitizing over a lifetime or joint lifetimes is a conservative strategy because it practically ensures that you will not outlive your money. Although you lose access to the large lump-sum of money immediately after purchasing the annuity, and the lifetime-based payments stop after your death, the payments will not run out in your lifetime, no matter how long you live.

Annuitizing a large amount of money is sometimes an emotionally hard choice to make. It feels like you are "giving it all away" despite the fact that you are actually ensuring a secure income source. One solution to the fear of annuitizing is to annuitize only a portion of the available funds. Annuitizing a portion, but not all, of your assets is probably sound for many situations. Jonathan Clements, a great financial writer and defender of the consumer, wrote the following in his September 3, 2003, column for the *Wall Street Journal*:

> I often suggest that income-hungry retirees take maybe a quarter of their nest egg and use it to purchase an immediate-fixed annuity, thus buying a lifetime stream of income. But if you really want to generate a lot of income and you think you will live to a ripe old age, here is an even better strategy. Buy that immediate annuity—but wait until age 75, so you get a generous income stream based on your shorter life expectancy.

There are also some products that offer guarantees that provide some return of the capital invested if you die early. For example, one option would be to choose payments for life with a guaranteed 10-year payout to your heirs if you die prematurely. Sometimes, a policy will specify that a large portion of the original cost will be returned to the family if the owner dies early. Alternatively, you might want to consider forgoing the extra expense of an annuity guarantee feature, and instead buy a life insurance contract with money not spent on any guarantee feature. My personal preference is to keep it simple: If you choose to purchase an immediate annuity, make it for your life or the lives of both you and your spouse. The common advice among financial planners and attorneys is, "Don't sell a client an immediate annuity without a guarantee feature, because if the client dies early, the heirs might sue you or at least

Please note: Annuitizing a portion of your assets is a method that ensures your money lasts at least as long as you do.

give you plenty of grief." From a financial planner or insurance agent's viewpoint, that is probably good advice. For the client, however, it might not be the best advice.

If you haven't done it yet, please get out a pad of paper, a pen or pencil and/or your computer spreadsheet. This is a good time to start looking at your own figures. Remember, nothing is written in stone, and this is for your eyes only.

I'd like to remind you to find a professional who is qualified and experienced in distribution and estate planning for IRAs and retirement plans and inspires your confidencce.

I know I sound like a broken record, but I hate to think you'll make a mistake and then really regret doing this completely on your own.

MINI CASE STUDY 6.1

When Annuitizing the Majority of Your Assets Is a Good Choice

Ida is a retired 65-year-old woman in excellent health with no children and no heirs. After her daily yoga and meditation routine, she enjoys her steamed organic tofu and broccoli sprinkled with ground flax seeds. After her breakfast, she swallows a host of vitamins and supplements with wheatgrass juice. Then she walks three miles to visit with her 95-year-old parents who are also in excellent health.

She has a $400,000 CD and no other considerable assets. She receives $15,000 a year in Social Security. She hates thinking about money, but fears that she will become destitute or at least miserable if she invests unwisely and another downturn in the market takes place. She spends $34,000 per year before taxes. Though she would prefer to spend a little more, she never wants to be in a position where she has to spend less. Her five-year CD, however, is about to mature, and she discovers from her bank that she would only get 3.5% interest if she renews it.

If she continues the investments in 60-month CDs, based on a 3.5% interest rate, she would earn and receive only $14,000 of interest income plus her Social Security of $15,000 for a total income of $29,000 per year. Because her Social Security is nontaxable, she pays only a small amount of taxes—($1,041, federal and Pennsylvania state income taxes, based on 2005 rates)—and she is left with only $27,959 of net income. So she must eat into the principal amount every year if she wants to spend $34,000. With principal deterioration and inflation to worry about, she fears she will outlive her money. Though she has been advised about the advantages of diversification, she is not comfortable owning stocks and doesn't want to be an investor. Even with a diversified portfolio, there are no guarantees that she would meet her financial goals, and her fear of being forced to reduce her spending could become a reality.

Alternatively, she could also purchase a $400,000 lifetime annuity. She will discover that there are an overwhelming number of varieties and choices. She could take an annuity over her lifetime only, or over both her and a beneficiary's lifetime if she chooses to name a beneficiary. She could have fixed payments or increasing payments at a flat interest rate of increase, or payouts that could increase by various amounts based on stock market returns to some degree. Based on recent rate quotations, she could choose one of the following guaranteed fixed annuities that would pay her the following amounts no matter how long she lived:

	Monthly Payment	**Annual Total**
Fixed payments, no increases	$2,573.64	$ 30,883.68
Payments increasing 4% per year	1,929.16	23,149.92
Joint lives, fixed payments, no increases	2,334.75	28,017.00
Joint lives, payments increasing 4% per year	$1,713.33	$20,559.96

Taking inflation into account, Ida feels that increasing the payments by 4% per year should provide her with adequate safety, and even improve her financial situation over time if the current low inflation rates continue as expected. She has a boyfriend, but she chooses not to name him as a beneficiary because it would reduce her income. She decides to purchase the increasing single life annuity providing $23,149.92 initially, which, combined with her Social Security, gives her an income of $38,150; it also generates a better cash flow and less tax than the CD option because with the annuity only about 37.4% of the annuity payment will be taxable to her. A comparison of the CD option and the annuity option follows:

	CD Option Without an Annuity	**Annuity Option**
Social Security income	$ 15,000	$ 15,000
Interest income	14,000	0
Guaranteed annuity income	0	23,150
	29,000	38,150
Less income taxes	(1,041)	(314)
Less spending needs	(34,000)	(34,000)
Amount available for savings (or required savings withdrawal)	($ 6,041)	$ 3,836

The annuity meets her needs. She will have a guaranteed income stream that, with the 4% inflation adjustment protection, should be sufficient to meet her needs for the rest of her life. She realizes an initial return of 5.78% on her $400,000, and it will increase annually by 4%, which is probably better than she could do with any safe investment. If she had to continue with CD investments, future interest income would be reduced since the principal is deteriorating at $6,041 per year, and the deterioration will increase. On the other hand, with the annuity option, she is able to put $3,836 in savings.

Comparing the annuity option with the CD option, her annuity payments are always increasing 4% annually while the CD interest income decreases. This causes the CD balance to become fully depleted when Ida is about 86 years of age, at a time when there is a surplus balance of about $154,000 under the annuity option. Figure 6.1 shows the principal balance remaining under these two options.

Figure 6.1

Balance of Funds Available
CD Investments versus Lifetime Annuities

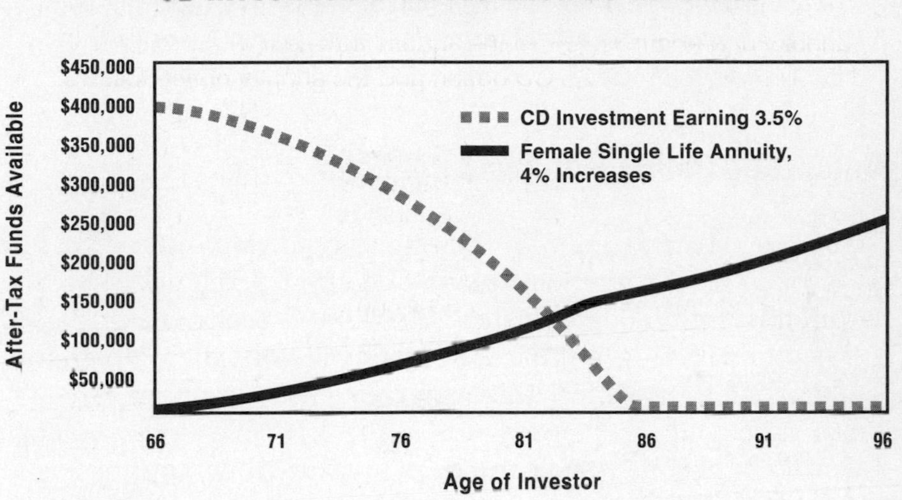

Figure 6.1 assumes that Ida's spending increases at a rate of 4% per year. You may be able to see that the annuity option levels off slightly when Ida is about 84 years old. This is due to a slight increase in the income taxes associated with the annuity. Only 37.4% of the annuity is taxable income initially, but when the nontaxable amounts received exceed the annuity cost of $400,000, the entire annuity payment becomes taxable. Most of Ida's Social Security income, however, is still not taxable even when this happens, and her taxes never exceed 10% of her income.

Though the annuity will end when she dies, she doesn't care because her needs are met and she has no heirs. This plan not only meets her psychological need for security, but it also is probably the best course of action for her.

Perhaps your investment goals are somewhat more aggressive than Ida's. In other words, you feel that to make the example more meaningful, we should compare the annuity with after-tax investments earning a rate of return of 5% or 6% instead of just a 3.5% CD. Using the same assumptions as in the above example, except that a 5% or a 6% rate of return on investments is achieved, the after-tax investment pool would be fully depleted by the time

Ida was 88 or 93 years old (for 5% or 6% rates of return), when there would still be either $197,000 or $304,000 remaining with the annuity option. Even Ida would flatly reject these more optimistic alternatives. She has no plans of dying before 88 or 93 and certainly does not want to live with investment worries or run the risk of running out of money.

Annuitizing Retirement Accumulations

Many people are faced with taking required minimum distributions from their retirement plans once they reach age 70½, the required beginning date. Instead of taking these payments based on the annual value and life expectancy factors, they can choose to annuitize the balance. This way, they no longer have to worry about managing the money and what happens if the balance dwindles or becomes depleted. In many situations, annuitizing at least a portion of the retirement assets is a good choice. In the late 1990s, when the market was up and you could smell confidence in the air, annuitizing was frowned upon. Why annuitize when you can make 25% in the market? Even if the market levels out at 10%, you could still do better than annuitizing.

In many real-life situations, annuitizing a portion of your retirement holdings is consistent with a desire for security. It provides a stable income that, combined with Social Security, will provide a minimum "base" of income and a sense of financial security not available with other strategies.

After three years in a row of significant losses in the stock market in 2000 to 2002, heightened fears of terrorism, federal deficits, and future stock market downturns, there is a new attitude. Many people just want to make sure they have financial security for themselves and their spouse. I rarely recommend that someone with large accumulations annuitize everything. Even with Ida, I would probably advise that she reserve $50,000 for another type of investment to give her a little liquidity.

In many real-life situations, annuitizing a portion of your retirement holdings is consistent with a desire for security. It provides a stable income that, combined with Social Security, will provide a minimum "base" of income and a sense of financial security not available with other strategies.

MINI CASE STUDY 6.2

When Annuitizing a Portion of the Retirement Plan Is Appropriate

George and his wife, Susan, both 65, retired in 1999 with $1.1 million in their combined retirement plans. George didn't do a good job of diversifying their holdings and to make matters worse, against Susan's wishes, he invested too much of their money in S&P large-cap growth stocks. After the market decline, they now have $800,000. No longer do George and Susan talk of a worry-free retirement. At the moment, they are more concerned about themselves than the stretch IRA for their grandchildren.

They have seen financial planners who have recommended a diversified portfolio striking a balance between income-bearing and growth investments. Still, Susan worries. The planners explain that if George and Susan invest too conservatively in an all-income portfolio, inflation will reduce the value of the principal and their estate will decline in purchasing power, something that makes Susan uneasy. George isn't as worried as Susan, but he would also like a long-term solution that would provide the possibility of an upside but with the assurance they will always have a roof over their head, food on the table, and gas in the car.

Although not all the investment forms of deferred annuities are available as immediate annuities, many investment choices for immediate annuities with qualified funds are available for George and Susan. Chances are they will purchase a fixed annuity because increasing annuities are often not available with qualified funds. That is, they will choose an annuity that is fixed in amount and will not go up with time. The payments, though level, will likely lose purchasing power with inflation. They may, however, choose a one-life annuity, a two-life annuity with full benefits to the survivor, or three-quarters or half benefits to the survivor, an annuity with a guaranteed payment for 5 years or 10 years, and so on. My purpose here is not to analyze all the annuity choices but to let you know that annuitizing a portion of a retirement plan is often a reasonable option that can be customized for your needs and goals.

My preference for George and Susan is to combine the concepts of annuitizing and maintaining a retirement plan. If George and Susan annuitize one-fourth of their $800,000 in retirement funds for a fixed income annuity, they would then be free to invest the remaining $600,000 of funds in a well-diversified portfolio and still look to enjoy the benefits of any future gains in the market. A $200,000 annuity would provide them with a retirement annuity income of $14,009 per year for as long as either of them lived.

Changes in interest rates and inflation may affect the economic outcome of annuitizing. If interest rates are low, the quoted annuity payout amount may be lower in anticipation of lower investment returns by the annuity issuing company. If interest rates are low and going higher, and you like the idea of annuitizing, you may want to consider waiting for the interest rates to rebound somewhat so the payout gets better before annuitizing a portion of your retirement plan. The advantages are, however, not as great as you may think, because the issuing insurance companies anticipate these long-term trends in interest rates.

Would you like to determine if you are a good candidate for an immediate annuity for a portion of your portfolio? If you are a Pennsylvania resident, either I or someone in my office will be able to advise you whether an immediate annuity would be appropriate for your situation. If so, we would be most pleased to provide quotes for interested readers. Please remember this is a completely different beast than a tax-deferred annuity.

Annuitizing Has Worked Out Well for Many Investors

Annuitizing has worked out well for many of my older clients who were forced to annuitize. For example, most TIAA-CREF participants who retired in the 1980s or before were forced to annuitize most of their significant TIAA (bond) and CREF (stock) holdings (they may also have been able to take some taxable withdrawals). They currently enjoy both a fixed payment stream from the TIAA annuity and a variable payment stream from the CREF annuity. (In most other retirement plans and commercially available qualified immediate annuities, such variable payment streams are not even available.) The retirees, in addition to whatever they saved, have their TIAA-CREF annuities and Social Security. They may not be rich, but they are usually comfortable. Usually they don't worry about money and, barring any unforeseen events, don't have to. There is no need for any trusts, no money management, and no messing around. When the market is up, they get larger distributions from CREF but still enjoy a steady income from the TIAA fixed annuity that has outperformed the guarantee. Although the CREF annuities were subject to large declines in the 2001–2003 timeframe, the payment amounts greatly exceed the TIAA payments based on growth over the last 20 years. This income, combined with their Social Security, will be something on which they can rely.

Annuitizing: A Risky Strategy?

Another view of annuitizing is that it is not conservative, but rather a gamble. Since most annuities are based on an actuarial life expectancy, you are gambling that you will outlive your actuarial life expectancy, and the company holding the annuity is gambling that you won't.

Evaluate the potential for you according to these criteria:

- If you have reason to believe that you will not survive your actuarial life expectancy, then annuitizing is probably a mistake.
- If you think, however, that you and your spouse are going to substantially outlive your actuarial life expectancy, then annuitizing will provide an assured income stream for a long life.

- If you have terminal cancer and your wife has a long life expectancy, consider having your wife purchase an immediate annuity on her life only.

Although annuitizing will provide fixed monthly amounts for a lifetime, there are other risks involved that make this conservative strategy a gamble. One risk is that the issuing insurance company will go bankrupt and be unable to meet its obligations to pay the annuity. Although the state governments provide some guarantees to protect against their insolvency, you could also choose insurance and annuity companies with quality ratings such as Standard & Poor's ratings of at least AA or preferably AAA to minimize this risk.

Another way to reduce your risk exposure is to buy immediate annuities from more than one company. For example, if you want to purchase an immediate annuity of $300,000 which represents 25% of your portfolio, consider three separate annuities of $100,000 each from three different companies.

Another risk involves the effect of inflation and the fixed nature of the fixed annuity payments. If the payout results in the same payment amount every month, the long-term effects of inflation can lead to the annuity income becoming inadequate to meet growing expenses. Some options are available to offset inflation risks when purchasing an annuity. One is choosing a payment stream that increases every year by a fixed rate of interest, although this option is not available for most retirement plan annuities, just after-tax annuities. This fixed rate of increase, however, is not directly tied to inflation, and could become insufficient in times of high inflation.

CREF annuities, for those in a TIAA-CREF plan, or any similar plan may help to protect your annuity payment stream from inflation by providing a payment that changes based on market investment returns. This can be both good and bad. If the stock market (or other investment index) does well, then you will be better off, but if the market returns are negative, you face the risk of the payments decreasing. Either can happen in times of high inflation. Pick your poison—do you risk the effects of inflation or of a market decline? Although there is no single correct answer, diversification may be the key to help in such decision making.

Another problem with annuitizing a retirement fund is that money is paid out on a regular schedule, and this may not be in tune with your needs.

Another problem with annuitizing a retirement fund is that money is paid out on a regular schedule, and this may not be in tune with your needs.

- If you do not need the money, then annuitizing retirement plan assets needlessly accelerates the payment of income taxes on your retirement accumulations. In theory, at least in the early years, the annuity payment will be somewhat higher than required minimum distributions since it reflects a return of principal. This is unlike the favorable tax situation we saw earlier in Mini Case Study 6.1 where Ida annuitized after-tax assets.
- If you need more than the annuity payment amount and you have annuitized everything, then you are just plain out of luck unless you can borrow from a bank or other lending institution. If you are taking minimum required distributions from a retirement plan, you can always eat into the principal for a large distribution when and if you need it. This is, of course, the fundamental risk of annuities.

Special Idea: Using Annuities for Spendthrift Children

Over the years, our legal practice has drafted many spendthrift trusts for adult children as beneficiaries of wills and trusts and retirement plans (see Chapter 14 for more details regarding spendthrift trusts). We usually draft these trusts when a parent feels that one of their adult children is not capable of handling money responsibly. Sometimes it is drafted to make sure the no-good son-in-law doesn't get one red cent of Mom and Dad's hard-earned money. The trust is set up for the benefit of the irresponsible child (or spouse of no-good son-in-law). A trustee is named to invest the funds and make distributions according to the terms of the trust.

Many times naming a spendthrift trust as a beneficiary is a good solution. Sometimes it isn't. There are multiple problems with trusts, including aggravation, an additional tax return, and legal, accounting, and trustee expenses. Perhaps the biggest problem with the spendthrift trust is choosing a trustee. Usually, the parents of the adult child make the decision of who should be the trustee of the spendthrift trust. One logical choice of trustee is one of the spendthrift's siblings because the sibling is likely to have a greater understanding of the situation than a bank or other corporate trustee. Do you, however, really want to set the stage for family strife? What happens when the trustee doesn't give the spendthrift what he wants? What would Christmas dinner be like after Brother Trustee just said, "No, Sister Spendthrift, you can't use the money from your trust fund for a vacation." Or "No, Sister Spendthrift, paying for tuition and room and board at the University of the Sun Devil Worshiper doesn't qualify as funds for education."

Naming a bank as trustee is often a problem too. Often there isn't enough money in the trust for a bank to be willing to serve as trustee. Even if there is a sufficient balance, there are fee issues, and ultimately many clients just don't want a bank involved.

The Solution to Providing for the Spendthrift Adult Child

Let's assume the goal is to provide an income stream for the spendthrift child for the rest of the child's life. Mom and Dad want the assurance that the child will be properly provided for. They may not see the need for the child to accumulate money. They also may not care about what happens to the money after the child dies.

One potential solution to the problem is to eliminate the trust entirely. Assume the parents have three children, and they want to treat all three equally. The parents could give a direction in the will or other document that the spendthrift's share would be used to purchase a lifetime annuity for the benefit of the spendthrift. An annuity will assure a future income stream and provide protection against the spendthrift's creditors.

MINI CASE STUDY 6.3

Using an Annuity in Lieu of a Spendthrift Trust (a True Story)

Concerned Parent is trying to figure out how to provide for his son, one of three children. He trusts his daughters completely and is planning to leave both of them their one-third of the inheritance directly. The issue is how to leave money to his son, whom he doesn't trust with money. If he leaves it to his son outright, he is afraid his son will deplete the principal through excessive spending or be vulnerable to potential creditors of both his son and his daughter-in-law. He also fears his daughter-in-law will put pressure on his son to spend more than he might be comfortable spending, or what may be prudent to spend, but he doesn't want to be too controlling from the grave or jeopardize his son's marriage.

If he leaves the money in some type of spendthrift trust, the money is tied up and perhaps overprotected. He would also have to choose a trustee. If the bank is a trustee (a corporate fiduciary), there will be fees and extra layers of administration. If he names one of his daughters as trustee, there is a good chance that he will totally ruin the relationship between the son and the daughter. Then he would have to decide among the terms of the trust. Should the trust have a mandatory distribution? How much judgment "license" is the trustee given? Should it be a total return trust?

Does Concerned Parent really want to control from the grave? *No!* The Concerned Parent doesn't want to control his son's life. He just wants to provide him with the highest degree of financial security.

At the Concerned Parent's death, the executor is directed to take all or a portion of what would have gone to the son directly to purchase an annuity with monthly annuity proceeds going to the son. Son gets an annuity for the rest of his life and most likely ends up with a larger monthly or annual distribution than he would have received had the inherited money been left in a trust.

Disadvantages include reduced flexibility for the son and the same disadvantages of annuitizing as were listed previously.

This idea of directing the executor to purchase an annuity has been used in practice to the total delight of the Concerned Parent setting it up. I recommend giving the executor the right to shop for the best deal on an annuity at the time of death.

Protection from Creditors

Another advantage of the immediate annuity is that it provides some protection from creditors. Once the annuity is purchased, the principal itself will be protected from creditors because it is gone—that is, outside the control of the annuitant. In some situations, a creditor may be able to reach the proceeds (a payment) of the annuity, but that is unlikely. For example, a creditor can't get an order directing an annuity company to pay the son's annuity directly to the creditor. It could, however, strategically levy a checking account where the proceeds of the annuity check would be deposited, in which case the son should learn to be an effective sleazebag or pay up.

This idea of buying an annuity is also a good idea for the father of a child who has substantial debts or who practices in a profession where there is significant personal liability, such as medicine. Of course, one of the downsides of annuitizing for the benefit of a child is that there will be nothing to pass on to the grandchildren.

To address that flaw, I offer several responses.

1. So what? With the exception of providing for education, most grandparents are much more interested in providing for their children than their grandchildren. Of course this isn't always the case, but it is in my experience.
2. You don't have to have the executor annuitize all the proceeds. You can have the executor annuitize just a portion.
3. Something could be set up for the grandchild directly. If you purchase an annuity for your child, you could leave some portion of the inherited IRA to a trust for the grandchildren to allow the greatest stretch.

A Key Lesson from This Chapter

Annuitizing a portion of your retirement plan or purchasing an immediate annuity for roughly 25% of your retirement assets is often a good strategy to help ensure that you never run out of money.

Withdrawing Retirement Plans Funded with Company Stocks and Net Unrealized Appreciation (NUA)

If you do not know how to ask the right question, you discover nothing.

— W. Edwards Deming

Main Topics

- What is NUA?
- Limits on funding qualified plans with employer stock
- Case studies (that save a bundle)

KEY IDEA

The difference between the market value of your company stock still invested in your retirement plan at the time of the distribution and its value at the time your employer made the contribution to your plan is called net unrealized appreciation or NUA. At retirement, it is critical to check for NUA before rolling money into an IRA. NUA qualifies for favorable tax treatment.

The difference between the market value your company stock still invested in your retirement plan at the time of the distribution and its value at the time your employer made the contribution to your plan is called net unrealized appreciation or NUA.

The underlying premise of this book is that the key to significantly greater overall wealth accumulation for you and your family is delaying for as long as possible the taxation on the distribution of any amounts from the tax-deferred environment—in other words, pay taxes later. There may be situations in the pension area, however, where we should make an exception to the rule. Paying tax on NUA now is one of the exceptions to the "don't pay taxes now—pay taxes later" rule. This is particularly true with the capital gains and qualified dividends tax at 15%.

What Is NUA, and Why Should I Care?

When an employee retires and takes a lump sum distribution from a qualified plan, such as a 401(k), the distribution may include employer stock that is worth more than its fair market value at the time it was contributed to the plan. The difference between the market value of the stock at the time of the distribution and its value at the time it was contributed is called *net unrealized appreciation* (NUA). You should care because NUA receives favorable tax treatment.

Employers have been and are still allowed to fund qualified plans with their own stock, using the fair market value of the stock to value the contribution. Though this practice is frowned upon since the Enron fiasco, it is still common and exists in many of the older plans. A pension plan may not have more than 10% of its assets invested in employer stock. For certain plans, such as stock bonus plans, all contributions are in employer stock. Profit-sharing plans may have 100% of their assets invested in employer stock.

If the stock was contributed by the employer, the employee gets to treat the NUA portion specially as long as the distribution initially qualifies as a lump sum distribution as described in Chapter 5. If the proposed distribution qualifies as a lump sum distribution, then the NUA is not taxed at the time of the distribution. The employee pays tax only on the original value of the stock from the time his employer contributed it to the plan. That amount becomes the basis of the stock in the hands of the employee. Employees do not pay tax on the NUA portion until they sell or otherwise dispose of the stock in a taxable transaction. Also, the employee then pays taxes at capital gains rates instead of ordinary income rates. No matter how long the employee has held the stock, the NUA portion is taxed as a long-term capital gain. The essence of the advantage of the NUA is that distributions will be taxed at capital gains rates rather than ordinary rates as with traditional IRAs. If the employee dies, there is no step-up in basis for NUA, which means that tax is still due on the total amount of the long-term capital gain.

MINI CASE STUDY 7.1

When Checking for NUA Saves a Bundle

Joe Employee retires and takes a lump-sum distribution from his company's stock bonus plan, consisting totally of his company's stock, which had been contributed by his employer. The total value of the stock at the time of the distribution is $500,000. The company's cost basis in the stock is $100,000.

Joe gets a Form 1099-R from his employer showing a total distribution of $500,000 and a taxable distribution of $100,000. The amount in Box 6, NUA, is $400,000. Joe pays tax on $100,000 of ordinary income at the time of the distribution. If Joe sells the stock immediately for $500,000, he will also report a $400,000 long-term capital gain.

Already, Joe is better off than if he cashed in a $500,000 traditional plan or even an IRA. If he cashed in a $500,000 IRA, he would have to pay income taxes on the entire amount at ordinary income tax rates. At the top marginal rate, the tax is $500,000 × 35% = $175,000 of income tax on an immediate cash out. This leaves Joe with $325,000 after taxes.

If, instead, the transaction qualifies for NUA, he sells $400,000 at capital gains rates of 15% and $100,000 at ordinary income tax rates:

$400,000 × 15% = $60,000, plus $100,000 × 35% = $35,000,

or a combined tax of $95,000. This leaves Joe with $405,000 after taxes. Better yet, Joe can take his NUA, keep track of the NUA status, and not pay immediate income taxes.

- If Joe holds the stock for three months and then sells it for $550,000, he will report a $400,000 long-term capital gain (the NUA portion) and a $50,000 short-term capital gain on the stock.
- If Joe holds the stock for a year after the distribution, and then sells it for $600,000, then the entire $500,000 of gain on the stock, not only the NUA, qualifies as long-term capital gain.
- If he just sits on the NUA, the account will continue to accumulate, but some day he will be subject to capital gains taxes. Even death can't escape the capital gain, and there is no step-up in basis.

In most cases, it is beneficial to roll over a distribution from a qualified plan into an IRA to get the benefits of tax-deferred growth. But Joe has done even better! While he holds the stock, all the appreciation is accumulating in a tax-deferred manner, since gain on the stock is not taxed until he sells it. And he will pay tax on the gain at capital gains rates when he sells the stock, rather than ordinary income rates like distributions from an IRA. Joe also has the option of keeping part of the stock and rolling over the balance of the shares to an IRA. In this situation, Joe would pay income taxes only on the basis of the shares he keeps and would maintain NUA status on those shares. If Joe rolls the stock over to an IRA, and later takes a distribution in stock from the IRA, the taxable amount of the distribution is the fair market value of the stock, and Joe is taxed at ordinary income rates. Rolling shares into the IRA is a bad idea for Joe, because he loses the tremendous benefit of the capital gains rates for the NUA portion.

This is why it is critical when you retire and are considering an IRA rollover that you check to see if there is any NUA in your retirement plan. If you do not have company stock in your plan, and there was no type of stock swap, you will not have NUA. If you do own employer stock in your retirement plan, then you will have to find out from the payroll department whether you have NUA. If some of the NUA on employer stock is relatively small due to the difference in the stock basis and fair market value at the time of the contribution, a rollover of those shares into an IRA may be a better approach. Preserving the tax-deferred status of those shares may outweigh the minimal long-term capital gain benefits derived from taking the distribution.

Getting a handle on NUA could present a tremendous savings opportunity. When you calculate how much money you can save in taxes, you will find you may be in a much better situation using the NUA rules to your advantage.

MINI CASE STUDY 7.2
A Typical NUA Opportunity

It is rare for an employee to have a retirement plan funded 100% with employer stock. More typical is the case of Bob, who retires from his company and receives a lump-sum distribution from the company's pension plan consisting of $450,000 in cash and other securities and employer stock worth $50,000, of which $40,000 is NUA. That is, the value at the time the company contributed to Bob's retirement plan was $10,000. This is a reasonable range that you might find for an employee who has worked for many years for the same company.

- Bob should roll over the noncompany stock portion (the $450,000) to an IRA and keep the stock while still excluding the NUA portion from income—the best of both worlds.
- Bob will end up with a $450,000 IRA and $50,000 in company stock and will have current taxable income of $10,000. The $40,000 in NUA won't be taxed until Bob sells the stock.

If the employer contributed the distributed stock to the plan, then the deferral and capital gain treatment apply only if the distribution meets the qualifications for a lump-sum distribution, other than the subsequent rollover of a portion of the plan to an IRA. Such a partial rollover would prohibit the ten-year averaging treatment as discussed in Chapter 5, but would not prohibit the special tax treatment for NUA. If the distribution does not qualify as a lump-sum distribution, then only the NUA of stock that the employee himself contributed to his plan would qualify for this special treatment of income deferral and capital gains.

A Key Lesson from This Chapter

The most important thing you can walk away with from this chapter is that before rolling money into an IRA, please check to see if there is any NUA, and if so, please either get professional advice or dig further into the matter. The difference between the market value of the stock at the time of the distribution and its value at the time it was contributed is called net unrealized appreciation or NUA, which receives favorable tax treatment.

Part Three

ESTATE PLANNING

It Is Never Too Early to Start

Overview

I find it hard to draw clear lines between retirement planning and estate planning because I view both retirement and estate planning as on one continuum. Optimal estate planning for IRA and retirement plan owners usually involves the same principle I have been consistently preaching throughout: Don't pay taxes now—pay taxes later.

In this part of the book, I expand on that concept and present what many experts and I feel is the ideal beneficiary designation of an IRA and/or retirement plan, known as Lange's Cascading Beneficiary Plan™. I published the first article on this plan in *Financial Planning* magazine in March 2001, right after the change in the tax law made this plan so favorable. A similar article was published in the peer-reviewed *The Tax Adviser* of the American Institute of Certified Public Accountants, and I have given talks on the subject at some of the top tax seminars in the country. Since then, Lange's Cascading Beneficiary Plan™ has been widely quoted with attribution to me in such sources as *Kiplinger's Retirement Reports* and the *Wall Street Journal*, and by Jane Bryant Quinn in *Newsweek*.

Well, you made it over the hump; you've accumulated well and planned your retirement. What happens next? You need an estate plan for your heirs. Please picture yourself after the necessary changes have been made, knowing that you have set things up in the most beneficial manner for your family. Your spouse may not be immersed in the details now, but he or she will be thrilled with the gift of security you are providing. Imagine how good you'll feel knowing that you have protected your estate from both the IRS and that no-good son-in-law who you never trusted!

If all your documents are in great shape (and now after reading the book you will be in a better position to know), you should be applauded! If, however, things aren't in great shape or if you have questions, please read on and take action so that your legacy won't be decimated by taxes.

As much as I like the plan, it isn't for everyone, so I also present a more traditional estate plan. A certain core of information is important to truly understand the benefits of Lange's Cascading Beneficiary Plan™ and the traditional plan. After learning the core information, you will be in a better position to know how to approach estate planning for you and your family.

Finally, a trend has emerged. With the continuing escalation of exemption equivalent amounts, many clients who would have been subject to or at least worried about estate taxes when the exemption amount was $600,000 today do not have that fear. Even if you don't anticipate estate taxes and the federal estate and gift tax structures aren't important to you, the concept of disclaimers and the stretch IRA are still critical.

The three critical concepts of this plan are:

1. The federal estate and gift tax structure
2. The concept of using disclaimers in the planning stages
3. The concept of the stretch IRA

The next four chapters address those topics in some detail. The first chapter in this part presents an extended case study of a sophisticated retirement and estate plan to optimize wealth for a professional married couple when the bulk of the money (more than $1 million) is in the husband's IRA or 401(k).

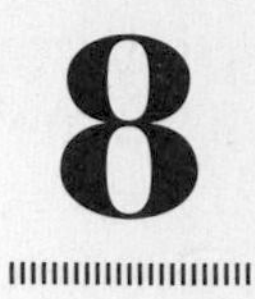

Eddie and Emily: A Retirement and Estate Planning Case Study

You can always amend a big plan, but you can never expand a little one. I don't believe in little plans. I believe in plans big enough to meet a situation which we can't possibly foresee now.

— Harry S. Truman

Edward J. Engineer ("Eddie"), age 68, is a retired engineer who worked for Westinghouse Corporation for 35 years. Eddie is married to Emily, age 65. They have two married children and four grandchildren. Their son Bill is doing quite well financially and is in a solid marriage. Their daughter Sarah, unfortunately, has significant marital problems and, to make life even more difficult, her finances are a concern to Eddie and Emily. To be perfectly frank, Eddie doesn't trust his son-in-law. Period.

Though Eddie made a reasonable salary at Westinghouse, it was difficult to save money. Taking care of the mortgage and maintenance on the house, buying groceries, and raising their children took most of his paycheck. They also paid for their children's college education. Eddie did make regular contributions to his retirement plan, and when it was deductible, to a voluntary IRA. Emily has a small IRA.

Just 10 years ago, Eddie only had $400,000 in total retirement assets. He was just hoping that the accumulations would provide for his and Emily's comfortable retirement. With time and compounding, however, Eddie's retirement assets have grown to roughly $900,000 in his 401(k) plan and $100,000 in several IRAs (his assets stood at $1.2 million three years ago.) The Engineers do not think of themselves as wealthy, and they have not changed their spending habits. Eddie continues to drive his 10-year-old car. He would consider it absolutely foolish to spend money on a new car. His current one is reliable and certainly serviceable.

Eddie and Emily remain in their modest house where they raised their children. They haven't remodeled the kitchen or bathrooms. Emily still clips coupons. Now Eddie and Emily are facing enormous taxes on their retirement assets both during their lifetimes and at their deaths.

Eddie and Emily have wills that are several years old. They were drafted when there was a greater risk of federal estate taxes when Eddie and Emily died. Eddie's will reflects traditional planning decisions that were quite common when there was a concern about paying estate taxes. It includes a trust that basically says that in the event Eddie predeceases Emily, a significant portion of his money will go into a trust from which Emily will receive income, and she will have the option to invade the principal for health maintenance and support.

Eddie was never really comfortable with the planning for his retirement plan or IRA. For instance, he wasn't sure how the beneficiary form of the IRA and 401(k) plan should be filled out.

The Engineers have an approximate net worth of $1.5 million, including life insurance. A detailed list of the Engineers' assets is as follows:

Eddie's 401(k) Plan	$900,000
Eddie's IRA	100,000
Emily's IRA	30,000
After-tax Investments and Savings	130,000
House	185,000
Cars and Personal Property	45,000
Whole Life Insurance	50,000
Term Life Insurance	60,000
Total Estate	$1.5 million

Eddie and Emily were never confident of the advice they received until they met Frank, a financial planner who worked closely with Larry, an estate attorney who did a lot of work in the IRA and retirement plan area. When Frank saw where Eddie and Emily stood financially, he proposed that he work with the Engineers to develop a comprehensive retirement and estate plan that would incorporate the best ideas from both Larry and him. What follows is a summary of some of Eddie and Emily's concerns and the resolution they developed with Frank and Larry.

Eddie and Emily's Retirement and Estate Planning Issues

- Eddie and Emily's first concern is providing for a comfortable retirement as long as they both live. Their second concern is providing for the survivor upon the first death.
- Though Eddie and Emily would prefer leaving money to their children rather than paying taxes, avoiding taxes is secondary to providing for each other.
- Eddie and Emily's Social Security and other income do not cover their expenses, and they must make withdrawals from their portfolio. They wonder if they should spend their IRA or 401(k) funds first, or whether they should spend after-tax money first—money they have already paid taxes on.
- Eddie and Emily trust each other completely, though Eddie is a little tighter about money than Emily.

Eddie is pretty sharp and he realizes that the years between entering retirement and being required to take minimum distributions will give him more control over his income than he has ever had. After 70½ his minimum distribution will be taxed for federal income tax purposes and his tax rate will increase. From now until then, his taxable income is relatively low. If he chooses not to make any IRA or 401(k) withdrawals and he lives off his after-tax funds (money not in his 401(k) or IRA) his income and his taxes will be extremely low. He wonders if these "low tax years" create an opportunity for him and his family.

- One of the issues the low tax years bring up is whether Eddie and Emily should convert a portion of their IRA or 401(k) into a Roth IRA. If they choose to convert a portion of their 401(k) and/or IRA into Roth IRAs, what is the optimal amount to convert? When should the conversion take place? Which assets should they use to pay the taxes on the conversion?
- The reason Eddie never rolled the money out of his 401(k) into an IRA: one-third of the money in the 401(k) is invested in a guaranteed income fund that is paying 6%, which makes Eddie happy. Was it really smart to leave the money in the 401(k)?
- Despite the fact that their children have widely disparate needs, Eddie and Emily want to treat the children equally.
- Eddie and Emily want to know more about optimal beneficiary designations for their retirement plans to pass that money on to their children and possibly their grandchildren.
- Eddie recently learned that with the higher exemption amounts (the amount you are allowed to die with, without having to pay federal estate taxes), the traditional trusts that were part of his wills and retirement plan and IRA beneficiaries might not only be unnecessary, but possibly financially disastrous.
- Eddie, even more so than Emily, doesn't want to see his no-good son-in-law get one red cent of his money. The thought of that no-goodnik living off his inheritance makes Eddie sick. This problem, though not his primary concern, weighs heavily on Eddie's mind.

Retirement Planning

Eddie knew the maxim: Don't pay taxes now—pay taxes later. He recognized the benefits of spending his after-tax dollars before his IRA dollars. He wondered if there were exceptions to that rule. He also knows minimum distributions are around the corner, and he wants to know what impact that will have on his planning. Specifically, he knows his income tax bracket is lower now than it will likely ever be again. Eddie decided to make Roth IRA conversions up to the top of the 15% bracket as per the advice in Mini Case Study 3.4.

Calculating the Minimum Required Distribution (MRD)

Fortunately for Eddie and Emily, the massive changes passed by Congress in 2001 actually simplified projecting Eddie's minimum required distribution. Though we are oversimplifying for this case study, using the minimum distribution calculator and examining the IRS tables found at www.PayTaxesLater.com/calculator and www.PayTaxesLater.com/book/irs_tables.htm and in the appendix of this book using Table III, Eddie realized that when he turned 70½ his minimum required distribution would be roughly 4% of the balance of his account. As he and Emily age, they will be required to take out more and more money from their IRA and 401(k) and pay income taxes on those withdrawals, whether they like it or not.

Estate Planning[1]

Eddie's new estate planning/attorney team was quick to stress that the beneficiary designation of his IRA and his 401(k)—not his will or living trust—determines the disposition of the retirement plan funds upon his death. Most of Eddie's assets were in retirement accounts. Thus, focusing on the design of Eddie's retirement plan beneficiary designations was the single most important portion of Eddie and Emily's estate plan.

[1] A discussion of taxation at the state level is beyond the limited scope of this case study; thus, all references to taxes refer to taxes at the federal level.

Eddie and Emily also wondered whether the trusts they had drafted when the exemption amount was $600,000 were still appropriate today with the higher exemption amounts. In addition, their previous attorney wasn't able to satisfy Eddie's concerns about the beneficiary designation of his 401(k) and his IRA. Eddie now realizes his planning was completely inadequate.

Eddie and Emily found out that their will and retirement plan and IRA beneficiary designation severely limited the options available to survivors and/or heirs upon either Eddie's or Emily's death. In fact, given the increases in the exemption amount, Eddie's and Emily's current documents are a disaster waiting to happen. They have the old A/B system whereupon if Eddie dies first, his IRA and other assets in his name go into a trust for Emily's benefit. True, Emily can draw income and invade principal for health maintenance and support, but as it turns out the trust as drafted for them would be a monumental mistake. Please read the section in Chapter 9 called "The Nastiest Trap of All."

Eddie's attorney looked at Eddie and asked him point blank, "Do you trust your wife?" After a little kidding he answered, "Yes." The attorney asked Emily if she trusted her husband and Emily also answered affirmatively. The attorney then took the opportunity to explain to Eddie and Emily the keystone of an estate planning technique that seemed tailor-made for their situation, "Lange's Cascading Beneficiaries Plan." (See Chapter 12 for more details.) In addition to the main features of Lange's Cascading Beneficiary Plan™, Eddie also wanted a spendthrift trust for Sarah's benefit to protect Eddie and Emily's assets from their no-good son-in-law.

Eddie also heard that it might not be a smart thing to keep the majority of his retirement plan in his 401(k). Larry, the estate attorney, asked something none of the other advisors asked. He asked to see the plan document, which has the rules that govern Eddie's 401(k) plan at work. The attorney explained that Eddie, or more accurately Eddie's children and grandchildren, had a big problem if Eddie and Emily died before the money was rolled into an IRA. Eddie found out that if he and Emily died, his heirs would have to pay income taxes on $900,000 the year after he and Emily died. The attorney also explained that though you can never get out of paying income taxes on those retirement plans and IRAs, it was usually advantageous to pay the taxes later via a stretch IRA. The stretch IRA can defer income taxes for 40 or even 80 years after Eddie and Emily's death. Westinghouse's 401(k) retirement plan will not accommodate stretching Eddie's 401(k) distributions over the lives of his children—a critical component of Lange's Cascading Beneficiary Plan™. Eddie learned that this difficulty with the Westinghouse's 401(k) was typical of many retirement plans—that is, the required distribution of the entire plan balance to a nonspouse beneficiary after the plan owner's death causes an enormous and otherwise unnecessary acceleration of income taxes. (Please see the section in Chapter 5 called "Tax Advantages of Transferring a 401(k) into an IRA.")

Though Eddie was reluctant to let go, with the exception of the fixed income account, he decided to roll his Westinghouse retirement plan into an IRA that he could direct so that he could take full advantage of Lange's Cascading Beneficiary Plan™.

As I was putting my 11-year-old daughter to bed one evening we talked about the most important thing about *Retire Secure!* She asked, "Dad, what about all of the people that will be able to live better lives because of your book? Isn't that the most important thing?" My daughter made me stop and think. I often get so lost in the material that I forget about the impact *Retire Secure!* is having on people's lives.

Many engineers and other analytical thinkers will enjoy reading this book as an intellectual exercise. You may see it as playing a game of accumulating wealth, cutting your taxes, and eventually passing on more money for your heirs. That's fine. But what you might not think about is that taking action on these points will make a real difference for you and your family.

So, please don't just read this book as an intellectual exercise. After reading the material, either on your own or preferably with the help of the appropriate advisor, please implement the appropriate strategies and put yourself and your family in a better position for the future.

Conclusions

With expert guidance, Eddie and Emily designed a retirement and estate plan that optimized their assets for themselves and eventually their children. The Engineers were relieved. Finally they had made the decisions they had been delaying for years.

The information contained in this case study is not intended as legal advice. Due to the personal nature of retirement and estate planning, the fictional estate plan discussed in this case may not be appropriate for another situation.

We get more excellent suggestions on our case studies from our readers than any other topics discussed in this book. If you have suggestions on how we could improve planning for Eddie and Emily, please give us your suggestions. The best suggestions will be published and acknowledged in our next edition. Please go to www.PayTaxesLater.com/book/suggestions.htm and thank you in advance for your efforts.

A Key Lesson from This Chapter

There is a reason that the words "retirement and estate planning" seem to just roll off the tongue—they belong together. It is important to understand that the consequences of your decisions may have immediate, short-term, and long-term tax ramifications. Plan with the big picture in mind, and keep things flexible when you can. Integrated planning always beats out something that is cobbled together.

How to Reduce Your Federal Estate Tax Burden

Collecting more taxes than is absolutely necessary is legalized robbery.

— Calvin Coolidge

Main Topics

- Defining estate and gift taxes
- Avoiding estate and gift taxes
- The importance of annual giving
- Different types of gifts
- Tax traps on the death of the second spouse
- The problem with B trusts intended for the benefit of the spouse
- The nastiest trap of all
- Funding trusts with retirement assets

KEY IDEA

For married couples whose assets exceed the Applicable Exclusion Amount (currently $2 million in 2006 through 2008), the concern is not with the estate tax at the first death, but rather the estate tax at the second death. For single or married taxpayers, simple gifts of $12,000 per year per beneficiary may save your heirs a bundle.

Defining Estate and Gift Taxes

In its simplest form, the federal gift and estate tax system is a transfer tax levied when individuals transfer assets during their lifetime or at their death. It is rare that individuals pay gift taxes during their lifetime. Therefore, it is much more common for the transfer tax to be imposed on the transfer of assets at their death.

With respect to transfers to spouses, the unlimited marital deduction allows you to transfer an unlimited amount of property to your U.S. citizen spouse, during his or her lifetime or at death, free of transfer taxes. If the spouse is not a U.S. citizen, the situation is more complicated and is beyond the scope of this book.

With respect to transfers to nonspouse beneficiaries, the IRS sets the upper lifetime limit on how much money individuals are allowed to transfer out of their estate before they incur a transfer tax. The amount an individual is allowed to transfer without incurring a federal transfer tax to nonspouse beneficiaries is referred to as the *Applicable Exclusion Amount*. The Applicable Credit Amount (formerly, and now often incorrectly, referred to as the Unified Credit Amount) is the amount of federal estate tax that would be due on the Applicable Exclusion Amount but for the existence of the credit.

The amount an individual is allowed to transfer without incurring a federal transfer tax to nonspouse beneficiaries is referred to as the Applicable Exclusion Amount.

In 2006, the Applicable Exclusion Amount equals $2 million. The Applicable Credit Amount (the amount of federal estate tax that would be due on $2 million but for the credit) equals $780,800. Married individuals may each transfer an amount equal to the Applicable Exclusion Amount to nonspouse beneficiaries. The amounts vary by year as follows:

The Applicable Credit Amount (formerly, and now often incorrectly, referred to as the Unified Credit amount) is the amount of federal estate tax that would be due on the Applicable Exclusion Amount but for the existence of the credit.

Applicable Exclusion Amounts

Year	Amount
2006, 2007 and 2008	$2 million
2009	$3.5 million
2010	Estate tax is repealed
2011	$1 million [a]

[a] *Unless Congress takes action.*

This schedule is a mess, and chances are that this is only the tip of the iceberg. It is likely there will be many more major changes during your lifetime. I firmly believe that no one can accurately predict what will happen with the estate tax exemptions. Even if Congress repeals the estate tax entirely, they could easily bring it back, as they have on three separate occasions during times of war when Congress needed more money. My objective is to show you how to build a flexible estate plan that accommodates all the scheduled changes and adapts for those changes about which we can only speculate.

Prediction is very difficult, especially if it's about the future.

— Niels Bohr

The groundhog is like most other prophets; it delivers its prediction and then disappears.

— Bill Vaughan

Given that the Applicable Exclusion Amount is a moving target, I think the safest way to plan is to recognize that your family may or may not be subject to the federal estate tax in the future. Whether your estate will be subject to federal tax will be determined by the combination of what your estate happens to be worth, what the Applicable Exclusion Amount equals in the year of your death, and how well you plan.

How You Can Save Millions without Spending a Nickel on Attorney Fees: The Importance of Annual Gifting

A lawyer is a learned gentleman who rescues your estate from your enemies and keeps it himself.

— Henry Peter Brougham

I had an uncle who planned to take his money with him. Why else wouldn't he make annual gifts to his deserving children and grandchildren? Why would he allow that money to be taxed at 50% and make his family wait to enjoy those funds?

I have a client whom I have nagged for years to make annual gifts to his children and grandchildren. The last time I was even firmer and strongly recommended family gifting and said now was a great time for a gift. He agreed that now was a great time for gifts and he stood ready to receive any gifts his children wanted to give him.

Control is nice, staving off the fear of running out of money is important, but saving what could be millions of dollars in estate taxes for your children is also important. Of course you have to consider your own individual circumstances. If you are in a position where gifting is advisable, I offer a short description of the most basic types of gifts.

my parents

Different Types of Gifts

I like to focus on three important forms of gifts:

1. The classic $12,000/year per beneficiary, usually children
2. Gifts of education
3. Gifts of insurance

The most important estate planning tool for many people is simple gifting. Before you even look at all the more sophisticated gifting models, seriously consider plain old, nonsexy gifts of $12,000 per year per beneficiary.

James Narron, an excellent estate attorney I met at the Heckerling Institute, likes to say, with a strong southern accent, "Keep your eye on the pine." He tells the story of when he was a little boy and his father was teaching him to drive a tractor. His father would tell him to "keep your eye on the pine." When he did, James would travel in a straight line toward the pine. When he looked around, he veered off course and lost his straight line. When he returned to keeping his eyes glued to that pine off in the distance, he would get back on course.

Most of my wealthy clients need to be told and then later reminded to "keep your eye on the pine." What is "keeping your eye on the pine"? It is making annual tax free gifts of $12,000 per year per beneficiary. If you are married, that means both you and your spouse can give each of your children a gift of $24,000 per year without incurring a gift tax penalty. It is simplest for the money to come from a joint account showing the gift came from both spouses.

MINI CASE STUDY 9.1

The Measurable Benefits of Simple Gifting

Tom and Judy, both 60 years old, have two children and four grandchildren. Though they have grown their estate to $4 million they are relatively frugal. They live comfortably on their pension and Social Security. They don't want Uncle Sam to get any of their hard-earned money at their deaths. At the very least, they want to drastically reduce their children's taxes at their death. Let's assume they reject all of the more sophisticated gifting techniques. They opt for simple gifts of $12,000 per year per beneficiary (with adjustments for inflation). They have six beneficiaries and each parent may give $12,000 per year per beneficiary. Thus they give away $144,000 (6 × $24,000 per donee) per year. Their plan is to continue making these gifts as long as they are comfortable with their own finances. They know that if they do nothing, they run the risk of growing too old and too rich to effectively use simple or even more complex gifting techniques.

The gifts continue for 24 years in annual amounts increasing with 3% annual inflation. Over time the amount gifted comes to $5,112,000. Assuming a 45% estate tax rate, the savings to the family, not including appreciation, would be $2,300,400. That is really significantly less than the savings if we assume that the cash gifted will appreciate at an after-tax rate of 4%. If the cash appreciated at 4%, then the projected value of the gifts at life expectancy would be $8,014,860, for a total savings to the family of $3,606,687. If we assume a 6% after-tax rate, the savings are approximately $4,617,886. If we use an 8% after-tax rate, the savings are approximately $5,991,569.

The most important estate planning tool for many people is simple gifting.

Of course, one of the reasons this example is questionable is because we really have no way of predicting what estate taxes are going to be. This lack of predictability is a terrible problem for estate planners, and planners have different methods of handling the problem.

Whether you will have a taxable estate for federal estate tax purposes will depend on the year of your death and the taxable balance of your estate. I do not like to assume there will be a tax, nor do I want to ignore the possibility that estates over $1 million may be taxed. I like to make wise choices that work out well for the family, whether there is an estate tax or not.

The Gift of Education: A Favorite for Grandparents

Economists report that a college education adds many thousands of dollars to a man's lifetime income—which he then spends sending his son to college.

— Bill Vaughn

Most grandparents who can afford it (convincing them they can afford it is a different matter) like the idea of at least partially funding their grandchildren's college education.

Grandparents as well as parents can pay tuition (as well as medical expenses) directly for their children or grandchildren, and these payments do not count against the $12,000 per year limit.

Section 529 College Saving Plans are really a variation of a gift. Section 529 Plan contributions are unique in that when you die, the proceeds of the gift and the appreciation of the gift are outside your estate. But while you are alive you retain the power to take the money back if you like. Though I have never seen anyone take back a Section 529 plan contribution, the assurance that the donor has that option appeals to practically every grandparent.

Section 529 plans accomplish the following:

- Provide income-tax-free growth.
- Give you the freedom to change beneficiaries within the family, including first cousins.
- Offer substantial control over the asset allocation of the investment.
- Allow you to divert the fund from the beneficiary back to the contributor and use the proceeds for nonqualifying purposes (subject to a 10% penalty).
- Are excluded from the estate of the contributor.

These five factors make the decision to invest in a Section 529 plan compelling, particularly for wealthy grandparents who want to provide for their grandchildren's education. For more information on Section 529 plans please visit www.savingforcollege.com.

Gifts of Life Insurance Premiums

Many planners recommend second-to-die life insurance to pay the estate tax at the second death. I agree that this is a great way to use second-to-die life insurance. What if the second death comes in a year when there is a high exemption amount or in a year when there is no federal estate tax? Second-to-die insurance is still usually a good deal and is an effective method of transferring assets to the next generation (or two generations). Therefore, if you can afford the premiums and are looking to pass money to the next generation, second-to-die insurance is worthwhile whether there is an estate tax or not. Of course, there are many types of insurance besides second-to-die that are worthwhile variations of a gift. I emphasize second-to-die insurance because it is the well-deserved classic. Please note, however, I would only recommend second-to-die life insurance if the underlying investment in the insurance policy seemed like a reasonable investment with or without the tax benefits.

Variations on Gifts

There are a number of sophisticated estate planning techniques that are really variations of making a gift. They include:

- Applicable Exclusion Amount–consuming gifts
- Family-limited partnerships
- Grantor-retained annuity trusts
- Grantor-retained unitrusts
- Intentionally defective grantor trusts
- Private annuities
- Qualified personal residence trusts
- Irrevocable trusts, including life insurance trusts
- Life insurance without trusts but owned by the heir, not the client
- Generation-skipping trusts
- Trusts for handicapped children

I leave discussions of these and other legitimate estate planning techniques for another day—or another book.

Gift Taxes

If your gifts exceed the $12,000 annual exclusion amount, the excess is subject to a graduated gift tax with rates ranging from 18% to 46% in 2006. To avoid owing gift tax, you may elect to deduct the excess over and above the $12,000 from your $ 1 million Applicable Exclusion Amount. For example, Daddy Donor chooses to give his son a gift of $62,000. Of that money $12,000 takes advantage of the annual exclusion. The $50,000 is subject to the gift tax. Daddy elects to have the $50,000 deducted from his $1 million lifetime Applicable Exclusion Amount rather than pay the gift tax. This leaves him with $950,000 that can be used for additional gifts.

It is important to make this election by filing a gift tax return, Form 709. That tells the IRS that the gift consumed part of the $1 million lifetime Applicable Exclusion Amount. Please also note that filing the gift tax return starts the statute of limitations on the gift. This is particularly important in the event that the value of the gift could be open to interpretation, such as a gift of an interest in a family-limited partnership, a piece of land, a business, or any other asset that by its nature is difficult to value.

It is conceivable that some people could use up part or all of their Applicable Exclusion Amount during their lifetime, depending on the nature of their lifetime gifts to nonspouse beneficiaries. After that point the portion of the estate that will be subject to estate tax depends on the year in which you die, how much of the exclusion has been used up, how much money remains, and how much of the money is tax sheltered.

The best strategy for wealthy clients who could end up in a taxable estate situation is to take advantage of the annual $12,000 per year per beneficiary exclusion, assuming they can comfortably afford to make the gifts. If the annual gifts of $12,000 per year are not sufficient because there is still too much money in the estate, further gifts that consume a portion of the entire Applicable Exclusion Amount can still be a good idea. Though annual gifts above $12,000 will eat into the Applicable Exclusion Amount and reduce what may be passed at death without tax, it also transfers out of the estate all the appreciation that would have been in the estate had the gift not been made.

MINI CASE STUDY 9.2
Gifts That Use the Total Applicable Exclusion Amount

Jill, a widow with a pension and Social Security that covers her needs, has $4 million and only one beneficiary, her daughter Lucky. Giving away $12,000 per year to the beneficiary is fine, but it hardly makes a dent in the potential estate tax at Jill's death. The $12,000 per year gifts will not be part of this example. Let's compare Jill giving Lucky $1 million in year one vs. making no gift. Also, assume Jill gets 7% on her investments and she lives 10 years.

To simplify the math, use the rule of 78s—which roughly holds that Jill's money will double in 10 years. Let's also assume a flat 50% estate tax. If Jill makes the $1 million gift and is left with $3 million, her estate will double to $6 million at her death. If the applicable exclusion is $2 million at that time, Lucky will have to pay estate tax on $5 million. (Total estate of $6 million plus $1 million [the amount of the applicable exclusion amount–consuming gift] minus $2 million [the Applicable Exclusion Amount at Jill's death]). Assume a flat 50% estate tax. Lucky pays $2.5 million in taxes. In the meantime, Lucky also earned 7% on her $1 million, which is worth $2 million at Jill's death.

Lucky will have $6 million less $2.5 million estate tax plus her $2 million = $5.5 million.

If Jill did not make the gift, her estate would have grown to $8 million. She would have a $2 million exclusion, so she would have to pay tax on $6 million, which would be $3 million. Lucky would be left with $5 million. By making the applicable exclusion amount-consuming gift (commonly referred to as a credit-consuming gift) in the prior example, Jill managed to reduce Lucky's taxes by $500,000.

In the real world, Jill would probably be well advised to make a leveraged gift such as a grantor retained annuity trust (GRAT), a family-limited partnership (FLP), a gift of life insurance, or one of the other gifting techniques. Lawrence Katzenstein, an excellent estate attorney with a head for figures and a heart for charity, presented wonderful original analysis at the Heckerling Institute. He showed that in many cases under the previous law it was even prudent to make a gift so large that it triggers gift tax while the donor is still alive but the result of the gift and the gift tax paid is that there will be a reduction of the overall tax burden at death. The problem with the analysis today is the uncertainty of future investments and, perhaps more importantly, future changes in the law. I would hate to see someone pay gift tax now, yet later, through changes in the law and/or in their portfolio, find out that they would not have been subject to estate taxes anyway.

Freezing the Gift Tax Exclusion Amount at $1 Million

Be aware that in 2004, the gift tax exclusion amount was frozen at $1 million, while the Applicable Exclusion Amount for estates rose to $1.5 million in 2005, and increased to $2 million in 2006. The gift tax exclusion will remain at $1 million, as the Applicable Exclusion Amount for estates increases. This is different from all previous years where the gift and estate tax exclusion amounts were the same. We now have lost the unified system where the gift and estate tax exclusions were the same; thus we can no longer properly refer to the "unified credit shelter amount."

This is important for gifting strategies. Don't get caught thinking that because the estate tax exclusion is $2 million that you can give away $2 million without paying a gift tax. In the prior example, had Jill given Lucky $2 million, that would have triggered immediate gift tax on $1 million ($2 million gift minus $1 million gift tax exclusion amount).

Once your "excess" lifetime gifts are greater than $1 million, the amount over $1 million cannot be applied to the Applicable Exclusion Amount, but rather you must pay the gift tax. Thus,

Be aware that in 2004, the gift tax exclusion amount was frozen at $1 million, while the Applicable Exclusion Amount for estates rose to $1.5 million in 2005 and increased to $2 million in 2006.

you can die with more than $1 million and not be subject to estate tax; but if you give away more than $1 million you will be subject to gift tax.

If taxable lifetime gifts exceed $1 million, the following gift tax rates apply:

	Rate	For Years
Taxable gifts between $1 million and $1.25 million	41%	All except 2010
Taxable gifts between $1.25 million and $1.5 million	43%	All except 2010
Taxable gifts between $1.5 million and $2 million	45%	All except 2010
Taxable gifts over $2 million	48%	2004
Taxable gifts over $2 million	47%	2005
Taxable gifts over $2 million	46%	2006
Taxable gifts over $2 million	45%	2007–2009 and 2011 and on
For all taxable gifts over $1 million	35% [a]	2010

[a] Rate is based on highest individual income tax rate

The Importance of Having After-Tax Dollars to Pay the Estate Tax

Inheritance taxes are so high that the happiest mourner at a rich man's funeral is usually Uncle Sam.

— Olin Miller

There is an entire world of literature just on gifting, both simple and sophisticated techniques. I include this brief summary because it is such an important area. It is also particularly important for large estates that are "IRA heavy." If clients follow my advice and spend (or give away) their after-tax dollars before their IRA dollars, they will be left with IRA dollars at the end of their lives. Likewise, many clients are already in that stage of having a lot of IRA dollars and not much else. If you die with nothing but IRA dollars, and your heirs need money after you die for expenses, taxes, or even their own personal needs, they will have to go into the inherited IRA for the needed funds. When they go into the inherited IRA the distribution triggers income tax. In addition to the immediate income tax on the withdrawal from the inherited IRA, beneficiaries lose the opportunity to stretch the IRA over their life expectancy.

In the case where a beneficiary must make withdrawals from the IRA to pay estate taxes, you end up in the horrendous situation where the withdrawal from the IRA to pay the estate taxes triggers an income tax, and the only source of paying the income tax that you have to pay because you withdraw money to pay the estate tax is further withdrawals of the IRA—withdrawals and taxes ad nauseam. This is a circular calculation that makes you want to weep. For clients who will be subject to estate taxes, it is particularly important that there be some after-tax dollars available to pay the estate taxes. Preferably, the money available to pay the estate taxes would be in the hands of the heir no later than when the client dies. That is, during the life of the IRA owner, he makes gifts (either simple, sophisticated, or through life insurance) so the beneficiary will have a stack of money to pay any estate tax. In the event the IRA owner dies in a situation where, because of the increased exemption equivalent amount, there is no tax, there is nothing lost; in the case of second-to-die life insurance, it can be wonderful for the family with or without the estate tax.

For clients who will be subject to estate taxes, it is particularly important that there be some after-tax dollars available to pay the estate taxes.

MINI CASE STUDY 9.3

Using Life Insurance to Pay Estate Taxes

Joe and Carol, both 70 and in good health, have an estate of $2 million. In addition to their portfolio, they have a pension and Social Security income. Depending on a number of factors, there is a reasonable chance that their family will never pay estate taxes when Joe and Carol die. On the other hand, they might.

They are interested in passing on a significant amount of money to their heirs. They examine the benefits of a second-to-die life insurance policy. They decide they can safely afford the premiums for $500,000 worth of coverage. They know that one of the benefits of the coverage is that upon the second death, their beneficiaries will receive $500,000 free of income and estate taxes. If they have a taxable estate, that $500,000 could go to pay the taxes and expenses, and the beneficiaries would be able to preserve the stretch IRA. This is a classic and effective planning strategy.

Suppose that at the second death, the amount of the survivor's estate is less than the Applicable Exclusion Amount so that the only costs will be the expenses of administering the estate and the state inheritance tax. The $500,000 purchase of the second-to-die policy will still have been a good decision because, assuming a good and appropriate choice of policy, it is a good way of passing on wealth even in the absence of the estate tax.

Gifting, particularly with large estates that are "IRA heavy," is particularly important, and individuals who are extremely interested in passing on wealth to the next one or two generations are encouraged to examine the numbers in the second-to-die analysis before rejecting the idea out of hand.

Why Should I Care about the Applicable Exclusion Amount If I Have Less Than $4 Million in My Estate?

You may be asking yourself why you need to be concerned about the Applicable Exclusion Amount if your and your spouse's assets are worth more than $2 million but less than $4 million in 2006. "Didn't you just tell me that each spouse could shelter $2 million in 2006 from the federal gift and estate tax?" Yes, each spouse can shelter $2 million in 2006 from the federal gift and estate tax. However, planning must be done to ensure the proper ownership of assets to maximize the use of the Applicable Exclusion Amount for each spouse.

For example, suppose that husband and wife jointly own assets worth $2.5 million. If the husband dies in 2006, there will be no taxes due at his death because all of the joint assets passing to the surviving spouse will qualify for the unlimited marital deduction, provided that she is a U.S. citizen.

If the surviving spouse accepts all of the assets, she will have $2.5 million in her name, which is more than the current applicable exemption amount of $2 million. (For this example, I am assuming that she only spends the growth and earnings on her assets and that the amount of her assets remains level during her lifetime.) If the surviving spouse dies later in 2006 or in 2007 or 2008 when the exclusion amount is $2 million, or after 2010 when the exclusion is back to $1 million (assuming no permanent repeal of the federal estate tax), her estate will be subject to federal estate tax.

I recommend, to the extent possible, that husband and wife divide their assets equally or as close to equally as possible by transferring some of the joint assets to the husband's name and some of the joint assets to the wife's name. That way, each spouse can pass the maximum amount possible, free of federal estate tax, by properly using their Applicable Exclusion Amount. Of course, the advice might change if there is a significant difference in life expectancy or amount of assets in one spouse's retirement plan.

I have seen far too many situations where assets were not equalized and the family was unable to capitalize on both parents taking advantage of his and her own Applicable Exclusion Amount. As I explain later in this chapter, proper ownership of assets prior to the first spouse's death enables the surviving spouse to have the maximum amount of possible options to reduce the total amount of transfer taxes ultimately due from both estates.

The Dreaded Double Tax on IRA Assets at Death

Though we attempt to provide you with tips to avoid this problem, heirs of IRA owners with significant estates often face the dreaded combination of estate taxes and income taxes at the IRA owner's death. The combination of income taxes and estate taxes can be more than 50% of the estate.

If you leave more than $2 million to a grandchild (a "skip" person) the grandchild may face a triple tax of income taxes, estate taxes and generation skipping taxes. The combined taxes could be as high as 70% or more of the estate.

If the IRA owner provides funds other than the IRA to pay the estate tax, the income tax on the inherited IRA, if everything else is done right, may be deferred over the life of the beneficiary. If the only money available to pay the estate tax is the IRA itself, withdrawals from the IRA to pay the estate tax will trigger income taxes. Then, the income taxes must be paid from distributions from the IRA and this cycle continues depleting the IRA very rapidly.

The recommendations you will read about in the section on gifting offer solutions to this problem. Some financial advisors have programs they refer to as "pension rescue." Under the right circumstances, these programs are a good idea. They are variants of what is recommended in the gifting section. The pension rescue involves taking a portion of your IRA, paying tax on the IRA distribution while you are still alive and giving the proceeds to your beneficiaries. This serves to reduce your estate and to provide your beneficiaries with after tax dollars to pay any estate taxes. This strategy is often combined with the purchase of life insurance (often a second-to-die policy) where the proceeds from the IRA distributions are given as gifts to children (usually through a trust) to purchase life insurance on the parents. "When the policy matures" (or, in other words, when both parents die), the insurance proceeds are distributed to the children who can then use the proceeds to pay any estate taxes or other expenses.

Income in Respect of a Decedent (IRD)

There is an important concept that your heirs should know about if they do end up paying estate taxes on an IRA or other type of retirement plan. The concept is called income in respect of a decedent (IRD).

Though the double taxation is draconian, the alert IRA beneficiary (or advisor of the beneficiary) can take advantage of this concept that many attorneys or tax preparers don't know about. IRD is a special deduction the IRA beneficiary is entitled to with every taxable distribution he receives from the inherited IRA. The deduction is taken as a miscellaneous itemized deduction and is not subject to the 2% of AGI limitation.

Let's look at this with a simple example. Bill dies in 2006 leaving an estate of $2.5 million, $1.5 million in after tax money and $1 million in an IRA, to his son. His son must pay $230,000 in estate taxes.

Eventually his son will have to pay income taxes on the $1 million inherited IRA and its growth when he takes distributions. However, the IRD deduction allows for an income tax deduction calculated as follows. Since there would not have been any federal estate tax if there had not been any IRA (just $1.5 million of after tax money) the $230,000 of estate taxes paid can be attributed entirely to the inherited IRA. The $230,000 divided by the value of the IRA in the estate of $1 million is 23%. This means that for every dollar that the IRA beneficiary withdraws from the inherited IRA, he can deduct 23 cents as an itemized deduction until his total deduction from the inherited IRA equals $230,000. Though it is still exceedingly painful to pay the double taxes, the income in respect to a decedent deduction (IRD) takes out some of the bite.

Avoiding Estate and Gift Taxes

In the United States there are several common ways to avoid gift and estate taxes. The first way is to simply die with less than the Applicable Exclusion Amount (subject to exceptions) in your estate! That sounds obvious, but with the shifting Applicable Exclusion Amount, it becomes extremely problematic, and planning for individuals with total estates over $2 million, or estates that have the potential to grow greater than $2 million, becomes more challenging—although we have discussed the effectiveness of gifts.

The second way is to leave money to a spouse taking advantage of the unlimited marital deduction. U.S. citizens (it is the citizenship of the beneficiary spouse, not the deceased spouse that is important) are entitled to inherit an unlimited amount of money from their deceased spouses, without paying any U.S. estate taxes. This applies to retirement plans, IRAs, and every other type of asset.

Simultaneous Death

What happens if there are simultaneous deaths? The challenge is to think out what the various possibilities are. You work out *who* you wanted to die first (from a financial perspective). So, let's say you have $3 million in an IRA. If you die when the Applicable Exclusion Amount is scheduled to be $2 million (in 2006) and we choose to say that your spouse has predeceased you, then there is a big estate tax. Let's say your IRA beneficiary designation is set up properly. Instead we can choose to say that you died first. We could then have the beneficiary's executor make a disclaimer that would result in your spouse getting $1 million and your children getting $2 million. The $2 million from you that goes to your kids won't be taxable. The $1 million that just went to your spouse (briefly) will also go to the kids. Since that comes from your spouse, there's no tax on that either. So if you have it set up properly, you avoid tax on the whole thing. If you don't have it set up properly, then there's a big tax.

The Exemption Equivalent Amount Trust (the B Trust, or the Unified Credit Trust)

One method of minimizing federal estate taxes has been to draft a trust which, upon the first spouse's death, protects from estate taxation one exclusion amount, currently $2 million (and going up after 2008). This traditional estate plan uses two separate trusts, the A trust (Marital Trust) and the B trust (Unified Credit Trust). The surviving spouse has the right to use any and all income and principal from the A trust. Typically the B trust is limited so that the surviving spouse is only permitted to use the income from the trust and may invade principal for health, education, maintenance, and support. When the surviving spouse dies, money remaining in the A trust will be subject to federal estate taxes, if the surviving spouse has more than the Applicable Exclusion Amount. On the other hand, because of its spending limitations, the B trust is not considered part of the federal estate of the surviving spouse and is therefore not subject to estate tax at the second death.

The B trust is funded with an amount up to, but not greater than the Applicable Exclusion Amount. Typically, these trusts are drafted without specifying an amount. Instead there is a funding formula that often does not provide the most beneficial results for the surviving spouse. Basically, the standard old-fashioned formula says that whatever the Applicable Exclusion Amount is in the year of death, that amount should go into the trust for the surviving spouse.

If you have one of these estate plans, you could inadvertently and unnecessarily be under-providing for your surviving spouse by transferring too much money to the trust. In fact, the full use of this B trust may be downright stupid. In the above example, with a total estate of $2.5 million, if we had traditional documents using the B trust, only $500,000 would go outright to the surviving spouse since $2 million would be required to fund the trust. Under the previous tax laws, an estate attorney may have drafted this type of trust to save estate taxes at the second death. The intent was to minimize federal estate tax at the second death.

Now, however, with portfolios down and the exclusion amounts up, your surviving spouse's estate may not be subject to federal estate tax. Do you think he or she would want all the money in the estate going to a trust? These traditional plans pose harm to the comfort and/or convenience of your surviving spouse, and many people don't even realize what their estate planning documents invoke. That is a tragedy. It would be wise to take a look at your own plan after finishing this book.

Wow! This can be a confusing chapter . . . but it's very important to see this through. Properly preparing this can mean the difference between being comfortable versus having to watch every dollar. Take your time and read this chapter; reread it a second time if you need to. While it's not pleasant to think about your passing on, it's important to prepare for your heirs. After all . . . none of us gets out alive. You want to be sure your family will continue to be taken care of after you are gone.

The Nastiest Trap of All

What follows is an analysis of how bad it can be if you have fairly standard wills and trusts. The quick analysis: it is nasty. The quick conclusion for clients with traditional documents and less than $2 million—it is time to review the will and trust.

If your will and/or trust uses a formula indicating the maximum marital deduction as "the spouse shall receive an amount equal to the maximum marital deduction amount available after taking into account the applicable credit amount," chances are that the document requires the dreaded mandatory funding of the B (exemption equivalent) trust, regardless of whether such funding is necessary under current law. Many wills and trusts contain this language, but with the new tax laws you must take action. Don't let your inertia compromise your spouse.

The Details of the Nasty Provisions

Let's assume the will or revocable trust or beneficiary designation of the IRA or retirement plan creates a trust (B trust, Unified Credit Amount Trust) as described above. Upon the death of the first spouse, the Applicable Exclusion Amount is automatically

Nastiest trap of all

paid into this trust. Though this isn't mechanically accurate for the purpose of the IRAs or retirement plans, it is conceptually accurate. The trust will pay income to the surviving spouse for his or her life and provide the right to additional money for the health, maintenance, and support of the spouse. The trust may even allow the spouse to invade the principal for $5,000 or 5% of the trust, whichever is greater, and may have additional provisions allowing invasion of principal for children or grandchildren if needed. At the death of the surviving spouse, the trust is usually distributed to the children equally.

Under the old law, this type of trust helped save on estate taxes, but unfortunately, under the new law, it creates a trap. Most of these trusts are structured so that:

1. The Applicable Exclusion Amount (it was $1 million in 2003, and now is $2 million in 2006, increasing to $3.5 million in 2009) is distributed to the trust.
2. The balance of the estate (if any) is distributed to the surviving spouse.

The complication is that, as the Applicable Exclusion Amount increases, fewer and fewer second estates will be large enough to be subject to federal estate taxes. Thus, if the first spouse leaves everything to the second spouse, at the death of the second spouse the combined estates may still be under the threshold of the amount subject to federal federal estate taxes. The raised exemption amounts mean fewer estates will be subject to estate tax, which means more estates will not benefit from this trust. Just because the spouse or family may not benefit from this trust, that does not mean the trust will not be activated.

...as the Applicable Exclusion Amount increases, fewer and fewer second estates will be large enough to be subject to federal estate taxes.

Presuming an individual has the type of documents that will force an amount equivalent to (or less than) the Applicable Exclusion Amount into the B trust, this may mean that existing documents will put most—if not all—of the first spouse's assets into the trust at the expense of the surviving spouse. While funding the trust was critical when saving estate taxes was the issue, depending on the size of the estate and year of death, that logic may no longer apply, given today's higher federal exclusion amounts. An individual's current documents may ensure that a huge amount of money goes into the B trust and that only a small amount, or maybe no amount, will be left directly to the surviving spouse.

Unintentionally Disinheriting the Surviving Spouse

Consider an estate consisting of Husband's $1.3 million IRA with the exemption—equivalent-type trust as the primary beneficiary. If he dies in 2006, all the money would go into the trust (because the Applicable Exclusion Amount is $2 million in 2006). If that is the couple's main asset, we have just created a financial catastrophe.

Many surviving spouses will be unhappy to find that as a result of the increased exemption amounts, more money is going to a trust for their benefit and less money is going directly to them. There is a strong chance the surviving spouse would prefer to have the money directly rather than in trust, particularly where there is no tax-savings benefit of the trust. In this instance a simple "I love you" will or beneficiary designation of the IRA or retirement plan would have been sufficient to avoid estate taxes at the second death.

"I love you" wills are quite common and serve an important purpose. The will says, "I leave everything to my spouse, and my spouse leaves everything to me." At the second death the money is divided equally among the children.

In this example, having a simple "I love you" will would have been sufficient to avoid estate tax. At the first death, the surviving spouse would have received the $1.3 million and used the unlimited marital deduction to avoid estate taxes. At the second death, the surviving spouse's total estate would have been less than the exemption equivalent amount. Thus, there would be no estate tax and no messing around with an unnecessary trust. Not only was the entire complicated estate plan misguided and unnecessary, it also poses serious problems for the surviving spouse and the rest of the family.

Though it is not overly costly to draft these trusts, living with them after the death of the first spouse until the second death is far more costly in terms of fees (at a minimum you have to prepare a special annual trust tax return), aggravation, and restrictions on the surviving spouse. With the rapidly changing estate tax exemption amounts, the vagaries of the stock market, and the big unknowns such as "when you will die?" and "how much money will be in your estate?" you could incur burdensome and unnecessary expenses. Worse yet, there is no benefit at all from the estate plan for that couple. Individuals who have plans similar to the one referenced above are advised to consider the benefits of revising their estate plans.

What If Retirement Assets Will Fund the Trust? Yuck!

What if the assets that fund the trust are retirement assets (IRAs, 401(k)s, 403(b)s, etc.)? Then, after the IRA owner dies, the minimum required distribution from the trust is based on the life expectancy of the surviving spouse. At the death of the surviving spouse, the children are required to maintain distributions at the rate established when the surviving spouse was alive. The result is an enormous acceleration of distributions from the retirement plan. This produces taxable income for the family, and an increase in taxes, and the family is deprived of the enormous potential they could have from a stretch IRA, which I cover in the next chapter.

A Key Lesson from This Chapter

Don't get caught with an estate plan that automatically transfers the Applicable Exclusion Amount into a B trust for the benefit of your spouse without making sure that is the best choice.

Laying the Foundation for Estate Planning: Using the Minimum Required Distribution Rules after Death

Generosity lies less in giving much than in giving at the right moment.

—Jean de la Bruyere

Main Topics

- What is an inherited IRA and how does it work?
- How do beneficiaries calculate and stretch minimum required distributions?
- Why beneficiaries should continue to take the least possible amount out of their inherited IRA.

KEY IDEA

Individuals profit from deferring income taxes during their lifetime; so can their heirs.

Most people want to incorporate some planning for their heirs, beyond that of their spouse. Providing for the surviving spouse is usually the highest priority. Ultimately, after the second death, you might hope to offer a cushion to children and/or grandchildren with the remaining funds. So, how does maintaining money in the IRA environment accomplish those two objectives?

Just as it was advantageous for you to keep money in your IRA, it is best for the beneficiaries of IRAs to retain the money in the tax-deferred environment for as long as possible.

Don't pay taxes now—pay taxes later. Just as it was advantageous for you to keep money in your IRA, it is best for the beneficiaries of IRAs to retain the money in the tax-deferred environment for as long as possible. Starting with that premise, let's examine planning for two types of beneficiaries.

What Is a Stretch IRA?

A stretch IRA is an IRA that has a beneficiary designation that provides for the possibility of maintaining the tax-deferred status of the IRA after the death of the IRA owner. You might be thinking, "I wish I had a stretch IRA. I only named my spouse as my primary beneficiary and my kids as my successor or contingent beneficiary." Well, guess what? You have a stretch IRA. After your death, your spouse and/or your children could continue to defer income taxes for many years after your death, as long as no one does anything really stupid. Before we get into the mechanics of avoiding doing something stupid, first, let's look at likely beneficiaries.

A stretch IRA is an IRA that has a beneficiary designation that provides for the possibility of maintaining the tax-deferred status of the IRA after the death of the IRA owner.

Who Can Inherit an IRA?

Just as at some point the IRA owner must take minimum distributions of his IRA, the beneficiaries of an IRA must also take minimum distributions after the death of the IRA owner. The

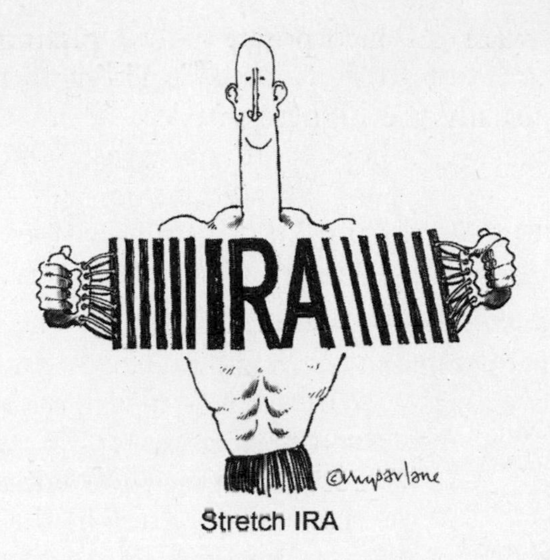

Stretch IRA

minimum distribution rules for inherited IRAs can be divided into two basic categories for individual beneficiaries:

- Spousal beneficiary
- Nonspousal beneficiary

Later sections of this chapter discuss the application of minimum distribution rules to estates and trusts.

Spousal Beneficiary

If the surviving spouse is the beneficiary, there are options to consider:

1. Treat the IRA as their own
   a. Trustee-to-trustee transfer to spouse's own new or existing IRA
   b. Spousal IRA rollover to spouse's own new or existing IRA
   c. Retitle the IRA (if not changing institutions)
2. Act as beneficiary of a Spousal Inherited IRA

It is generally best for the surviving spouse to treat the IRA as their own rather than as an Inherited IRA. By making it his or her own, the surviving spouse will be able to generate a greater amount of tax-deferred growth because he or she will be able to:

- Defer distributions if she is younger than 70½.
- Take the lowest possible minimum required distribution based on the Uniform Life Table.
- Name new beneficiaries on the account and give the newly named beneficiaries the ability to stretch the IRA after the spouse dies. (Providing the newly named beneficiaries with the ability to stretch the IRA is a unique right provided only to the surviving spouse.)

If the surviving spouse is unhappy with the institution holding the IRA or with the investment choices, he or she can complete a trustee-to-trustee transfer. An IRA spousal rollover is also a possibility. I prefer the trustee-to-trustee transfer over the spousal IRA rollover for the same reasons that I like the trustee-to-trustee transfer while the IRA owner is alive (see chapter 5). If he or she is happy with the institution and the current investments, the surviving spouse can inform the institution holding the IRA of the desire to retitle the account and treat the IRA as their own.

If a surviving spouse decides to treat the IRA as his or her own, ultimately the tax treatment is similar to the treatment of the deceased IRA owner. The difference is that the future minimum required distributions will be calculated from the Uniform Life Table based on the surviving spouse's age. The one exception occurs during the year that first spouse dies. If there is a minimum required distribution for that year, it will be based on the deceased spouse's previous distribution schedule and must be withdrawn by the surviving spouse prior to completing the trustee-to-trustee transfer. That specific minimum required distribution becomes the property of the beneficiary, not the estate (that goes for nonspousal beneficiaries also). By assuming ownership of the IRA, you can name your own beneficiaries (usually children and/or grandchildren who will become eligible to stretch the tax-deferral period over their individual life expectancies).

If the IRA is to be split among the surviving spouse and other beneficiaries, separate accounts should be established. Special care should be taken with the titling of the beneficiary accounts. Also, take care to change Social Security numbers.

Spousal Beneficiary Who Chooses the Spousal Inherited IRA Option

There are situations when the surviving spouse might choose not to assume ownership of his or her deceased spouse's IRA.

Perhaps the surviving spouse is younger than 59½ and he or she wants or needs the distributions.

- If the surviving spouse takes over the IRA as their own and is younger than 59½, he or she must comply with Section 72(t)—Premature Distribution Exceptions to avoid the 10% penalty on early distributions.
- A spousal beneficiary who treats the IRA as a Spousal Inherited IRA rather than treat it as their own can take out as much as needed before age 59½ without penalty. The surviving spouse will not be required to take a distribution until their deceased spouse would have turned 70½.

There is a risk with this alternative: if the surviving spouse chooses to treat the IRA as a Spousal Inherited IRA it preempts any possibility of a long stretch for the ultimate beneficiaries, usually the children. When the spouse acts as a beneficiary of an inherited IRA, the MRD will be based on the single life expectancy of the surviving spouse. After the surviving spouse reaches 70½ the surviving spouse's life expectancy will be recalculated each year. With the Inherited IRA when that spouse dies, the beneficiaries who inherit the assets will be locked in to taking distributions based on the surviving spouse's remaining life expectancy, and the divisor will be reduced by one for each subsequent year. A full explanation of the rules and regulations for this option can be found under the heading "Nonspouse Beneficiary" (page 169).

Compromise Solution

In my practice we have come up with a compromise. When surviving spouses are younger than 59½ and need the proceeds from the IRA for their normal living expenses, we make a projection of how much money he or she will need until turning 59½. I include in the calculation some growth of the assets. Then, we treat that amount (the combination of her needs and the assumed interest and appreciation of those funds) as the inherited IRA, and for the rest we do a trustee-to-trustee transfer. The advantages are clear:

- He or she has access to the entire inherited IRA without penalty.
- There are allowances for immediate distributions.
- The portion that is rolled over into her IRA will continue to grow tax-deferred, stretching the IRA both before she is 70, and after she is 70½.

Sometimes it is a delicate calculation to figure out how much the surviving spouse will need and what interest rates are likely to do. I would probably prefer to err on the side of over-providing for the surviving spouse until 59, even at the expense of some income tax acceleration.

If you are uncomfortable with that approach because you don't want to pay any extra taxes, you could underestimate and then plan to do a Section 72(t) periodic payment schedule before 59½ for a portion of the IRA that would be rolled over into the surviving spouse's IRA.

Spouses younger than 59½ who have a need for considerable money before they turn 59½ should seek professional help from someone who will run the numbers to help determine how to split up the IRA.

What If the Younger Spouse Dies First?

Another time when a spouse might choose to act as a beneficiary rather than assume ownership of the IRA occurs when the younger spouse predeceases the older spouse. The advantage here is that he or she may defer taking distributions until the IRA owner would have turned 70½. However, even though there might be some additional deferral period until the surviving spouse has to take the money out, I generally do not like this election. Unfortunately, when the time arrives to begin taking distributions, the surviving spouse must take out minimum distributions based on his or her sole life expectancy—once again, you lose the potential for the stretch for the beneficiaries after the second death.

Nonspouse Beneficiary

If the beneficiary is a nonspouse, and assuming no one botches it, the beneficiary has a new type of asset called an Inherited IRA. The nonspousal beneficiary may not roll the Inherited IRA into his or her own IRA; thus it isn't an IRA. Assuming proper drafting of the beneficiary designation and proper follow-through after the death of the IRA owner, the beneficiary of the Inherited IRA will also not have to pay income taxes on the Inherited IRA, at least not all at once. He will be able to stretch the Inherited IRA and take his own minimum required distributions based on Table I (Single Life Table) found in IRS Publication 590. Alternatively, that information can also be found at www.PayTaxesLater.com/beneficiary.htm, along with a calculator that will make the theory and the actual calculation quite easy.

The minimum required distribution for the beneficiary of the Inherited IRA is based on the beneficiary's life expectancy as of December 31 of the year following the year the IRA owner died. Please note, however, that the beneficiary must be determined no later than September 30 of the year following the year that the IRA owner died. The reason for the September 30 deadline is to give the IRA custodian sufficient time to make the minimum required distribution before the end of the year.

For example, assume that Judy (from the Tom and Judy example described in Mini Case Study 11.1) dies at age 88 and that her nonspouse beneficiary is then aged 63. The beneficiary would have a deemed life expectancy of 21.8 years (the life expectancy for a 64-year-old using the Single Life Table) for the first distribution, which would have to be withdrawn by December 31 of the following year. The minimum required distribution for the Inherited IRA is calculated by dividing the balance in the account as of December 31 of the previous year by the life expectancy of the beneficiary. For this example, assume an IRA balance of $1 million on December 31 of the year the IRA owner died. The minimum required distribution for the survivor would be $1 million divided by 21.8, or $45,871.56. As the beneficiary (survivor) ages, the factor is reduced by one year, that is, the next year's factor would be 20.8, then 19.8, and so on. Naming a younger beneficiary means a larger life expectancy factor and a lower minimum required distribution.

Thus, a younger beneficiary who inherits an IRA will have a greater potential for long-term tax deferral than would an older beneficiary. Stated another way, the present value of the future cash flows to a younger beneficiary is greater than that to an older beneficiary. Even when the surviving spouse uses a joint life expectancy (his or her life expectancy and a beneficiary 10 years younger) to calculate the minimum required distribution, the Inherited IRA has a greater tax deferral potential for the surviving spouse's child than for the surviving spouse. The inherited IRA would have its greatest tax deferral potential in the hands of a grandchild (preferably via a well-drafted trust). A younger beneficiary means a longer life expectancy. A long life expectancy equates to lower annual minimum required distributions; the greater the portion of assets that remains in the tax-deferred environment, the greater the accumulation.

A young beneficiary who inherits an IRA will have the greatest potential for long-term tax deferral.

Later chapters tie the minimum required distribution rules for Inherited IRAs into the estate planning process.

Estate as Beneficiary

A long life expectancy equates to lower annual minimum required distributions; the greater the portion of assets that remains in the tax-deferred environment, the greater the accumulation.

Naming an estate as the beneficiary of your IRA is almost always a mistake because the beneficiaries of an estate do not qualify as designated beneficiaries for purposes of the minimum required distribution rules. Thousands of misguided souls will cause their beneficiaries massive income tax acceleration unless someone or something intervenes.

- If the current beneficiary of your retirement plan or IRA is your estate, you should revise the beneficiary designation immediately.
- If you have not named a beneficiary and the default beneficiary of your IRA is the estate, then you must name a beneficiary.

In order to achieve the stretch for the beneficiary, you must have a designated beneficiary for your IRA. That used to be easier said than done. Now, it is hard to avoid, assuming you fill out the beneficiary form as recommended in Chapter 13. A limited stretch for the remainder of the owner's unused life expectancy is available if the owner dies after the required beginning date without naming a designated beneficiary.

Trust as Beneficiary

There are many situations when a trust will be a good choice for a beneficiary of an IRA. The most obvious reason is if the beneficiary is still a minor. Another reason to name a trust as beneficiary of an IRA is to reduce or eliminate estate taxes. Finally, you may want to use a trust if your beneficiary is not responsible with money and you want to make sure your beneficiary doesn't do anything stupid with the money. If you want to ensure that the beneficiaries stretch the IRA, naming a trust as the beneficiary of an IRA will achieve your goal.

Generally, we assume that a rational beneficiary will want to continue to defer income taxes after the IRA owner's death. We also know that a drafting error in the trust or a procedural error could prevent this from happening and lead to a massive acceleration of income taxes.

It is important that any trust that will serve as the beneficiary of an IRA or retirement plan be drafted with extreme care to ensure that:

- The retirement plan or IRA beneficiary designations are properly in place.
- The trust qualifies as a designated beneficiary.

If those two qualifications are met, the life expectancies of individual beneficiaries of a trust can be used for purposes of the MRD.

Technical Requirements for a Trust to Get the Stretch IRA Treatment

For the trust to qualify as a designated beneficiary (and get the stretch treatment) it must meet the following five requirements:

1. The trust must be valid under state law, or would be but for the fact that it is not yet funded.
2. The trust is irrevocable or will become irrevocable at the creator's death.
3. The trust beneficiaries must be identifiable—that is, by the last day of the year following your death, it must be possible to identify all the persons who could possibly be beneficiaries of the trust.
4. All the trust beneficiaries must be individuals.
5. Documentation about the trust must be provided to the plan administrator by October 31 of the year following your death. This consists of a copy of the trust instrument or a final list of all the beneficiaries.

Depending on the ages of the beneficiaries, the amounts, and the individual's situation, it may be worthwhile to establish a trust as the beneficiary of an IRA. If so, please be sure to comply with all the requirements so the beneficiary can enjoy tax benefits as well as the protection provided by a trust.

This is an area where an attorney's input is advisable. Unfortunately, most attorneys just don't know this stuff. Since it is so easy to botch one of the requirements above, choose your attorneys with care, and be sure to ask specifically about their experience with drafting a trust as a beneficiary of an IRA.

A Key Lesson from This Chapter

While you are alive, don't pay taxes now—pay taxes later. The same advice holds true for your beneficiaries. I encourage you to discuss this concept with your beneficiaries so that they are aware of the material advantages of stretching an IRA. Now, on to the ultimate solution for estate planning with IRAs and retirement plans.

The Answer to the Problem: Using Disclaimers in Estate Planning

If you cannot accurately predict the future, then you must flexibly be prepared to deal with various possible futures.

— Edward de Bono

Main Topics

- How disclaimers work
- Mistakes to avoid
- Advantages of disclaimers
- Comparing the disclaimer approach to the traditional approach

KEY IDEA

An individual who disclaims an inheritance simply steps aside and the next person in line (the contingent beneficiary or beneficiaries) inherits. Planning with this option in mind allows a family to assess and respond to the actual financial needs of the family after the death of the first spouse.

How Disclaimers Work

You can't force someone to accept an inherited IRA. In traditional families, the standard procedure is for the IRA owner to name his or her spouse as the primary beneficiary and their children equally as contingent beneficiaries (the same ingredients of the "I Love You" will). Here's the key: The surviving spouse always has the option to choose not to accept the inherited IRA and disclaim her entire interest or a portion of her interest in the inherited IRA.

Let's assume the surviving spouse's disclaimer meets the federal requirements for a qualified disclaimer and the applicable state law requirements for a valid disclaimer (as described later in this chapter). The IRA can be divided into as many inherited IRAs as there are children, and the surviving spouse will not be treated as making a gift for federal gift or estate tax purposes. Subsequently, each child can take minimum distributions from their inherited IRA based on their own individual life expectancy. Under the current rules, the beneficiary, whose age will determine the minimum required distribution, does not have to be determined until September 30 of the year following the year of the IRA owner's death.

The surviving spouse always has the option to choose not to accept the inherited IRA and disclaim her entire interest or a portion of her interest in the inherited IRA.

Please do not misunderstand this concept. You cannot change beneficiaries after the IRA owner dies. If the three children were named equally as the contingent beneficiaries, the surviving spouse could only disclaim to all three children in equal shares. The surviving spouse could not pick and choose among the children nor alter amounts or percentages. If she disclaims, the children must receive equal shares. Disclaiming simply means that one beneficiary steps aside in favor of the next beneficiary. Should the first beneficiary disclaim, the contingent beneficiary is able to use his or her own life expectancy to calculate the minimum required distribution of the inherited IRA, allowing the IRA to be stretched.

Under most state disclaimer laws, the surviving spouse has nine months to decide whether or not to accept, disclaim, or partially accept and partially disclaim his or her interest. The requirements for a qualified disclaimer under federal law (which are generally the same requirements as under state law, although you must always review applicable state law to confirm that the proposed disclaimer meets the requirements) include the following:

You cannot change beneficiaries after the IRA owner dies... Disclaiming simply means that one beneficiary steps aside in favor of the next beneficiary.

1. The disclaimer must be irrevocable, unqualified (unconditional), and in writing.
2. The written disclaimer must be delivered to the owner of the interest or the owner's legal representative (i.e., executor or retirement plan administrator).
3. The disclaimer must be received by the owner of the interest no later than nine months after the date of death or nine months after the disclaimant attains age 21, whichever is later. (While the beneficiary is not finally determined until September 30 of the year following the year of the IRA owner's death, the disclaimer must be filed within nine months to be effective.)
4. The disclaimant has not accepted the interest (the interest can be either a partial interest or the entire interest) or any of its benefits. Also note that a disclaimer to a B trust for the benefit of a surviving spouse is a common exception to this rule because the surviving spouse's interest in the B trust is not considered to be an acceptance of any of the benefits of the IRA.
5. The property must pass to the alternate beneficiary without any direction on the part of the disclaimant.
6. The property must pass to either the spouse of the decedent or to a person other than the person making a disclaimer.

The death of a spouse is an emotional time. It's easy to make big mistakes when you're in an emotional state. Discuss, plan and prepare ahead of time, and please make sure you have a flexible plan that will survive changes in both the tax code and how your investments do over time. Then, after a death, your surviving spouse will have all the options at his or her disposal and will have an entire nine months to make a decision on what to do.

Avoid This Mistake

After a death, if the named beneficiary is even considering a disclaimer, the most important thing is *to do nothing!*

The surviving spouse should not take control of the assets. Do not transfer or roll the assets into the spouse's name until you have made a final decision not to disclaim any portion of the account. Although the IRS has still permitted disclaimers in certain situations after the spouse has partially accepted the assets, it is more prudent and considerably less expensive not to accept any assets until after you have consulted with a qualified advisor. I recently had a situation where the surviving spouse, in an attempt to save money, tried doing some of the estate administration on her own. She figured she could take care of making the trustee-to-trustee transfer of her husband's IRA over to her own name before she came in to see us. She filled out paperwork to put into motion the trustee-to-trustee transfer; later that month, she informed us of her husband's death and came to see us regarding the rest of the estate administration. I immediately saw the potential for the benefits of a disclaimer, something she forgot about. Unfortunately, I was too late. Before our office became involved, she took control of the IRA and transferred it into her own name. We could not do a disclaimer on any portion of her husband's IRA, something that would have provided great benefits to the family.

Advantages of Disclaimers

Trying to predict the future is like trying to drive down a country road at night with no lights while looking out the back window.

— Peter F. Drucker

A disclaimer offers several potential advantages. When reading about the examples, please assume that the surviving spouse is named as the primary beneficiary and the children equally as contingent beneficiaries of the first spouse's IRA. There are, of course, circumstances when disclaiming is not appropriate, and the surviving spouse would be wise to choose to retain the entire IRA. If, however, the surviving spouse has significantly more money than she needs, choosing to disclaim the IRA could be a powerful course of action. If the surviving spouse disclaims the IRA to the children, it accomplishes two objectives.

There is a good chance that the best solution will be for the surviving spouse to keep a portion of the IRA and disclaim the remaining portion.

1. The IRA is not included in her estate, which could reduce estate taxes for the children at her death.
2. The second and perhaps more important advantage is that the minimum required distribution of the inherited IRA would be based on the life expectancy of the children rather than the shorter statutory joint life expectancy of the surviving spouse (longer life expectancy = longer tax deferral).

There is a good chance that the best solution will be for the surviving spouse to keep a portion of the IRA and disclaim the remaining portion.

The beauty of this disclaimer arrangement is that the decision of whether or how much to disclaim can be made after the death of the first spouse when a clearer picture of the surviving spouse's financial situation is available.

Comparing the Disclaimer Approach to a Traditional Approach

If you have the traditional retirement plan that includes a B trust, the following information is enormously important and similar to the analysis presented on page 159 under the heading "The Nastiest Trap of All." The problem with the "fixed in stone" traditional approach is that no one can predict:

- The future value of the investments
- Which spouse will die first
- The needs of the surviving spouse
- What estate tax laws will be in force at the death of the first spouse and/or the death of the second spouse

The traditional approach only allows you to guess at what might be an optimal plan for the surviving spouse and family.

The appeal of the traditional approach is that the bequeathing individual exercises control; he or she decides how to leave money at death and sees that the appropriate documents are drafted. This approach does not allow the surviving spouse to make discretionary decisions. With a traditional plan, the IRA owner need not worry whether the surviving spouse is going to make appropriate choices. The thinking has been done, and the decisions are made.

One problem with this approach is that any traditional plan that is put in place today will likely be far from optimal within one or two years. As the laws change and the balances in the estate and other factors change, the will or beneficiary designation must be redrafted. Please keep in mind that under the current law, the exemption amounts vary significantly from year to year.

Applicable Exclusion Amounts

2006, 2007 and 2008	$2 million
2009	$3.5 million
2010	Estate tax is repealed
2011	$1 million [a]

[a] *Unless Congress takes action.*

Please note that the shifting target of the exemption equivalent amounts (the amount of money you can die with before you incur federal estate tax) creates chaos for the estate planner. Traditional estate planners not using disclaimer-type planning will be forced to revise the will, trust, and beneficiary designation of the IRA every year to achieve the optimal result. (Of course, perhaps the traditional planner should not complain. All this revising brings in lots of revenue. The shifting exclusion amounts could have been called "The Estate Planners' Full Employment Act" because it creates a steady need for redrafting and tinkering with the estate plan.)

The shifting exclusion amounts could have been called "The Estate Planners' Full Employment Act" because it creates a steady need for redrafting and tinkering with the estate plan.

I suggest that the decision of whether the surviving spouse should keep all the funds or whether the children should receive some portion of them (not to mention other choices) can be most effectively made when the spouse is in possession of "current facts and figures." Properly drafted documents and beneficiary designations using possibilities of disclaimers can provide the surviving spouse with options—not carte blanche—after the death of the first spouse.

Many planners use the exclusion amount trust to avoid estate taxes without considering disclaimers. That traditional planning can be harmful, even devastating, as shown below in Mini Case Study 11.1.

MINI CASE STUDY 11.1
The Income Tax Hit of IRAs in the B Trust

Suppose Tom dies at the age of 70 with $1 million in an IRA. He had a family. His wife Judy is 68 and has $1 million in after-tax assets. They have one child who is 43 years old, and one grandchild who is 13 years old.

Let's assume Tom went to a traditional estate planner. The planner named a revocable trust with the traditional A/B trust as a beneficiary of Tom's IRA, forcing the $1 million IRA to fund the B trust prior to the funding of the A trust. The minimum distributions from Tom's IRA will be distributed to the trust (technically the inherited IRA will not be transferred to the trust; the distributions from the inherited IRA go to the trust). Since Judy has her own $1 million and she doesn't want to accelerate income taxes, she elects to take only the minimum required distribution of the inherited IRA.

Since Tom's IRA is funding a spousal trust rather than going directly to Judy, the minimum required distributions will be higher than necessary. They will be based on Judy's single life expectancy, rather than on a combination of her life expectancy and the life expectancy of someone who is 10 years younger. In determining these distributions to the trust, Judy's single life expectancy will be reduced by one year for every year throughout her lifetime and after her death. If Judy lives beyond her life expectancy, there will be nothing left in the trust. The consequences are accelerated income taxes for the family and probably no estate tax savings.

Assuming a 7% growth rate and that Judy will survive until age 88, it will take 19 years for the balance in the plan to be distributed to the trust, and distributions will stop before Judy's death. The total distributions received by the trust would equal $2,122,088, with a value of $1,488,070 in today's dollars as adjusted for 3% inflation (shown in the following table). Judy doesn't want to pay the trust's higher income tax rate and doesn't want the income from the inherited IRA to remain in the trust, so she makes annual withdrawals from the trust to transfer the income tax burden to her. Judy receives the distributions and pays her taxes. Whatever she doesn't spend over the course of her life is included in her estate.

Year	Distributions	Inflation-Adjusted Value of Distributions	Ending Trust Balance
1	$ 53,763	$ 52,151	$ 1,016,237
2	$ 57,741	$ 54,328	$ 1,029,632
3	$ 62,026	$ 56,609	$ 1,039,681
4	$ 66,646	$ 59,001	$ 1,045,812
5	$ 71,631	$ 61,512	$ 1,047,388
6	$ 77,014	$ 64,150	$ 1,043,691
7	$ 82,833	$ 66,927	$ 1,033,917
8	$ 89,131	$ 69,856	$ 1,017,160
9	$ 95,959	$ 72,951	$ 992,403
10	$ 103,375	$ 76,231	$ 958,496
11	$ 111,453	$ 79,723	$ 914,138
12	$ 120,281	$ 83,456	$ 857,846
13	$ 129,977	$ 87,478	$ 787,919
14	$ 140,700	$ 91,854	$ 702,373
15	$ 152,690	$ 96,691	$ 598,849
16	$ 166,347	$ 102,179	$ 474,422
17	$ 182,470	$ 108,720	$ 325,161
18	$ 203,226	$ 117,455	$ 144,697
19	$ 154,826	$ 86,797	$ -
TOTAL	$ 2,122,088	$ 1,488,070	

Using the same assumptions, however, if Tom names Judy outright, instead of the B trust, and Judy rolls the $1 million IRA into her own IRA and names her child as the beneficiary, total distributions to the family will be deferred over 43 years and increased by more than $3 million to $5,202,805 or, in inflation-adjusted dollars, $2,279,550—an increase of $791,480.

Using the same assumptions as above, except that Judy names her 13-year-old grandchild as beneficiary of her rollover IRA, the total amount of distributions from the IRA will be stretched over a period of 71 years (the life expectancy of the grandchild) and total $15,608,663 or $3,490,597 in inflation-adjusted dollars. Figure 11.1 shows the value of the distributions in inflation-adjusted dollars using these three beneficiary choices.

Figure 11.1

Graph Value of Distributions

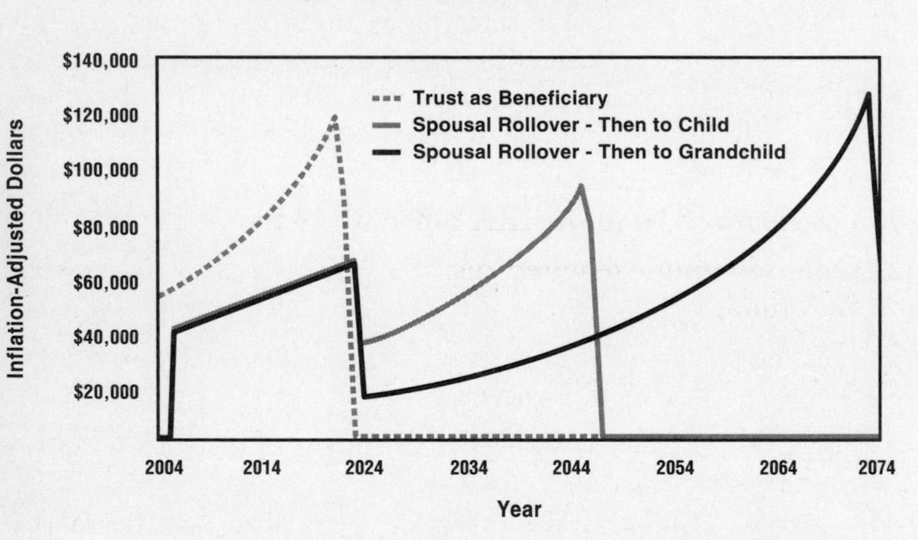

The reasons for the significant additional deferrals of distributions when Judy rolls the IRA over into her own name are:

1. There will be no MRD for Judy until she is 70½, so the IRA continues to grow fully tax-deferred.

2. When Judy is 70½, the MRD divisor factor will be based on a combination of her life expectancy and the life expectancy of someone who is deemed 10 years younger. That specific number is taken from an IRS table called the Uniform Life Table. As a result, Judy's MRDs will be much lower than the MRD for the trust that was based solely on her life expectancy.

3. Furthermore, if the IRA is rolled into Judy's IRA, the minimum required distributions after Judy's death are determined based on her child's single life expectancy, which allows for even lower distributions. If the IRA is transferred to the trust at the death of the IRA owner, and if in our case Judy were to die prematurely, the minimum required distributions will continue to be disbursed based on the original projection of Judy's life expectancy, even though she is dead!

Hark! Hark! One of our proper number-crunching reviewers is yelling "I object." He screams we are not presenting a fair picture. We must consider the value of the distributions from the IRAs and the potential growth even after income taxes have been paid. To do this, we look at the numbers using the following assumptions:

1. Distributions from the IRA funds are all taxed at a 25% rate.
2. Only minimum required distributions are taken from each IRA fund.
3. IRA distributions, net of this tax, are invested in after-tax funds to also yield 7% growth.
4. The after-tax fund is subject to net taxes of only 15% due to capital gains rules and rates.
5. Spending is made from each scenario's after-tax funds in the same amount beginning in 2006 when MRDs are required in Judy's (rolled-over) IRA. The spending amount is $30,000, increased 3% annually for inflation.
6. The remaining retirement assets are measured with a 25% income tax allowance.
7. The value of total remaining funds, both IRA and after-tax, are measured using 3% inflation-adjusted dollars.

Figure 11.2 shows the value of total funds using the trust, spouse and then child, and spouse and then grandchild, as beneficiaries:

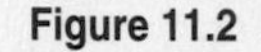

Figure 11.2

Graph Value of IRA Inheritance Using Different Beneficiaries and Taking Only MRDs

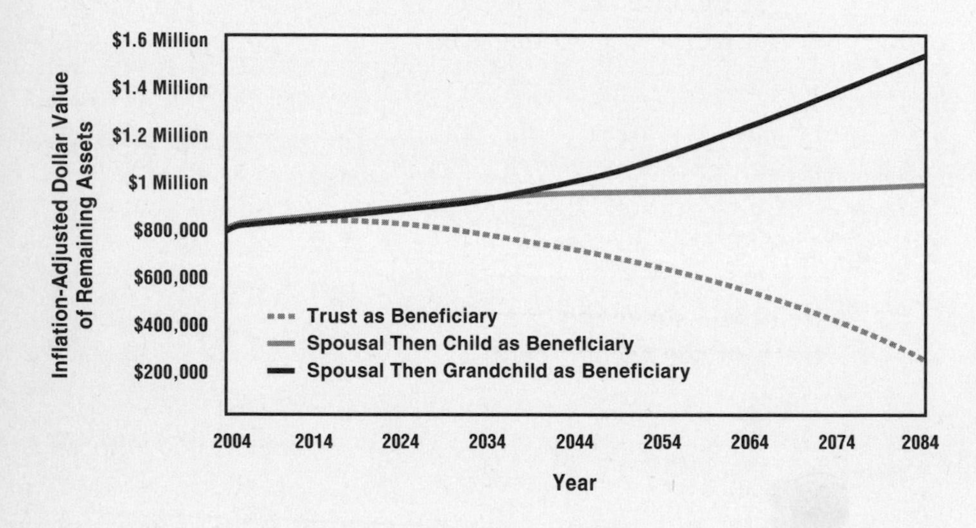

The supporting calculations show that the trust alternative begins becoming less favorable than the rollover IRA after the first year. After Judy's death, using the grandchild as beneficiary begins to become more favorable than using the child. Over time, due to the additional tax deferral in the IRA, this graph shows that it is better to use assets other than IRAs as assets to fund a B trust if possible. Please note, however, that this approach does not consider the potential estate tax savings. In some cases, there would be an estate tax savings if we used the B trust because we would avoid the double taxation of the estate tax and income tax in many situations. Because we do have a potential estate tax savings, we can't throw the idea of using the B trust as beneficiary of the IRA out the window.

Where does that leave us?

The Problem of Estate Planning in a Nutshell

- If we leave everything in the estate, including the IRA, to the surviving spouse, there might be an enormous estate tax at the second death. The damage will be compounded if there are no funds to pay the estate tax except by making distributions from the IRA that would trigger income tax—the payment of which would trigger more income tax, ad nauseam.
- If we use a traditional plan and fund the B trust before we leave anything to the surviving spouse, we may have the problem of not sufficiently providing for the surviving spouse. In addition, if the underlying asset is an IRA or a retirement plan, we have the additional problem of the accelerated distributions during both the life of the surviving spouse and for the children at the death of the second spouse.
- If there are sufficient assets to provide for the surviving spouse, we also may want to have children or grandchildren as beneficiaries of IRAs in order to take advantage of their long life expectancies that would stretch the IRA.

The problem, of course, is that there are too many variables, and we cannot predict which ones will be relevant at the time of death. How much money will be there at the first death? Who will die first? What tax laws will be operative in the year of the first death? What will the needs of the surviving spouse be? Now that we understand the problem, what is the solution? The answer lies in the next chapter.

Special note to financial professionals: understanding this concept is critical to your business. Please go to www.PayTaxesLater.com/finprof.htm for a special report designed to help you take better care of your clients and grow your business.

A Key Lesson from This Chapter

Any inflexible plan that we draft now will likely be in need of revision in a year or two. With constantly shifting circumstances, laws, and exemption equivalent amounts, it is extremely difficult to make a plan that will survive all the foreseeable and unforeseeable events.

The Ideal Beneficiary Designation of Your Retirement Plan

"Stretching and Disclaiming: Lange's Cascading Beneficiary Plan™" — Based on a Presentation Delivered at the National Tax Conference of the American Institute of CPAs in Washington D.C.

The circumstances of the world are so variable that an irrevocable purpose or opinion is almost synonymous with a foolish one.

— W. H. Seward (1801–1872), American statesman

Main Topics

- What the will does and does not control
- How the plan works
- Who should use the strategy?
- Who shouldn't use this strategy?

KEY IDEA

Lange's Cascading Beneficiary Plan™'s disclaimer strategy preserves the safety net for the natural heir of the IRA owner (i.e., the surviving spouse) by allowing complete discretion for the surviving spouse to keep funds for themselves, or to disclaim to children, or to trusts both for grandchildren or the surviving spouse. The decision of whether and how much to disclaim can be made after the death of the first spouse.

Critical Information: A Will or Living Trust Does Not Control the Distribution of an IRA or Retirement Plan

In my practice, clients often come with sophisticated and lengthy wills or revocable trusts covering every contingency, including a variety of trusts or subtrusts. When I ask clients where most of their money is, they often reply in their IRA or retirement plan. Then, when I ask about the beneficiaries of the IRA and retirement plan, I find that despite their long and complex wills, the beneficiary designation that controls the vast majority of their wealth is often two lines long:

1. Surviving spouse
2. Children equally

In this scenario, all the good planning that went into the will or revocable trust is of limited or no use to the client who has large retirement accounts, potentially the largest asset in the client's estate. This is because the will or revocable trust does not control the beneficiary designations of retirement plans.

...the will or revocable trust does not control the beneficiary designations of retirement plans.

This mistake is deadly and all too common. In my experience, effective planning for the retirement plan and/or IRA is the exception, not the rule. In the area of estate planning for IRAs and retirement plans, the difference between effective and ineffective planning can be hundreds of thousands, sometimes millions of dollars.

Why do the *Wall Street Journal*, *Newsweek*, *Financial Planning* magazine, *The Tax Adviser* (AICPA), and a host of other national periodicals sing the praises of Lange's Cascading Beneficiary Plan™?

It's simple. It's a secure way for you to easily, safely, and with maximum flexibility plan your estate and provide for your heirs before one of you dies. It's a plan that has passed the test of time! Read on and take notes, you'll want to implement this!

I have an idea for you. For discussion's sake, I am going to assume that you are married and that you are willing to answer the following question with an unequivocal yes. Are you ready for this? I love this. I do this in practice all the time. Do you trust your spouse? Seriously, do you *trust* your spouse?

Let's assume the answer is yes, that you trust your spouse. For discussion's sake, let's say that you have one of those traditional marriages: You're married and you have kids and grandchildren. You have four choices for beneficiaries when it really comes down to it. Number one, you have your surviving spouse. We love our spouse. We want to provide for the comfort and security of our spouse after we die. I'm happy to report to you that in 27 years of practice nobody came in and said, "My goal for my estate is to have my grandchildren so stinking rich that they'll never have to work a day in their life." Nobody ever said that. I'll tell you what people say. "I want to take care of my spouse." That even comes before saving taxes. That comes before everything. I want to take care of my spouse. Let's leave that as the number one option. But one of the problems with that is you might end up with a big estate tax. Let's say you have $3 million in an IRA. You die. At the second death, your spouse's estate will have a $2 million exemption and $1 million that is taxable. There will be a $460,000 tax.

Maybe what you need is a trust. The trust says income to the spouse and right to invade principal for health, maintenance and support. At the second death the trust goes to the kids equally. It might be a reasonable strategy. It might save $460,000 in taxes. But it might be bad. It might be *really* bad. Your surviving spouse could face significant limitations that are totally unnecessary. Traditionally the amount of money that would go into the trust would be equal to the Applicable Exclusion Amount. If that were the case, for a death in 2006 the trust would get $2 million. The Applicable Exclusion Amount has risen dramatically since a lot of these traditional plans were written. There are a lot of people who, if their spouses died right now, would be forced to have all their money transferred to the trust and nothing would go directly to the surviving spouse. It's called "the nastiest trap of all." I promise you there are hundreds, probably thousands of people reading this book who have that as their plan. So the trust might be good, but it might be a disaster.

The next beneficiary could be your children. They might be a good choice as beneficiaries, given that:

- You might have an estate tax if you leave it to your spouse and it might be a big one.
- The trust may or may not be good.
- The children may need the money.

But the children may not need the money, in which case you'd want to give it to your grandchildren and let them stretch it.

What are we going to do? How can we decide between these four choices? Maybe do a little bit of each? Maybe try to figure it out? I know. Let's do a projection! Let's project how much money we are going to have when we die! Oh . . . we don't know when we are going to die. I know, let's make a projection based on how much money we are going to have and what the tax laws are going to be! Oh . . . we don't know what the tax laws are going to be. Well, I'll tell you this, in 27 years I've done a lot of projections, and one thing is common to every single one of them. They are all wrong. Every time I've been wrong! We had *more* money than I thought. We had *less* money than I thought. The *tax laws* were different. The *wrong person* died first. So how can we handle this? How can we make this decision now if you don't want to come back and redo your will every year or two? I have an idea. Let's not decide. We just won't decide.

I refuse to decide.

Well, how do you refuse to decide? You let the surviving spouse make decisions within nine months after the date of your death. Then you'll have answers to all of these questions. You'll know how old the surviving spouse is. You'll know exactly how much money there is. There won't be any questions about what the tax laws are. If you were to look at my will or my IRA beneficiary designation, with the exception of money going to charity, if my wife wants it she can have it all. If she doesn't want it because she is worried about an estate tax, she could put it in a trust and get the income from it. If she doesn't even want the income from it, it will then go into a trust for our little girl. And if our daughter is grown up with kids of her own and she doesn't want it, it will go into a trust for her children. I'm not going to decide now, because I trust my wife. She can do whatever she wants. I'm going to suggest that if you trust your spouse, don't decide now. Let your spouse decide.

I've been drafting documents for Pennsylvania residents since the early 1990s, and it works beautifully. I can't tell you I'm happy when someone dies; it's always tragic when a client dies. But if they die with this plan in place, we almost always get a good result for the family. If you use a more traditional plan, decisions are fixed and set in advance. With the traditional plans that were drafted when the exemptions were $600,000, what's happening is that all this money is going into a trust and the surviving spouse is under provided for. It happens all the time. And it is going to get worse as the exemptions go up.

By the way, I have a really quick history for you. When they changed the law in 2001, I knew instantly, within days of Congress changing the law, that this was going to be the best estate plan there was. I was very excited. I had an email newsletter, which at that time was going out to 50,000 readers. I wrote this little article saying here's the ideal beneficiary of your IRA and I sent it out into email land. You never know what is going to happen. I was surprised by a call I received around two days later when I heard, "Hi. This is Jane Bryant Quinn." I talked to her at length and she put my plan in her column. Then *Financial Planning Magazine* asked me to write about this plan. I did, and they published my article. Later on, the American Institute of Certified Public Accountants (AICPA) said, "Hey this is greatest thing since sliced bread. Write an article about that. We'll peer review the article and we'll send it out to our 60,000 CPA subscribers." The *Wall Street Journal* also got a hold of this. They loved the idea. They've already written two articles on it. Cascading beneficiaries is all over the literature now, and we're seeing a lot of it. So you can see this isn't just some crazy, fluky idea. This is something you should seriously think about putting in place for yourself.

How the Plan Works

First, a bit of background on terminology. To the best of my knowledge, I am the first person to use the term "Cascading Beneficiary Plan™" to describe the layering of beneficiaries through the use of disclaimers. Furthermore, Lange's Cascading Beneficiary Plan™ takes the technique to a new level of sophistication and flexibility. It is not uncommon currently to see references to "cascading beneficiary plans" in estate planning literature. Journals and magazines which originally published my articles on Lange's Cascading Beneficiary Plan™ continue to promote the concept, although they have dropped my name and simply refer to a cascading beneficiary plan. Using the cascade or disclaimer technique is a

Lange's Cascading Beneficiary Plan™ (LCBP™) gives the spouse both the time to make decisions and the power to act on them.

sound and excellent solution for many estate planning problems. I cannot attest, however, to how other financial professionals use the concepts and would not know if all the advantages to my particular plan are incorporated in the work of others. So, for the sake of clarity and because I have a vested interest in maintaining the integrity of my Plan, I will refer to it as "Lange's Cascading Beneficiary Plan" or LCBP™ for short.

LCBP™ recognizes the importance of providing for the surviving spouse and also the advantage of keeping options open after the death of the first spouse. LCBP™ accommodates the surviving spouse's need to take stock of his or her financial situation before deciding whether or not to disclaim. If he or she does decide to disclaim, the next question is: how much? Relevant facts to consider include finances at the time of the first death, the future financial picture, tax laws at the date of the first death, family needs, and perhaps most importantly, the needs of the surviving spouse. LCBP™ gives the spouse both the time to make decisions and the power to act on them. Traditional families—that is, families without the complications of second marriages and stepchildren—would be wise to consider incorporating LCBP™ with disclaimer options into their estate plans.

Please note that LCBP™ can be used for wills and living trusts as well as IRAs or retirement plans.

Typically, to take full advantage of LCBP™, the IRA owner should name primary and contingent beneficiaries to their IRAs according to the following hierarchy:

1. The spouse
2. A unified credit shelter trust (or B trust)
3. A child (or the children equally)
4. A well-drafted qualifying trust for a grandchild (or grandchildren)

To preserve the surviving spouse's options, the participant should name the spouse as the primary beneficiary. The contingent beneficiary could be a unified credit shelter trust (or B trust) that is incorporated within LCBP™.

The unified credit shelter trust can be used to protect against a potential estate tax at the death of the surviving spouse. Money disclaimed to the unified credit shelter trust will not be subject to estate tax in the estate of the surviving spouse. As discussed in Chapter 11, a disclaimer to this type of trust will not violate the rule for a qualified disclaimer that says a taxpayer who disclaims can't directly benefit from the disclaimer. The surviving spouse could also avoid estate taxes at the second death if, at the first death, he or she disclaimed at least some of the inherited IRA to the children. That portion of the IRA would not be included in the surviving spouse's estate and would not be subject to estate taxes at the death of the surviving spouse.

LCBP™ contains provisions for the surviving spouse to disclaim some or all of his or her interest directly to the third contingent beneficiary, which would most likely be a child, or if there is more than one child, to the children equally. Then that child would be deemed a primary beneficiary, and the minimum required distribution of the inherited IRA would be based on the child's life expectancy.

I have written this chapter from the standpoint of the IRA or retirement plan owner who is planning his or her estate. What if you are the beneficiary of an inherited IRA or retirement plan? What should you do? At first, do nothing. I mean it. Don't do something quickly that you may later regret. If you inherit an IRA or retirement plan, it is absolutely critical to review your options with a qualified expert in IRAs and retirement plans. You might even need to take a couple of months to think over all your options and plan accordingly. Not only is this an area where thousands of people make mistakes, but the scope of the mistakes can often be measured in hundreds of thousands and even a million dollars or more.

When you are planning to leave your IRA and/or retirement plan to your heirs, you must impress upon them how important it is they get appropriate advice after your death.

Additionally, contained within the IRA beneficiary designation that I would recommend is language that allows an adult child to disclaim his or her interest in what had been disclaimed from his parent (the surviving spouse) to a trust for the benefit of his or her own child or children. Then, the trust for the grandchild would be deemed a primary beneficiary of the retirement account and could use the grandchild's own life expectancy for minimum required distribution purposes (the ultimate stretch).

The Ultimate "Cascade" of a Very Flexible Plan

In a perfect cascade, the surviving spouse:

- Could retain some of the participant's IRA, roll it over into his or her own name, and appoint his or her own beneficiaries.
- Would have the option to disclaim a portion to the B trust (it may be more likely to disclaim after tax funds into the B trust because of the income tax acceleration discussed earlier).
- Could disclaim a portion to an adult child, who would be the deemed primary beneficiary for that portion, which would allow him or her to use his or her own life expectancy for MRD purposes.

At which point, the adult child:

- Could retain some of the participant's IRA and take minimum required distributions based on his or her life expectancy; and/or
- Disclaim a portion to the trust for his or her own child, who would become the primary beneficiary for that portion and could then use his or her own life expectancy for minimum required distribution purposes.

If the surviving spouse chooses to roll the entire IRA into his or her own IRA, then the path of distributions is fairly straightforward (see column one of Figure 12.1.): The surviving spouse

Figure 12.1

Lange's Cascading Beneficiary Plan™

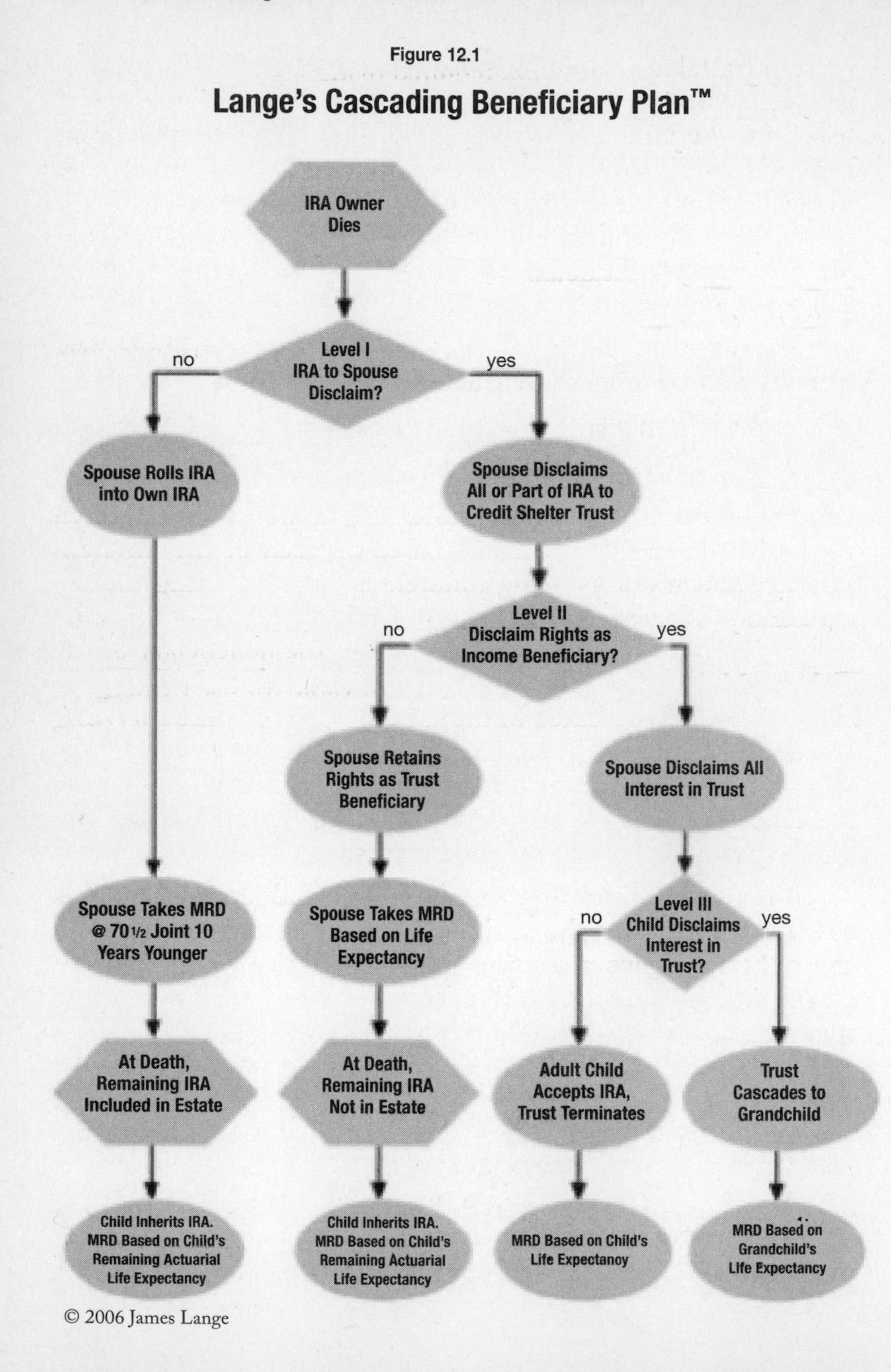

must begin taking minimum required distributions by April 1 of the year following the year that the surviving spouse turns 70½ based on the joint life expectancy of himself or herself and a beneficiary deemed to be 10 years younger. He or she would use Table III (Uniform Lifetime Table for use by owners, which is presented in appendix). Under this table, the surviving spouse's life expectancy is recalculated each year, which means he or she can never outlive the IRA.

The surviving spouse will also be able to name his or her own primary and contingent beneficiaries. At the surviving spouse's death, the remaining IRA is included in the surviving spouse's estate for estate tax purposes. The minimum required distribution for the ultimate beneficiary of the inherited IRA—in traditional families, the children equally, assuming none of the children further disclaims—is calculated based on each of the different life expectancies of as many children as there are using the life expectancy of each beneficiary as of December 31 following the year of the death of the deceased spouse. The beneficiary of the IRA would then use Table I (Single Life Table for use by beneficiaries, which is presented in the appendix). Unlike the surviving spouse, the beneficiary may exhaust his or her IRA even if only withdrawing minimum required distributions because his or her life expectancy is frozen as of the surviving spouse's death and reduced by one for each subsequent year.

If the spouse disclaims into the B trust and retains the rights as income beneficiary, he or she will receive a steady income and the right to receive discretionary principal for health, maintenance, and support. Depending how the trust was drafted, the surviving spouse could retain the power to withdraw the greater of $5,000 or 5% of the trust on an annual basis. Furthermore, those assets in the B trust will not be included in the estate of the second spouse to die, possibly saving estate tax at the second death.

From a minimum required distribution or income tax perspective, the B trust is the worst alternative for an inherited IRA. During the life of the surviving spouse, the minimum required distribution is based on the surviving spouse's single life expectancy, Table I (Single Life Table), which forces a higher distribution than if the beneficiary would be the surviving spouse outright (using Table III, a joint life expectancy factor). Furthermore, it is quite possible that over the life of the surviving spouse, the entire IRA may have to be distributed and thus be disadvantageous to the family. Remember that the surviving spouse cannot recalculate his or her life expectancy when the B trust is named as the beneficiary.

After the surviving spouse dies, the remainderman of the B trust (the person who receives the remainder of the trust, usually an adult child) must continue to take minimum required distributions if the IRA has not been exhausted during the surviving spouse's lifetime. These MRDs are based on his or her deceased parent's remaining single life expectancy, not his or her own much longer life expectancy. (See column two of Figure 12.1.) Thus, by utilizing the B trust as a beneficiary of an IRA, the stretch is greatly reduced and the planner is condemning the survivors to accelerated income taxes.

As a practical matter, many people like the security of the B trust option because it provides for the living needs of the surviving spouse while ensuring that the trust assets will not be included in the estate of the surviving spouse, thus saving estate taxes at the second death. Though many attorneys often draft B trusts as the contingent beneficiary of an IRA, in practice upon the death of the first spouse, it is often wiser to attempt to find better alternatives than the B trust for the disposition of the IRA.

If the spouse is financially secure and chooses to disclaim either all or a portion of his or her interest as primary beneficiary to the contingent beneficiary, the B trust, and then simultaneously disclaims some or all of his or her income interest in the trust to the remainderman (the child), this continues the cascade. The long-term advantage of the lower minimum required distributions then moves to the foreground. The child, or the grandchild (assuming the child disclaims to the grandchild), can then take minimum distributions over the course of his or her own life expectancy (see columns three and four of Figure 12.1). A longer life expectancy means a lower minimum required distribution, which in turn means that a greater percentage of the assets in the inherited IRA can continue to compound and grow tax-deferred.

LCBP™ protects or overprotects the surviving spouse. It allows the greatest flexibility to stretch the IRA and allows decisions to be made after the death of the IRA owner. However, this flexibility is a two-edged sword. By giving the surviving spouse that much power, the planner risks the surviving spouse making inappropriately conservative decisions, such as failing to disclaim. The family could end up with less-than-optimal results.

You can see why this plan might not work well in families with the complications of second marriages and stepchildren. The potential exists that your spouse will have no motivation to pass the money on to your children from your first marriage. Rather than disclaim any of the money to your children, your surviving spouse might be more inclined to keep all of the money and eventually leave it to his or her own children and grandchildren.

Perhaps the best short explanation of LCBP™ comes from Jane Bryant Quinn in *Newsweek*:

> For moneyed families, where the heirs won't need the IRA right away: When you die, your spouse could refuse to accept ("disclaim") all or part of the IRA. That money could go to a trust that pays your spouse a lifetime income and then passes to the children. Alternatively, your spouse could disclaim the IRA proceeds directly to your children, who could either take the money or disclaim to your grandchildren. They'd still have to take their minimum distributions, but the bulk of the IRA could be tax-deferred for generations.

Kiplinger's Retirement Reports writes:

> If you're looking to stretch out your IRA's life but want to make sure your spouse is provided for when you die,

you can use what Pittsburgh attorney and CPA James Lange calls a "cascading beneficiary" strategy.

Lange paints this scene: You are married with children and grandchildren. You name your wife as the primary beneficiary and a bypass trust as first contingent beneficiary. The second contingent beneficiary is the children equally. The third is a trust for the grandchildren. At your death, your spouse could roll over all or part of the IRA into her IRA and could also disclaim a portion into the bypass trust.

The advantage of disclaiming to the bypass trust is that upon your wife's death, the proceeds of the trust are not included in her estate. She could also disclaim all or part to the children, who could then take withdrawals based on their longer life expectancy. Finally, if neither your spouse nor your children need all the money, they could disclaim all or a portion to a trust for the grandchildren.

Another interesting feature of LCBP™ is that it is also suitable for wills and revocable trusts. If you want the entire spectrum of options open for your surviving spouse, then drafting LCBP™ for the will (and/or revocable trust) and the IRAs and retirement plans is an excellent plan.

Are People Happy with Lange's Cascading Beneficiary Plan™?

I developed and employed an early version of the cascade in the early 1990s. It has been tested and proven worthy. After determining that the fundamentals of the cascade were sound, I added the full Cascading Beneficiary Plan™ in January 2001, immediately after the overhaul of the IRA and retirement plan distribution rules, which increased the options for a "stretch IRA." Most of my clients are still kicking. We have, however, been writing these plans long enough to have had some deaths. The surviving spouses have appreciated the flexibility of our plan, and several of them who made decisions based on the state of the law at the time of their spouse's death were able to make better decisions—that is, more advantageous to them and their families—than the decisions that would have been forced upon them with the traditional A/B trust estate planning. People always say hindsight is 20/20. This plan offers a unique opportunity to actually use hindsight in deciding the best way to divide up the estate.

If you are a Pennsylvania resident and are interested in having Lange's Cascading Beneficiary Plan™ for your family, please call 412-521-8007 to explore implementing this plan for you.

Are you from another state other than Pennsylvania? For more information on retiring secure and paying taxes later, please email me at book@PayTaxesLater.com.

What If the Federal Estate Tax Laws Are Repealed?

As this book goes to press, there is proposed legislation to repeal or radically change the federal estate tax laws. Interestingly enough, no matter what the outcome or changes finally put into effect, LCBP™ is still sound. My advice regarding what type of will, revocable trust, or even beneficiary designation you should have for your IRA and retirement plan would be the same. That is, even in the event there is a full repeal of the federal estate tax, I would still advocate LCBP™ for most readers.

Please remember, the B trust is one of the options in the LCBP™. Why would I still include the option of the B trust when apparently there would be no federal estate tax? Isn't the main point of the B trust to avoid federal estate tax at the second death? If there is no federal estate tax, why bother with the B trust? Yes, that's true. However, please keep in mind that whatever tax law changes are made, there will be more changes after this set of changes.

Three times our country eliminated the federal estate tax and three times it has been reinstated. So, even if it is repealed, who is to say that in five years it is not brought back again?

So, if you have the LCBP™ in place and they subsequently repeal the estate tax, I would do nothing. There would be no reason to make any changes. Even if there is repeal and no need to have the B trust, it can't hurt to have the B trust as an option.

If you were drafting a new document, would I recommend you retain the B trust as an option in the will and/or living trust? Yes. Why?

In short, why not? Other than the minor additional cost of including the B trust as part of the LCBP™ compared to leaving it out, which is minimal, why not give the surviving spouse all the options that might be relevant?

In addition, you may live in a state that has separated their state death taxes from the federal estate tax and calculates the tax based on older rates. In those states, the LCBP™ is especially relevant because of the flexibility it provides for the beneficiary to disclaim the ideal amount calculated based on that state's law rather than having a more traditional estate plan forcing all assets into a B trust.

The last two administrations had relatively little respect for precedent in estate taxation. Why would we think any changes that will take place will be permanent? My best guess is that whatever Congress does, they will change it again, probably a number of times, in your own lifetime.

If you have the LCBP™ and they change the law, you can shrug and say, I don't have to redo my documents. If they change the tax laws again after the first set of changes, you can shrug and say, I still don't have to redo my documents.

If you don't have the LCBP™ but rather have a traditional estate plan and want to keep traditional estate planning documents (the A/B trust format), you have to make changes if they repeal the law and you have to make changes again when they change it again.

In the event that the tax is not repealed but the exemption amount is raised, the B trust could be drafted as a precautionary measure and presumably would not be an important option. It would likely end up being an unnecessary option that will never be utilized.

On the other hand, in the event the federal estate tax is repealed and then brought back, the fact that you have a document that allows for those changes in the law would mean that you would not have to redo your wills, trusts and other documents again. Also please note that, in the event of repeal, the impact of the nastiest trap of all will certainly be more widespread than it is today.

The argument for a simplified LCBP™ without the B trust is also reasonable for smaller estates. If your estate is $2,000,000 or less, the LCBP™ without the B trust would seem to be a reasonable choice.

In conclusion, in the event of repeal, I would still recommend Lange's Cascading Beneficiary Plan™ for wills and trusts. For larger estates, I would still include the B trust possibility, even for IRAs and retirement plans, knowing that it will probably never be utilized. For estates of $2,000,000 or less, you could do the LCBP™ without the B trust. That way if the client and the drafting attorney prefer to keep things as absolutely simple as they can, you could leave the B trust out of the LCBP™ and have all of the options except the B trust. The overriding thought, however, is that the LCBP™ would survive a federal estate tax repeal and you should not have to continually change your documents every time there is a federal estate tax law change.

A Key Lesson from This Chapter

Having a flexible estate plan offers several advantages including providing the surviving spouse with multiple options for distributing the inheritance based on the family's circumstances at the time of the first death. By incorporating the cascade into an estate plan you give yourself the best chance to "stretch" an IRA and pay taxes later.

13

Changing Beneficiaries for Retirement Plans and IRAs

When at last we are sure,
You've been properly pilled,
Then a few paper forms,
Must be properly filled.

— Dr. Seuss

Main Topios

- Filling out the beneficiary form
- Complex designations incorporating the cascade
- Trusts as beneficiaries
- Hazards of naming different beneficiaries to different accounts

KEY IDEA

Even the simplest beneficiary designation requires more than just a cursory review.

A Caution

Though I have a disclaimer at the beginning of the book, I want to reemphasize that you should not rely on this information for filling out the beneficiary designation of your IRA or retirement plan.

I shudder at books and computer programs that help readers draft wills and fill out beneficiary change forms. There is often considerable judgment involved in filling out IRA beneficiary change forms and/or a will, and a generic book or software program cannot supply that judgment. Some of these consumer resources may be relevant for people who can't afford an attorney and need these documents. If, however, there is money at stake, professional guidance is needed, and a careful vetting of the professional is recommended.

Plenty of people fill out the form incorrectly. Let's say you have a really simple beneficiary designation. I leave the money to my two sons: Jack and Tom. My secondary beneficiaries are my grandsons: Bob and John who are Jack's boys. Unfortunately something happens to Jack. Where is Jack's money going to go? Is it going to go to your grandsons Bob and John? No, it's going to go to your son Tom. You don't want to disinherit your grandsons. Poor Bob and John don't have a parent. Now they don't even have any money. People simply don't fill out the forms correctly. It happens all the time with really bad results. By the way, it's not just people filling out their own beneficiary forms who make mistakes. Financial professionals, attorneys, and CPAs who are not knowledgeable in this area also make these mistakes. I don't even let clients fill out the forms. I'm not going to do a wonderful plan for people and then let them fill out the beneficiary form incorrectly. The whole thing could just blow up.

Filling Out the Forms

Even the simplest beneficiary designation requires more than just a cursory review. An individual who wants to name adult individuals in one's beneficiary designations needs to know the names, birth dates, and Social Security numbers of each beneficiary. But it goes beyond that. The individual must also decide where the money should go if a beneficiary predeceases the account owner.

Even the simplest beneficiary designation requires more than just a cursory review.

- If there is one primary and one contingent beneficiary and the primary beneficiary dies (or disclaims their interest), the contingent beneficiary inherits all.
- If the primary and contingent beneficiaries die before the account holder and if the form is not accurately completed, the proceeds could be paid to the estate of the account holder, or possibly to an intestate heir (the person who would have received the money had you died without a will). The problems include the wrong person getting the money and/or causing an acceleration of withdrawals and an income tax nightmare.
- If the children of the deceased first-named beneficiary are designated to inherit their parent's share, then the retirement account will be paid to those children, a much better plan. But again, you should probably have a trust for those children.

Clearly there are too many combinations to outline all scenarios. Furthermore, no two beneficiary forms and/or change forms that are issued by different financial institutions—such as Schwab, TIAA-CREF, or any of the major houses and the independents—are alike. It is critical to carefully read the form and instructions and develop, with the assistance of a qualified advisor, a strategy that is specific to your situation.

It is critical to carefully read the form and instructions and develop, with the assistance of a qualified advisor, a strategy that is specific to your situation.

MINI CASE STUDY 13.1

Filling Out the Forms—Simple Designation

Abe Account Owner is filling out his beneficiary forms. His first priority is to provide for his wife Wanda and, after her, his children Charlie and Charra. He also wants to ensure that, if either of his children should predecease him, their share will pass on to their children (his grandchildren). If the deceased child had no children, then the share would pass to his or her sibling.

1. He designates Wanda as the 100% primary beneficiary, inserting her Social Security number, date of birth, and where requested, her address. By designating her as 100% primary beneficiary, no other primary beneficiaries can be listed, and he will now move on to the contingent beneficiary section of the form.
2. He then designates his two children as the contingent beneficiaries, allocating 50% to each of them. As with Wanda, he inserts their Social Security numbers, dates of birth, and where indicated, their addresses.
3. He must now go one step further. Some forms (TIAA-CREF, for example) have a box that, when checked, directs that the money going to a child who predeceases the account holder should be paid to their children (the account holder's grandchildren) in equal shares. If the form does not have such a selection, then "per stirpes" should be written after the children's individual names. By using this term, the plan administrator will know to pay the share of that deceased child to the predeceased children's children in equal shares. This is true whether or not there is one beneficiary or two, and will ensure that the retirement account passes to the next generation rather than reverting to the estate of the account holder.
4. The account holder signs and dates the form where indicated and submits it to the plan administrator for processing. Usually within a couple of weeks the account holder will receive confirmation from the plan administrator that the changes have been effected.

An extra step must be taken if an account holder names someone other than his or her spouse as beneficiary of their qualified plan account. The spouse must consent to this designation on the form and must have the consent notarized. This section of the form is usually below where the account holder signs. This step must be taken before the plan administrator will accept the form. Most qualified plans are subject to this spousal consent rule (with exceptions that are beyond the scope of this book) while IRAs and Roth IRAs are not subject to the rule.

The biggest problem with the simple designation is that:

- It does not contain the B trust option. You want the option if you want to give your surviving spouse more flexibility.
- If money passes to a minor, the minor can use the funds to buy a fast car and have a party when they reach 21 or even 18 in some states—there is no trust for the benefit of the grandchildren.

Complex Designations: Incorporating the Perfect Cascade

Now we address more complex designations. Some people might want more sophisticated beneficiary designations that name trusts as the beneficiaries of their retirement plans. For the purposes of this chapter, we assume that the account holder has designated his or her spouse as their primary beneficiary but wants to designate a trust as the contingent beneficiary. (In chapter 14, we discuss the ramifications of designating a trust as the primary versus contingent beneficiary of a retirement plan.) This scenario is likely under three circumstances:

1. Where a credit shelter or B trust will be the contingent beneficiary for disclaimer and estate tax savings purposes.
2. Where we want to provide for a spendthrift child or want to ensure the child enjoys the stretch IRA to the fullest.
3. Where an individual wants to allow for grandchildren to receive retirement monies, but not outright. This can be accomplished with a standalone trust or a revocable trust or a trust within a will called a testamentary trust.

If the client wants to use a standalone trust (our office uses what is called a *Plan Benefits Trust*) to control the distribution of his or her retirement benefits, the beneficiary designation is relatively simple: the spouse is designated as the primary beneficiary and the LCBP™ is designated as the contingent. The Plan Benefits Trust incorporates the perfect cascade to provide the option of the B trust and the option of a trust for grandchildren.

Alternatively, a client can preserve all of the distribution options of a Plan Benefits Trust through a well-drafted beneficiary designation that includes all of the options. However, the designation is more complicated because not all of the options are contained within one standalone document.

To introduce one more level of control, in some situations an account holder might want the contingent beneficiaries to be their children, but the holder also wants their children to have the right to disclaim some part or all of their shares to their own children (the account owner's grandchildren). Rather than using the per stirpes designation, which would pay the money directly to the grandchild (though subject to a custodian's control until the grandchild becomes 21), the account holder may want to designate separate trusts for the grandchildren as the beneficiaries. It is important to set up separate trusts for each grandchild. Using separate trusts will ensure that each beneficiary can use his or her own life expectancy for minimum distribution purposes.

Using separate trusts will ensure that each beneficiary can use his or her own life expectancy for minimum distribution purposes.

One Consolidated Group Trust versus Individual Trusts for Grandchildren

If one "group" trust is used, then all beneficiaries are stuck taking distributions according to the life expectancy of the oldest beneficiary. Some clients, however, want to have one trust with several beneficiaries believing that there is no need for equalization and prefer having the flexibility to make unequal distributions.

For example, assume you are leaving money to three grandchildren, all children of your child. You could leave the money in three separate trusts, or you could leave the money in one trust. If you choose three separate trusts, you would get the longest stretch for the youngest beneficiary. In addition, you would make sure or close to sure that each grandchild would be treated equally. If one grandchild went to college, his trust could be used for college. If another grandchild didn't go to college, eventually he would get the money.

On the other hand, if you weren't worried so much about equality and just wanted to emulate real life where you spend money on your children and grandchildren without keeping track of each dollar and equalizing at the end, the single trust may work well for your needs even though you are slightly accelerating distributions from the IRA. Many families prefer the flexibility of one trust if one of their primary estate planning goals is to educate their grandchildren. In a separate trust scenario for grandchildren, it is possible that one grandchild's education costs may not be fully covered due to insufficient funds while another grandchild takes his inheritance and drinks beer and buys a fast car. Since this result is not desired by most families, our clients are split regarding whether they prefer separate trusts for grandchildren to maximize IRA deferral or a single trust for grandchildren to permit unequal distributions.

Finally, you want to think about how you want your retirement plan to be distributed in the event that neither your spouse nor your descendants survive you. Under these circumstances you might want to do something for charity or give the assets to your siblings. All of these considerations must be spelled out in the beneficiary form, or else the assets will pass through the estate.

Since no beneficiary change form allows for this kind of stepped planning, an attachment should be drafted that clearly spells out how the beneficiary designations should work. Most plan administrators are willing to accommodate such sophisticated planning when it is presented in a clear and concise manner.

The Hazards of Naming Different Beneficiaries for Different Accounts

It is quite common in my practice for clients to say they want one particular account to go to one beneficiary and a different account to another beneficiary. The accounts might reflect the relative proportionate value that the client wants each of the different beneficiaries to receive, but I think this can turn into a nightmare.

- You will have a terrible time trying to keep track of the different distribution schedules.
- As the different investments go up or down, the amount going to the different heirs would also go up and down, which is probably not the intent.
- A beneficiary designation may say, "I leave my Vanguard account to beneficiary B and my Schwab account to beneficiary A." If during your lifetime you switch or transfer money from Vanguard to Schwab, you have, in effect, changed who is going to get what, and that may not be your intention.

In general, I prefer one master beneficiary designation for all IRAs, retirement plans, 403(b)s, 401(k)s, and the like. In it I describe distributions as I would in a will or irrevocable or revocable trust. That way, we can avoid mistakes and simplify estate administration after the retirement plan owner dies.

I recognize that, for investment purposes, people use different accounts for different beneficiaries. For example, you might treat the investments of a grandchild beneficiary differently than those of a child or spouse. Under those circumstances I would be willing to bend and accept different beneficiaries for different accounts.

Submitting the Forms

For any trust that is a beneficiary of an IRA, the IRS requires that, by October 31 of the year following the year of the account holder's death, the plan administrator must be provided either with a copy of any trust designated as a beneficiary or a certified list of all of the beneficiaries. As a matter of practice, we submit the trust to the plan administrator at the time we file the form to give the plan administrator the opportunity to immediately lodge any objections to the trust, when the account holder can still make accommodations. Obviously, if the plan administrator does not get a copy of the trust until after the account holder's death and then makes a complaint, there could be problems. Then, after the account holder's death, we submit a final copy of the trust to comply with the IRS minimum required distributions rules.

A testamentary trust, where the contingent beneficiary is a trust contained in the account holder's will, is treated differently from a standalone trust. Then, a copy of the will should be provided to the plan administrator just as a standalone trust would be.

Where the trust is a tertiary beneficiary—that is, where the children are the contingent beneficiaries and the trusts for grandchildren receive money only at the death of the children or via the children disclaiming, then a copy of the will is generally not provided until it is determined that the trust will actually become a beneficiary.

On February 1, 2005, the IRS increased its fees to obtain a private letter ruling. to $9,000 In the past, when taxpayers made a mistake, they would ask the IRS to let them slide with a private letter ruling. Now, between the IRS fee and the professional fee to prepare the ruling, the cost could be $15,000 or more. Moral of the story: Pay close attention to the beneficiary form.

A Key Lesson from This Chapter

Do not underestimate the attention to detail that is required to fill out a beneficiary designation. For many people, their IRA or retirement plans constitute the bulk of their wealth, and the beneficiary designation, not the will, controls the disbursement of those funds.

Trusts as Beneficiaries of Retirement Plans

Put not your trust in money, but put your money in trust.

— Oliver Wendell Holmes

Main Topics

- Whether to consider a trust as a beneficiary to your IRA
- Young beneficiaries
- Spendthrift trusts
- Unified Credit Shelter Trusts
- QTIPs (Qualified Terminal Interest Property)

KEY IDEA

Using a trust as the potential beneficiary of a retirement plan and/or IRA can be an excellent method of protecting the beneficiary. Creating trusts for minors, trusts for spendthrifts, and trusts for spouses can be appropriate under certain circumstances.

There are many types of trusts, and each one serves a particular purpose.

Protecting Young Beneficiaries

The most prudent way to leave money to a young beneficiary is through a trust.

Typically I draft trusts for young beneficiaries with the following provisions:

- The trustee is given the discretion to make distributions for health, maintenance, support, education, postgraduate education, down payment for a house, seed money for a business, and if the parent or grandparent is a real sport, one summer in Europe.
- Then, at the age of 25 (not 21) the beneficiary is entitled to withdraw 33% of the principal of the trust.
- At age 30, the beneficiary is entitled to make a withdrawal of up to one-half of the remaining balance.
- At age 35, the beneficiary has unlimited access to the principal. This example provides a reasonable starting point, but is not the only way to draft a trust.

Obviously, it is easy to vary the terms of the trust according to personal preferences. The type of trust I described works well when the beneficiaries are young, usually for grandchildren when it is unclear how they will turn out as young adults. Trusts are the most prudent way to leave money to young beneficiaries or spendthrifts. If the beneficiary is already in his or her late teens or early 20s, you can alter the terms as seems prudent. Some 25-year-olds are perfectly capable of handling the money without the need for a trust. Some 35-year-olds are nowhere near ready for that type of responsibility. If your beneficiaries are old enough for you to make a judgment, then you don't have to rely on the general language recommended above.

Trusts are the most prudent way to leave money to young beneficiaries or spendthrifts.

Most of the trusts for minors that I draft are for the benefit of a grandchild (or grandchildren). The trust would take effect if the IRA owner dies and the child who was named before the grandchild either predeceased or disclaimed to their children.

MINI CASE STUDY 14.1
Protecting Junior

Tom, a retired IRA owner, has one son, Joe, and one grandson, Junior, age 3. He fills out his beneficiary form as follows:

1. My son, Joe
2. My grandson, Junior

Tom dies. Joe doesn't want or need the money. He disclaims. The money will then go to Junior. Since there was no trust, Junior will have complete access to the money when he reaches 21 (younger in some states). Tom's legacy might be a Corvette for Junior.

Assume, instead, that Tom names his beneficiaries as follows:

1. My son, Joe
2. The Tom Family Trust for Grandchildren under Articles V & VI of the Last Will and Testament of Tom dated January 1, 2005.

With this structure, Joe can be much more comfortable. He disclaims to the trust that has reasonable restrictions for Junior rather than disclaiming the assets outright to Junior. Now, Junior will not come into all the money at 21, but if he has legitimate needs they can be met. By going to the trouble of drafting the trust, Tom gave Joe a better choice with a better result for the family. He protected the money from premature taxation and frivolous spending. Another advantage is that the trust will protect the money from Junior's creditors. The trust money is protected from creditors of the beneficiary, which may range from an individual suing the beneficiary to the beneficiary's spouse if the beneficiary's marriage goes sour.

The Mechanics of Naming a Minor's Trust as Beneficiary

Please remember the basics. The beneficiary designation, not the will, controls the proceeds of the IRA at death. Therefore, the beneficiary designation of the retirement plan deserves attention.

In our office we draft a special document to be used as the retirement plan or IRA beneficiary designation. Within that long document (see Lange's Cascading Beneficiary Plan™) we draft a special trust or, more often, a series of trusts to be used as the beneficiary of the IRA.

An acceptable alternative is to direct the proceeds into a qualifying trust that complies with the five conditions listed in Chapter 10 (see page 172), and submit a correctly worded beneficiary designation form. If that is done correctly, we have the same result. If the beneficiary form is completed incorrectly or if the terms of the trust do not meet the five conditions described in Chapter 10, then we have enormous problems. Please refer back to Chapter 13 for details on actually filling out the beneficiary forms.

In my office, I do not allow a client to fill out their own beneficiary change form for their IRA or retirement plan. Granted, it takes us additional time. It requires even more work if there are IRAs and retirement plans in different companies, all of which are likely to have their own beneficiary change form. I have seen enough instances where the client and/or his attorney were cavalier about the IRA beneficiary form and the form was filled out incorrectly. I have also seen situations where the attorney's directions to the client were not clear, or the client didn't follow the attorney's instructions. With large IRAs or retirement plans, there is too much at stake for errors. My original intention was to include sample language with this book, but after thinking it through, I fear I would invite mistakes and bad results. Get help from a competent

With large IRAs or retirement plans, there is too much at stake for errors. . . . Get help from a competent attorney who understands drafting IRA beneficiary designations.

attorney who understands drafting IRA beneficiary designations. The attorney should understand your entire financial situation and have the core requisite technical knowledge of the law and the forms before being asked to properly fill out the forms. This is one instance when I think paying an attorney is money well spent. Some other financial professionals are competent to perform this task, but please make sure that filling out a beneficiary form is not incidental to a sale but rather is a job taken seriously by whoever is performing it.

MINI CASE STUDY 14.2

The Perils of Inaccurate Beneficiary Designations

Tom fills out the beneficiary form, "My grandchild Junior, in trust." There is a will with a trust for Junior, but there is no specific reference to that will in this beneficiary designation. The result is that Junior may be able to reach this money when he is 21 because, in effect, there is no trust as a beneficiary specific to the beneficiary designation. Although Junior's parents may successfully be able to argue that the trust mentioned in the beneficiary designation is the same as the trust under the will for Junior's benefit, considerable time and expense can be saved by initially completing the beneficiary designation properly.

Perils of a Trust That Doesn't Meet the Five Conditions

Tom fills out the beneficiary form, "The Tom Family Trust for Grandchildren, found in my will." Assuming the trust in the will meets all five requirements, the money will pass as intended in trust.

If, on the other hand, the trust in the will violates one of the five conditions, then we do not have a qualifying trust as a beneficiary. If that is the case, the income from the IRA is accelerated and Junior loses the ability to stretch the proceeds of the IRA over his lifetime.

Spendthrift Trusts

Please note this type of trust may also be referred to as a "forced prudence trust," or, and this is my personal favorite, the "I don't want my no-good son-in-law getting one red cent of my money trust."

The basic spendthrift trust is usually drafted because not every child, even those beyond 35 years old, will have developed sufficient maturity or sense of fiscal responsibility to make wise choices after the death of their parent or parents. Parents may feel their children may never be financially responsible and will want to control from the grave for the remainder of their child's life. Since the greatest value of an inherited IRA is to stretch the benefits over the lifetime of the beneficiary, it would be a financial disaster to have an inappropriate and premature withdrawal of these funds.

A spendthrift trust will put a trusted relative, friend, or financial institution in control of the beneficiary's money and will ensure that the inherited IRA is used as a lifetime fund rather than an "I want a brand-new Porsche fund." In more severe cases, where drug addiction or alcohol abuse comes into play, additional special provisions are often recommended. Spendthrift trusts typically also include creditor protection language, and while such language does not offer the beneficiary perfect protection, it does go a long way toward protecting the beneficiaries not only from themselves but also from their creditors or potential creditors. One set of common creditors for your children are your children's spouses in the event of a divorce. Other times, even without a divorce, a child's spouse may be pushing the child to act irresponsibly with the inherited funds. Sometimes a trust protects a child from his or her spouse's irresponsibility.

Our law firm is experiencing an ever-growing number of clients who love their kids, but who don't trust their kids' spouses.

True Story Ensuring the No-Good Son-in-Law Gets Nothing

One of life's greatest mysteries is how the boy who wasn't good enough to marry your daughter can be the father of the smartest grandchild in the world.

— Proverb

A couple came into my office, and the first thing the husband said was, "I don't want my no-good son-in-law to get one dime of my money." Only after discussing this issue could we proceed with providing for his wife, his other children, his grandchildren, and saving taxes. What we ended up with was, basically, leaving any money that his daughter might inherit to a trust for the benefit of the daughter. We named an independent trustee whose job is to make sure the money is protected from the son-in-law, even if the daughter wants to give her husband money. In terms of actual drafting, the language is similar to a traditional spendthrift trust.

While I have no hesitation drafting a trust when the client thinks there is a significant need to protect the beneficiary, other practitioners go much further in the direction of controlling from the grave. For some children, they are certainly right, and it is far more prudent to leave money to a child in trust. Some practitioners see leaving money for adult children in trust as the norm rather than the exception. I am personally a cheapskate and like to keep things simple if we can. Therefore, my "normal" situation is not to draft a trust for an adult beneficiary.

One noted expert who recommends using a trust for an adult child as the rule instead of the exception advocates putting virtually all of an adult child's interest from an inherited IRA into a trust. He claims this forces the child to stretch the benefits over their lifetime and protects the child from creditors. He claims that the adult children are happy with this arrangement.

One compromise might be to give the children optional, not mandatory, withdrawal opportunities. I prefer the simplicity of trusting the adult child's judgment unless there is a reason not to. The idea of forcing the adult child to stretch the IRA, and not permitting optional withdrawals, to maximize creditor protection is a reasonable idea under some circumstances. If you do choose to use this idea (or even in a spendthrift situation), the trust should go beyond just providing the minimum required distribution. It should also have a provision for health, maintenance, support, education, and so on.

A relevant issue when naming a trust as a beneficiary of an IRA is whether the drafter wishes to treat the minimum required distribution as income or as part income and part principal for trust accounting purposes. Pennsylvania and some of the other states in accordance with the Uniform Principal and Income Act of 1997 (the "UPAIA") have adopted tracing rules which require the Trustee to allocate the portion of the minimum required distribution determined to be income as income and the remainder of the minimum required distribution as principal. If the income portion of the minimum required distribution cannot be traced, the UPAIA states that a minimum required distribution payable to a trust will be treated as 90% principal and 10% income for trust accounting purposes. Accordingly, if the objective is for the income beneficiary of the trust to pay the income tax due on the minimum required distribution, drafters should opt out of the UPAIA by mandating that minimum required distributions payable to the trust be treated as income and paid out to the income beneficiary.

Unified Credit Shelter Trust or B Trust as Beneficiary

As mentioned at the beginning of the estate planning section of this book, a frequent contingent beneficiary of a retirement plan is the B trust, or the unified credit shelter trust. This type of trust gives the surviving spouse all of the trust income and the trustee the flexibility to distribute principal for the health, maintenance, and support of the surviving spouse. The surviving spouse is also often given a "5 & 5" power, meaning that each year the surviving spouse could withdraw the greater of an additional 5% of the corpus (assets excluding profit and interest) of the trust or $5,000. At the death of the surviving spouse, the trust proceeds generally go to the children equally. The purpose of this type of trust is to ensure that, for federal estate tax purposes, the proceeds of the trust will not be included in the estate of the second spouse to die.

As we previously discussed, despite the potential estate tax savings, using this trust will cause the minimum required distributions to be based on the age of the surviving spouse, thus accelerating income taxable withdrawals, both during the surviving spouse's life and after the surviving spouse dies. As a result, we never recommend this type of trust as the primary beneficiary of an IRA or retirement plan and only use it as a contingent beneficiary available for disclaimer purposes. For more about disclaimers, please see Chapter 11.

Assume an IRA or a 403(b) or 401(a) participant owner dies. Also assume that either a well-drafted B trust, or unified credit shelter trust, is the primary beneficiary, or that it becomes the beneficiary because the surviving spouse, who had been named as the primary beneficiary, disclaims and the B trust is the secondary beneficiary.

We have discussed the minimum required distribution rules for the inherited IRA owned by the trust both during the life of the surviving spouse and after the surviving spouse dies. What perhaps is not clear is the mechanics of how the account should be handled after death in order to avoid a massive acceleration of income taxes.

Mechanics of the B Trust as Beneficiary of the IRA

After death, the IRA will be transferred into an account titled something like "Joe Schmoe, deceased, for the benefit of Bill Schmoe, Trustee of the Joe Schmoe Plan Benefits Trust." However, the money is not actually transferred to the trust at that point. The name of the account is retitled, but this is not an income taxable event.

The money sits in this newly named account held by the plan administrator. The MRD rules for that inherited IRA are based on the life expectancy of the surviving spouse. If, for example, the surviving spouse has a 20-year life expectancy, we would divide 20 into the balance as of December 31 of the year the IRA owner died in order to calculate the minimum required distribution. In the subsequent year, the life expectancy factor would be 19, then 18, and so on. Even after the death of the surviving spouse, the children would still have to take withdrawals based on the surviving spouse's remaining life expectancy according to the tables, if any money remains.

When a trust is the beneficiary of an inherited IRA, income taxation occurs when the money is transferred from the IRA to the trustee of the trust, usually only on a minimum required distribution basis. The trustee will receive the check from the plan administrator and deposit it into a checking account in the name of the trust. If the money is retained by the trust, the trust must pay income taxes on the distribution at trust income tax rates. More commonly, the trust will distribute the MRD it received to the trust beneficiary, the surviving spouse. The reason for distributing the minimum required distribution amount (or other amounts withdrawn) in whole is to avoid income taxation to the trust, which is usually taxed higher than individual income tax rates.

Mechanically, you may choose to follow our example from a recent estate plan. We calculate the MRD for the year early in the year. We have a monthly automatic transfer of the minimum required distribution from the inherited IRA to a separate trust checking account. Then we have an automatic transfer from this trust account to the bank account of the surviving spouse.

At the end of the year, the plan administrator issues a 1099 (or multiple 1099s) to the trust. The trustee files a Form 1041 reporting the distribution as income and deducts the same amount as a distribution deduction via a K-1 issued to the surviving spouse, thus paying no tax. The surviving spouse includes the K-1 income on her own 1040 for the year and pays the income tax accordingly.

Therefore, what people had heard in the past—that when the money goes to a trust it becomes taxable—is accurate. However, what they did not understand is that after the death of the IRA owner, the money is transferred into an inherited IRA account and not a trust account until minimum distributions or other distributions are incurred. Simply renaming the account to the name of the trust is not a withdrawal of the entire IRA.

The QTIP (The A Trust of the A/B Trust)

I hate QTIP (Qualified Terminal Interest Property) trusts as beneficiaries of retirement plans and IRAs. It is typical to see QTIP trusts in second marriages. The trust basically says to pay the surviving spouse an income for life, but at the second spouse's death have the principal revert to the children of the first marriage.

The terms of the QTIP trust have provisions for the surviving spouse that are similar to the provisions for the surviving spouse in the B trust. Like the B trust, it provides income to the surviving spouse and the assets revert to the children at the surviving spouse's death. The purpose of the QTIP trust, however, is not to avoid estate taxes at the second death. Rather the purposes are to provide an income to the surviving spouse, to preserve a marital deduction at the death of the first spouse, and to preserve the assets for the children from the decedent's first marriage. The marital deduction allows the first estate to escape federal estate taxation on the assets transferred to the QTIP trust. But unlike the B trust, the balance of the QTIP trust is included in the estate of the second spouse to die. As a result, there is no estate tax savings with the QTIP trust.

It is natural to want to protect your second spouse and then have the money revert to the children. For after-tax assets, QTIP trusts, though not a perfect solution, are often the best solution. In reality, for IRA owners using this type of plan, the biggest question in my mind is who will be most unhappy: the surviving spouse, the children of the first marriage, or the poor trustee.

This type of trust accelerates income taxes by forcing both the surviving spouse and the children of the first marriage (generally the ones who inherit the remainder of the trust at the second death) to take minimum required distributions based on the surviving spouse's age. Because QTIP trusts are usually the primary beneficiaries, there are few disclaimer opportunities providing alternative ways to reduce income taxes.

As a result, during the surviving spouse's life, minimum distributions are accelerated faster than if the surviving spouse had been named outright. When the surviving spouse dies (assuming the surviving spouse predeceases the children), the children will also have an accelerated minimum required distribution schedule based on the life expectancy of their stepparent, not their own life expectancy (the same situation as the MRD of a unified credit shelter trust). (See Mini Case Study 9.1.)

An Alternative Solution to the QTIP

Instead of setting up a QTIP trust, provide:

- *x*% of your IRA to your surviving spouse
- *y*% of your IRA to the children of your first marriage

For example, if the value of an income stream for a 65-year-old surviving spouse based on a 6% rate of return is worth roughly 58% of the principal of the IRA (based on the life expectancy of the surviving spouse and depending on what tables you use), then it is simpler and preferable in the vast majority of cases to leave the surviving spouse 58% of the IRA and the children 42% of the IRA.

Upon the death of the IRA owner, the surviving spouse takes his or her share and rolls it into an IRA. Until the surviving spouse reaches 70½, there is no MRD. When she reaches 70½, she will take minimum required distributions based on the Uniform Life Table (see appendix). The children take their shares as an inherited IRA and stretch distributions based on their own life expectancies. Clean. Simple. Cheap. No trusts, no fuss, no muss.

This solution may not fit with the IRA owner's goal of making sure the surviving spouse always has an income. In some circumstances, particularly for an older and less sophisticated beneficiary spouse, it may be prudent to direct the executor to buy an annuity that will guarantee the second spouse an income for life (see Chapter 6).

Another solution is to buy life insurance. But please, no QTIPs for IRAs.

A Key Lesson from This Chapter

Establishing a trust as a beneficiary is most successful for protecting minors and spendthrifts. B-type and QTIP-type trusts, though sometimes an interesting option, are usually not best for IRA and retirement plan beneficiary designations.

How Greedy Givers Can Benefit Their Families While Also Benefiting Charity: Doing Well by Doing Good

As I started getting rich, I started thinking, "What the hell am I going to do with all this money?" . . . You have to learn to give.

— Ted Turner

Main Topics

- Charitable estate planning with IRA and retirement assets
- Charitable trusts in general
- Charitable remainder trusts
- Alternatives to charitable trusts
- Testamentary charitable trusts

KEY IDEA

By understanding a few concepts, you can do far more for charity than you may have expected while still providing for your family.

Charitable Estate Planning with IRA and Retirement Assets

Some people have charitable intentions, and regardless of any tax benefits, they plan on giving large amounts of money during their lives and at their deaths to worthy charities. Some people are not charitable at all and neither make lifetime gifts nor death transfers to charity. Then, there are the rest of us, including me, whom I will label, tongue-in-cheek, as greedy givers.

Greedy givers' primary concern is providing for our family and ourselves. We do, however, have charity in our soul and want to make some provision for charities both while we are alive and at our death. If we can make a large impact with our charitable dollars, particularly if we get Uncle Sam to significantly subsidize our charitable intentions, we are that much happier. To this group we address this chapter.

Sometimes simple planning goes a long way toward providing great value to the charity, great value to your heirs, and eliminates or at least reduces funds going to the IRS.

A Simple Example of Which Dollars to Leave to Charity

Assume you have an estate consisting of $500,000 in an IRA and $500,000 in after-tax money. Assume further that you want half to go to charity and half to your heirs. Many planners, in an attempt to keep things simple, would prepare wills and beneficiary designations leaving one-half of the IRA and one-half of the after-tax funds to the charity and one-half to the heirs. Or worse, they would leave their entire IRA to their heirs and make a bequest of their after-tax money to the charity.

Charities don't care in what form (IRA, after-tax, highly appreciated dollars, Roth IRA, etc.) they get their money, because they do not pay income taxes. Individuals do care because of the different tax ramifications of the different type of inherited funds.

In the above example, it makes sense to give the IRA to charity unless the beneficiary is 40 or under and would benefit from a stretch IRA. Then a young beneficiary could enjoy many years of tax deferred growth. In the more common situation, it is best to leave the IRA to charity. In that case, no one will ever have to pay income tax on the IRA or the growth on the IRA. Give the after-tax money to the heirs. That way, the heir will pay less income tax than if they received the proceeds as an inherited IRA. There is one exception. In cases where the beneficiary is able to stretch

Charities don't care in what form (IRA, after-tax, highly appreciated dollars, Roth IRA, etc.) they get their money, because they do not pay income taxes. Individuals do care because of the different tax ramifications of the different type of inherited funds.

the IRA for 40 years or longer, it may be more advantageous to leave the IRA to the beneficiary and the after-tax funds to the charity.

Likewise, Roth IRAs are the worst assets to leave to charity, but the best asset to leave to an heir, because the distributions to the heir, which can be stretched out over a lifetime, come out tax-free—which is a tremendous benefit to an individual but meaningless to a charity.

Charitable Trusts in General

Next, we graduate to split-interest gifts. Split-interest gifts are gifts where the donor or his family maintains some interest in the property and a charity (or charities) also receives an interest. They are often found in some form of a charitable trust. These trusts can be established and funded either during your life or at your death. The living or *inter vivos* trust involves a transfer of assets to a charitable trust while you are alive. Testamentary charitable trusts take effect at death and are created in a will, a revocable trust, or even the beneficiary designation of an IRA and/or a retirement plan.

The annuity interests maintained by either the donor or the charity are typically referred to as an "income" interest or a "remainder" interest. An income interest is the recurring annuity payments that last either a number of years or for the life of the donor or spouse or other noncharitable beneficiary or the joint lives of the donor and spouse or other noncharitable beneficiary. The remainder interest is what is left in the trust at the end of the term or live(s). If the charity gets the remainder interest, (which by far is the most common) it is a charitable remainder trust. If the charity gets the annuity but the donor's family gets the remainder, it is a charitable lead trust.

An annuity trust gives the income beneficiary a fixed amount each year. The term "unitrust" is used when the annuity amount is calculated as a percentage of the value of the trust assets, so unitrust payments typically vary in amount as the investment values grow from earnings and are reduced by the annuity payments. The four main kinds of charitable trusts are therefore referred to as:

1. Charitable Remainder Annuity Trusts (CRATs)
2. Charitable Remainder Unitrusts (CRUTs)
3. Charitable Lead Annuity Trusts (CLATs)
4. Charitable Lead Unitrusts (CLUTs)

A donor is entitled to a charitable income tax deduction based on the value of the income or remainder interest irrevocably pledged to the charity. In these trusts, the donor is only taxed on investment income of the trust as he receives payments from the trust. This can create income tax deferral advantages as shown in the following mini case studies:

MINI CASE STUDY 15.1

When a Greedy Giver Should Consider a Charitable Remainder Trust

Paul and Mary, a married couple, both 62, want to receive a regular income during their upcoming retirement which they anticipate will occur when they are 65. They have $500,000 worth of GE stock that has a basis of $100,000. (This is not IRA or retirement plan money, and they have other assets besides this stock.) They have been worrying about the lack of diversification and heavy concentration of their portfolio for years, but did not want to sell the stock and incur a large capital gains tax.

They are charitably inclined. They are approached by their local charity and told if they make a gift of the $500,000 stock using a charitable remainder annuity trust (CRAT), they will receive an income tax deduction of $86,650 on the value of the remainder interest and a fixed income of $30,410 per year for the rest of their lives. They received the maximum annuity amount permitted in this case (over 6% of the initial value of $500,000). At their death their heirs would not receive any of that money; it would go to the charity.

Paul and Mary figure if they sold the stock without the charitable trust they would have $440,000 left. (Capital gain of $500,000 − $100,000 = $400,000 gain × 15% = $60,000 tax.

$500,000 – $60,000 = $440,000.) If the $440,000 is invested at 6%, the income would be only $26,400, and they have no guarantee the money will earn 6%.

With the charitable remainder annuity trust, however, they receive:

- An upfront $86,650 income tax deduction of the remainder interest while avoiding the initial $60,000 capital gains tax.
- A fixed stream of income equal to 6% of the assets will continue even if the trust value declines. This annuity income will be taxed at capital gains rates if there is no ordinary income in the CRAT. While they are still working and in a high ordinary income tax bracket, they will invest the CRAT portfolio for capital appreciation and after they retire, when they plan to be in a lower tax bracket, they can invest the portfolio for income.

MINI CASE STUDY 15.2
When a Greedy Giver Should Consider a CRUT

Paul and Mary, from the preceding example, are more optimistic about potential investment returns, and want a higher annuity income. They are willing to risk lower future annuity receipts if the investments decline but want to get larger payments if the investments do well. They can choose a CRUT that will pay them 10.481% of the annual value of the trust each year, which yields $52,405 in the first year. This is the maximum percentage of the CRUT payment permitted in their case, based on their ages and a Section 7520 interest rate of 5.4%. This results in the minimum charitable deduction of $50,000 or 10% of the initial trust value. The future annuity payments will increase in amount if the CRUT earns over 10.481% or decrease in amount if earnings are less than that.

For people with charity in their heart, the CRAT and CRUT approaches are good deals. After the transfer of the GE stock to the charitable trust, the GE stock is sold and there is no capital gains tax to you, except for the annuity payments, and no federal income tax for the trust or the charity. (It should be noted that in states like Pennsylvania, which does not recognize charitable trusts as tax-exempt, there can be state income taxes on the trust earnings.) Then, with the proceeds of the GE stock, the trustee of the charitable trust purchases a well-diversified portfolio. The charitable remainder interest's value is a good current tax deduction and the annuities provide a great retirement income benefit.

MINI CASE STUDY 15.3

Using a NIMCRUT—a Variation of a CRUT

A Net Income with Makeup CRUT (NIMCRUT) is a CRUT which stipulates that the annuity payments are only to be paid to the extent of the current year's realized income. If the income is less than the payout percentage, the deficiency is withdrawn in addition to the annual percentage amount in future years when there is sufficient income. From the prior Mini Case Study 15.1, assume Paul and Mary funded the trust with cash. If the trust was a NIMCRUT, they could defer any annuity income while they are working and in a high marginal tax rate by investing only in appreciating securities. After they retire, and before they are again in higher tax rates due to MRDs on their retirement income, they can sell the appreciated securities in the NIMCRUT and get the annuity payments along with deficiencies of amounts not collected in prior years. Since they will be in a lower tax bracket between retirement and minimum required distribution years, this strategy, though more complicated than a regular CRUT is an interesting variation that should be considered. If there are remaining deficiencies at their deaths—(i.e., the actual returns were lower than the stated amount on the CRUT and they would have been entitled to take more money from the trust in future years)—the heirs of Paul and Mary are entitled to the deficiency amounts with the remainder of the trust value going to charity.

Here is a summary of possible scenarios for Paul and Mary and the charity (or charities) by using a CRAT, CRUT or NIMCRUT.

- If the donor and his spouse live long enough, there may be little for charity, and it will have been a major plus for Paul and Mary.

- If Paul and Mary don't live long, the charity will do quite well.
- With normal life expectancies, both Paul and Mary and the charity will do well, but Paul and Mary will do better than the charity.

Given a normal life expectancy, will Paul and Mary do better than if they had invested the money and left the proceeds to their children with no charity involved? Probably not. I don't encourage charitable trusts for people who are not at all charitably inclined.

CRTs work out so well in terms of taxes and what the family gets that you don't have to be extremely charitable to make this work for everyone. Typical charitable remainder unitrusts (CRUT) often retain 90% of the benefits (the projected value of the annual payments) for the family and the charity receives only 10% of the benefits (the projected value of the remainder interest). Not bad for a greedy giver. In addition, the donor:

- Receives a current charitable deduction for the percentage of the transfer to the trust to the CRUT allocated to the charity's remainder interest (10% in this case),
- Avoids a large capital gains tax on the sale of the appreciated assets used to fund the trust, and
- Receives a regular income for life (some or all of which may be taxable at capital gains or ordinary rates). However, the income to the donor can be much higher than many people realize.

At the donor's death (or subsequent to more than one income beneficiary, at the death of the last income beneficiary), the remaining proceeds go to a charity. The NIMCRUT election can also be used for CRUTs to provide additional tax deferral opportunities by careful investment planning.

Less commonly used are CLATs and CLUTs which can allow remainder interests transferred to heirs and result in lower estate taxes upon death by moving future appreciation out of the taxable estate. Since estate taxes are less common now, these are less frequently used. CLATs and CLUTs, however, also provide larger initial charitable deductions at formation, so they can become useful when current tax deferral is appropriate. Charitable trusts are often packaged together with life insurance like peas and carrots. The idea is the insurance proceeds constitute the "replacement trust," replacing what the children would have received. They go together well.

Alternatives to Charitable Trusts

Charitable trusts come with inherent administrative burdens including setting up the trust, preparing annual income tax returns for the trust, annual calculations of the withdrawal amount, and investment management. Although CRTs have advantages for large transfers of money, simpler alternatives are available for those who would rather avoid these burdens. These include charitable gift annuities and pooled income funds.

Charitable Gift Annuities

Charitably motivated individuals may enter into a charitable gift annuity contract with charitable organizations that offer the option—a common practice for many universities. This is an agreement contract between the charity and the donor. It is similar to a CRT in that:

- The donor transfers a sum of money to the charity.
- The donor gets an annual annuity income from the charity.
- The donor gets a partial income tax deduction for the gift.
- The charity gets the remainder interest.
- The agreement is irrevocable.

The charitable gift annuity differs from CRTs in that:

- Smaller amounts can be contributed. Minimums may be as little as $10,000 or $25,000, whereas CRTs are usually only done with hundreds of thousands of dollars or more.
- No annual tax returns have to be filed.
- No investment management by the donor is necessary.

The annuity income to the donor must be fixed in amount and does not vary from year to year. This is similar to the CRAT but unlike the CRUT, where the income could change with the change in value of the trust. The annuity payouts are often determined using guidelines set up by the American Council of Gift Annuities. For example, a 65-year-old individual transferring $25,000 would receive a $1,500 per year annuity (6% of the initial amount) and get an up-front charitable deduction of $8,882.

Charitable gift annuities are great for people who like the idea of CRTs but want to participate on a smaller scale. Charitable gift annuities are typically more generous to the charity than CRTs which are often more generous to the family.

Pooled Income Funds

Pooled income fund giving is similar to charitable gift annuities, except the annual income paid to the donor is variable and consists of the interest and dividends earned in a pooled investment account. The payout does not include capital gains income, so the payout is typically smaller, but the up-front charitable deduction is larger. Therefore, more money eventually goes to the charity. For example, a 65-year-old individual transferring $25,000 may receive a smaller annuity, $875 per year (3.5% of the initial amount) and an up-front charitable deduction of $13,564.

MINI CASE STUDY 15.4
Testamentary Charitable Trusts

May your charity increase as much as your wealth.

— Proverb

Now the fun really begins. Let's assume the parents of a 40-year-old child have a large estate including a substantial amount of money in their IRA.

Freddy and Frieda have given a lot of money to their child already. They think Frank is too carefree with his money, and they are worried that he may blow his inheritance. At the same time, they don't want Frank to end up under a bridge when he is age 70.

Freddy and Frieda are charitably inclined. When Frank was young they made sure he did volunteer work because they consider charitable involvement a blessing. They are not blind to estate planning nor do they scorn effective tax planning. They want all the tax benefits they can get. Though they ultimately want a significant amount of their money to go to a charity, they also want Frank to have access a regular income during his life. In addition, they want to encourage Frank to have the option to direct some of their money to the charity or charities of his choice at his death.

After a lengthy conversation with their advisor, they establish a charitable trust as the secondary beneficiary of their IRA. (They are each other's primary beneficiary.) Their advisor is a good woman so she clearly outlines all the benefits of their decision.

- During their lives, it is their money and they can do whatever they want with it.
- If they ever reconsider their decision, they can change the beneficiary to Frank, they can choose to give all the money to the charity, or they can devise something completely different.
- At their deaths, assuming they don't change the beneficiary, the money would go to a trust. If they die when Frank is 40, Frank will get an income of 7.29% of the principal every year for the rest of his life.

- At Frank's death, whatever is left can go to a charity of Frank's choosing.

The numbers work out pretty favorably, and Freddy and Frieda's wishes are respected. The charity must wait to get their money, but they will get it. The loser is the IRS because of all the income and estate tax they couldn't collect.

This chapter provides only a small glimpse into the window of charitable giving. It is one of my goals to present objective information and encourage individuals who would not have otherwise considered charity or charitable trusts to do so after realizing all the tax and other benefits.

If you haven't any charity in your heart, you have the worst kind of heart trouble.

— Bob Hope

A Key Lesson from This Chapter

I believe there are many greedy givers—people with charity in their hearts but whose interest in their families comes first. If this book provides you with some incentive to explore some charitable options, even if the charity has to wait, then there will be charitable value as well as commercial and educational value to the book.

16

A Point-by-Point Summary of the Whole Process

Money isn't everything, but it sure keeps you in touch with your children.

— J. Paul Getty

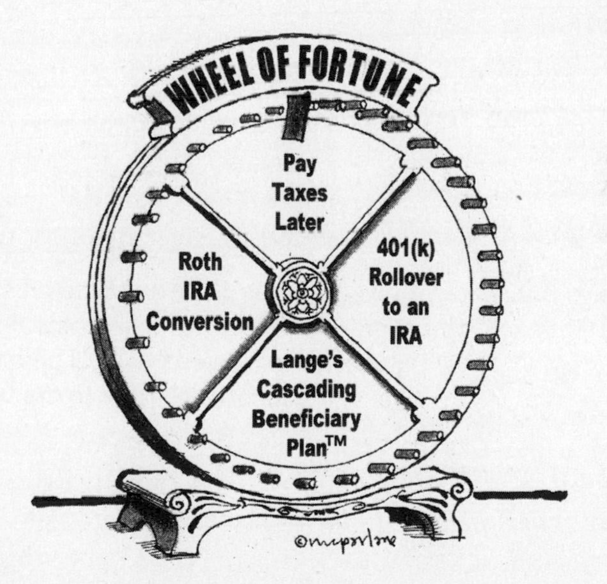

If you are still working, please:

1. Contribute the maximum amount to your retirement plan that your employer is willing to match or partially match.

2. Contribute the maximum allowed to Roth IRAs.
3. If you can afford it, contribute nonmatching funds to your retirement plan, a Roth 401(k) if available.
4. Deduct retirement plan contributions on your tax return, form 1040 (another way to look at it is that you don't have to pay income taxes on the wages earned that are contributed to the retirement plan).
5. Allow these funds to grow income tax deferred.
6. Continue to make new contributions.
7. Continue deferring taxes by deferring distributions.

At retirement when you need money:

8. Spend nonretirement assets (money you already paid income tax on) before you spend your retirement plan money.
9. Spend your Roth IRA last.
10. Plan for needed or required minimum distributions during your lifetime.
11. Keep your minimum required distributions to a minimum.
12. Pay income taxes only when retirement funds are distributed to you.

When you are ready for serious planning:

13. Put in place a specially drafted Change of Beneficiary Form for your retirement plan and IRAs. The plan recommended in *Retire Secure!*, Lange's Cascading Beneficiary Plan™, could allow continued tax deferral up to two generations after your death while at the same time providing or over-providing for your surviving spouse or other heirs.
14. Determine if you are eligible for a Roth IRA conversion, and if so, determine whether it would be advantageous.

A Letter to the Reader

Dear *Retire Secure!* Reader,

First, I want to thank you for purchasing the book and congratulate you for making it this far. It's no secret that plowing through this information can be challenging.

But . . . the most important decisions remain to be made. "What are you going to do with this treasure trove of newfound knowledge?"

You could respond in several ways after reading *Retire Secure!*

1. I am going to take action. Tax reduction and long-term security are important for me and my family.
2. This information is important, but (and then some excuse for not taking action).
3. I am really busy right now. I will get on this as soon as things calm down. (A variant of number two.)

You really can't afford to have the number two or three responses. You need to take the next step: find an appropriate advisor with a lot of experience in distribution and estate planning for IRAs and retirement plans, and set up an appointment.

Perhaps you could plan your retirement and your estate on your own and maybe it would turn out fine, but . . . maybe you would make a huge mistake that could be enormously costly.

And wouldn't you agree that your retirement and estate planning is the wrong place to gamble? True, you do have more knowledge now than when you started this book, but this is an area where one hole in your knowledge can be a financial disaster.

I can't tell you how many people have been to one of my seminars and decided to "wing it" on their own. Unfortunately, they come to me after they have made some huge mistakes and are now in trouble. Every time I see it happen it makes me wince. Once the mistakes have been made, it's hard to ever recover financially, especially if you are already retired.

If you already have a qualified, experienced and proactive IRA and retirement plan distribution expert who you trust, great, you're ahead of the game. Please make that call and carry through until your planning is complete.

If not, it is my most sincere recommendation that you seek out a qualified advisor. Please make sure they are qualified for your type of assets, which are IRAs and/or retirement plans. Many CPAs, attorneys, or financial planners are not IRA and retirement plan distribution experts so please be careful.

But since you bought this book and read it, you can approach the task of finding an advisor with some confidence. You now have the requisite information to be better able to judge your candidate's qualifications. Doing due diligence in choosing an advisor is absolutely crucial. The goal should be to enter into a long-term relationship where you can receive not only the best advice for your situation as it stands today, but proactively receive the best advice on an ongoing basis as time passes and your situation and the tax laws change.

You see, with your new knowledge you're uniquely able to *fully* participate in your retirement planning. No longer will you just have an uneasy feeling that you would like to understand why you are getting the advice you are getting.

Depending on your situation and the capabilities of your advisor, you may be best off with a CPA, an attorney, a financial planner or some other type of financial professional. You may even want more than one advisor on your team. My point is . . . don't read the book, pat yourself on the back for making it through, and then put it up on the shelf and do nothing.

If, however, you don't have a trusted advisor and can't find anyone that you feel has the appropriate expertise in retirement plans and IRAs, there is another option for some readers. I am offering a number of free consultations and taking on a very limited number of private clients who will work with me directly. If you are interested in working with me one on one and you are a resident of PA, CA, FL, OH, NY, or VA, please visit www.PayTaxesLater.com/book/freeconsultation.htm or refer to the end of the book for contact information.

If you would enjoy the benefits of *hearing* some of the material presented, please turn to the back of the book for the free CD offer. Don't forget to sign up for the free reports as well.

I wish you a long, happy, healthy and secure retirement!

To your prosperity,

James Lange

CPA/Attorney at Law

A Special Note to Financial Professionals

Thank you for taking your valuable time to read *Retire Secure!* I urge you to bring this information to your practice in a proactive way.

In the beginning of the book I urged you to have a printout of your clients with you as you read. I suggested that you think about how the different strategies could be used by individual clients to significantly improve their financial picture. If you did that, wonderful. Really, that is great. Now take the next step and plan how to communicate relevant ideas to your clients. Many advisors will make calls. Obviously, if you schedule appointments with clients, that will be significantly better.

If you didn't make notes for your clients while you were reading, I would encourage you to get your client list out now, and make some notes while the ideas are fresh. By reviewing the individual chapters and looking at a list of your clients it should trigger associations—different ideas that would work for different clients.

Finally, whether you made a list before or are doing so now, please don't read this book and go back to your old routine. Apply this information to your clients' situations and communicate with them.

Please sign up for my free email newsletter for financial professionals at www.PayTaxesLater.com/book/finprof.htm. Every financial professional who has clients with significant IRAs and/or retirement plans should have a copy of *Retire Secure!* If you have responsibility for other financial professionals, consider purchasing a copy of this book for all the financial professionals of your organization as well as using it as a premium for your favored clients.

Providing appropriate advice on IRAs and retirement plans is no longer a luxury. It is a necessity. Jerry Reiter, CEO/Chairman of Financial Advisors Legal Association, said that *Retire Secure!* will help provide the education that financial advisors need to reduce their potential liabilities.

If you found the information in this book helpful, you will certainly want to take advantage of the free CD offer. Also visit www.PayTaxesLater.com/book/finprof.htm for special offers and free reports specifically for financial professionals.

Thank you for your business. I hope you and your clients reap tremendous benefits from you reading and implementing the ideas in *Retire Secure!*

I wish you the best.

Appendix

Life Expectancy Tables

TABLE I

(Single Life Expectancy)
(For Use by Beneficiaries)

Age	Life Expectancy	Age	Life Expectancy	Age	Life Expectancy	Age	Life Expectancy
0	82.4	28	55.3	56	28.7	84	8.1
1	81.6	29	54.3	57	27.9	85	7.6
2	80.6	30	53.3	58	27.0	86	7.1
3	79.7	31	52.4	59	26.1	87	6.7
4	78.7	32	51.4	60	25.2	88	6.3
5	77.7	33	50.4	61	24.4	89	5.9
6	76.7	34	49.4	62	23.5	90	5.5
7	75.8	35	48.5	63	22.7	91	5.2
8	74.8	36	47.5	64	21.8	92	4.9
9	73.8	37	46.5	65	21.0	93	4.6
10	72.8	38	45.6	66	20.2	94	4.3
11	71.8	39	44.6	67	19.4	95	4.1
12	70.8	40	43.6	68	18.6	96	3.8
13	69.9	41	42.7	69	17.8	97	3.6
14	68.9	42	41.7	70	17.0	98	3.4
15	67.9	43	40.7	71	16.3	99	3.1
16	66.9	44	39.8	72	15.5	100	2.9
17	66.0	45	38.8	73	14.8	101	2.7
18	65.0	46	37.9	74	14.1	102	2.5
19	64.0	47	37.0	75	13.4	103	2.3
20	63.0	48	36.0	76	12.7	104	2.1
21	62.1	49	35.1	77	12.1	105	1.9
22	61.1	50	34.2	78	11.4	106	1.7
23	60.1	51	33.3	79	10.8	107	1.5
24	59.1	52	32.3	80	10.2	108	1.4
25	58.2	53	31.4	81	9.7	109	1.2
26	57.2	54	30.5	82	9.1	110	1.1
27	56.2	55	29.6	83	8.6	111 and over	1.0

TABLE II

Please See IRS Publication 590.

TABLE III

(Uniform Lifetime)
(For Use by Owners)

Age	Distribution Period	Age	Distribution Period
70	27.4	93	9.6
71	26.5	94	9.1
72	25.6	95	8.6
73	24.7	96	8.1
74	23.8	97	7.6
75	22.9	98	7.1
76	22.0	99	6.7
77	21.2	100	6.3
78	20.3	101	5.9
79	19.5	102	5.5
80	18.7	103	5.2
81	17.9	104	4.9
82	17.1	105	4.5
83	16.3	106	4.2
84	15.5	107	3.9
85	14.8	108	3.7
86	14.1	109	3.4
87	13.4	110	3.1
88	12.7	111	2.9
89	12.0	112	2.6
90	11.4	113	2.4
91	10.8	114	2.1
92	10.2	115 and over	1.9

Index

B

C

D

ABOUT THE AUTHOR

Photo: Karen Meyers

James Lange, CPA/Attorney is a nationally recognized IRA, 401(k) and retirement plan distribution expert. With over 27 years of experience, Jim offers unbeatable recommendations when he tackles the #1 fear facing most retirees: running out of money. Jim has also developed "Lange's Cascading Beneficiary Plan™," which is widely regarded as the "gold standard" of estate planning for IRA and retirement plan owners.

Jim's recommendations have appeared 20 times in the *Wall Street Journal.* Jane Bryant Quinn introduced the country to Jim's mantra, "Pay taxes later," in *Newsweek.* Jim's articles have appeared in the *New York Times, Journal of Retirement Planning, Financial Planning, The Tax Adviser (AICPA),* and other top financial, legal and tax journals.

Jim has a CPA practice, a law practice, and is a registered investment advisor. Jim's practices have 1,568 clients. Jim has presented 148 workshops for taxpayers and financial professionals throughout the country. He is also one of the country's most informed voices on Roth IRAs. In 1998, Jim wrote the definitive article on Roth IRA conversions for *The Tax Adviser*, the peer reviewed journal of the American Institute of Certified Public Accountants. That article is one of the few articles where the pros and cons of a Roth IRA conversion are analyzed in excruciating detail *and* his analysis was reviewed by the toughest peer reviewers in the country. Jim's website www.rothira-advisor.com is consistently in the top 10 sites when you Google "Roth IRA."

Not one to miss an opportunity to keep his loyal readers and clients up to date on matters of importance, Jim also maintains four Web sites. His flagship site is www.PayTaxesLater.com. His sites now have over 32,374,000 hits. He also sends out an email newsletter to 9,500 opt-in subscribers.

Jim lives in Pittsburgh, in the home he grew up in, with his wife, Cindy, and their daughter, Erica. When Jim is not devising new strategies for retirees to save taxes and accumulate wealth (which is most of the time), he enjoys bicycling, skiing, traveling with his family, and playing chess and bridge with his friends and online.

If You Qualify - You May Secure a FREE Consultation With CPA/Attorney/Registered Investment Advisor James Lange

Jim will be accepting a limited number of private clients. If you qualify, the free consultation will assess your needs and requirements to determine the viability of a successful working relationship with Jim.

The initial qualifications for the free consultation with Jim are:

- **you must be a resident of one of the following states PA, CA, FL, OH, NY, or VA (Registered Investment Advisor application pending in NY), and**
- **you must have a minimum of $1,000,000 in investable assets.**

If you live in one of these states but have less than $1,000,000 in investable assets, Jim may be able to refer you to another advisor either inside or outside of his organization.

Integrated Retirement and Estate Planning Services

- **Comprehensive planning for IRAs and retirement assets**
- **Money management services (in conjunction with affiliated firms)**
- **Unique strategies for Roth IRAs and Roth IRA conversions**
- **Strategic planning for TIAA-CREF participants**
- **Transfer of wealth to your spouse and/or succeeding generations**
- **Charitable giving**
- **Insurance recommendations, if appropriate**
- **Income tax preparation**
- **Drafting wills and trusts (PA only)**

To Pursue this Offer Please Visit

www.PayTaxesLater.com/book/freeconsultation.htm

or call 412-521-7857.

Explore the opportunity of working directly with Jim.

Public Speaking

Jim offers workshops and seminars for both taxpayers and financial professionals. For more information please see www.PayTaxesLater.com/book/speaking.htm

Here's How You Can Get ALL of the Valuable FREE Reports Highlighted in *Retire Secure!*

We mention a number of FREE reports throughout ***Retire Secure!*** Each report can be ordered from our website. Please visit www.PayTaxesLater.com/book/order.htm or call **412-521-8007** to obtain any of the following:

FREE Roth IRA Conversion Report

Should You Make a Roth IRA Conversion?

This report contains proven strategies and case studies from Jim's forthcoming book on Roth IRAs. It also contains his recommendations for capitalizing on the new provisions for Roth IRA conversions included in the *Tax Increase Prevention and Reconciliations Act* (TIPRA, signed May 17, 2006).

FREE TIAA-CREF Report

Distribution Planning for TIAA-CREF Participants

Most TIAA-CREF participants wonder, *"How should I handle my retirement finances? What do I need to do at retirement?"* Discover your options in Jim's TIAA-CREF guide.

FREE New Roth 401(k) Report

Save $20,000/Year Tax-Free Using the New Roth 401(k)

This original report can help you accumulate tens or even hundreds of thousands of dollars in tax-free funds!

Please visit **www.PayTaxesLater.com/book/order.htm** or call 412-521-8007. We also have other free offers and high value offers at this site.

Attention Financial Professionals!

If you're a financial professional interested in both technical and practice building information, I urge you to visit www.PayTaxesLater.com/book/finprof.htm **for a free report geared towards financial professionals, How to Develop IRA Rollover Business** and to see our specialized newsletter and products just for you.

FREE CD OFFER (Valued at $147)

Includes Free Shipping &Handling

"The Secrets to a Secure Retirement"

Our FREE full-length audio CD reinforces crucial concepts from ***Retire Secure!*** and gives you **many more tax-savvy strategies** not covered in the book. I recorded a special session consisting of the highlights from my most popular presentations—*the presentations that receive the highest evaluations from both laymen and financial professionals*—and produced a full-length audio CD.

Originally, I planned to send a less valuable CD for free and charge $147 for this one. Then, I decided to give away the best CD because establishing a continuing relationship with interested readers and or listeners is my primary objective.

I urge you to order this **FREE CD** so you can:

- **Improve your financial outlook with the tax-free growth of a Roth IRA, Roth 401(k), and/or a Roth IRA conversion, including the May 17, 2006 changes**
- **Cut taxes on your IRA withdrawals so you and your heirs keep more money**
- **Dramatically REDUCE your risk of running out of money by learning which assets to spend first and which to spend last**
- **Apply the best accumulation and distribution strategies for your IRA and/or retirement plan**
- **Explore how to use Lange's Cascading Beneficiary Plan™ to get the ultimate protection for your spouse, while preserving valuable "stretch IRA" options for your children and grandchildren (works for single individuals as well)**

To order, please go to
www.PayTaxesLater.com/book/freecd.htm,
Phone 412-521-8007
Or use the **Quick Order Form** on the reverse side this page.

I urge you to take the next step and request our free CD (valued at $147). There is **no risk** and **no charge**; it comes with free shipping & handling. Offer good while supplies last.